UNIONS, WORKERS, and the LAW

This material was prepared pursuant to Contract #99-8-1383-42-20 from the U.S. Department of Labor by the author, who was commissioned by the George Meany Center for Labor Studies, AFL-CIO, in partial fulfillment of its Tripartite Program for Apprenticeship and Associate Degree in Labor Studies. The opinions contained in this material do not necessarily reflect those of the George Meany Center for Labor Studies, the American Federation of Labor-Congress of Industrial Organizations, or the U.S. Department of Labor.

UNIONS, WORKERS,
and the LAW

Betty W. Justice

The Bureau of National Affairs, Inc., Washington, D.C.

Library of Congress Cataloging in Publication Data

Justice, Betty, 1948–
　Unions, workers, and the law.

　Bibliography: p.
　Includes index.
　1. Labor laws and legislation—United States.
　2. Trade-unions—Law and legislation—United States.
　3. Collective labor agreements—United States.　　I. Title.
KF3319.J87　1983　　344.73′01　　82-22826
ISBN 0-87179-400-4　　347.3041
ISBN 0-87179-393-8　　(pbk.)

Printed in the United States of America
International Standard Book Number: 0-87179-400-4 (hardbound)
0-87179-393-8 (paperback)

to my parents,

who taught me the dignity both of work
and of resistance to its oppression

Contents

Preface

This book is a textbook. It is neither a political commentary nor a discussion of utilization of the law to achieve social change. Its purpose is to introduce the reader to the legal framework in which workers relate to employers both as individuals and as a group through unions. The text examines major principles of labor law, as well as specific rules of law governing those relationships with some attention to the social policy decisions that underlie them.

This book is not intended to be a comprehensive treatment of all law impacting on the employment relationship. Because of space limitations, some important developments in the law are not covered at all. For example, neither criminal law as it may apply to activities that are a part of a labor dispute nor publicly imposed "just cause" limitations on an employer's discretion in making personnel decisions are discussed in this book. My selection of topics is not meant to suggest the unimportance of other topics which have been excluded. Even on those topics included in the text, the treatment is not always detailed and thorough. I have tried to illustrate, sometimes by extensively discussing a particular case, the legal process, labor-management problems that receive the attention of the legal process, the public response, and the mechanics of government regulation as expressed in specific rules.

I have not attempted to catalog rules governing the employment relationship, because a mere compilation of rules would have little long term utility for the student. The law is not etched in stone; it is a dynamic process, reflecting ever shifting balances of power between various groups within the society. Indeed, a major role of law (and of government) as seen by the framers of the Constitution was the resolution of disputes caused by the fact that "Those who hold and those who are without property have ever formed distinct interests in society." (James Madison in *Federalist Paper* No. 10). During the past and into the present, the rule of law has recognized the power of these two groups and has directed that they act toward each other in such a manner that the social peace and good is maintained.

Beyond this general framework of the law, its application often depends on the particular facts of each situation brought to the legal decisionmaker. While some definite rules can be confidently stated, it is a troublesome responsibility to state precise rules. While the author of a rule knows the factual situation that led up to its enactment, a reader may read the rule and think of a situation that has one additional, or one less, fact. For instance, one might think that the right of employees to communicate about union business on the employer's premises would be a simple one. But the rule, or more accurately the rules, in this instance change according to the presence or absence of a number of factors: whether it is an employee or a nonemployee organizer attempting to communicate; whether the employee is on the premises on his or her day off or during a shift break; whether the premises are open to the public; whether the communication is oral or printed; what the content of the communication is; whether or not the workplace is already unionized; and dozens of other such possibilities that can impact on the legality of the activity. Furthermore, the rules sometimes change for no other reason than that the judge(s) now deciding an issue believe that it was incorrectly decided the previous time around. Because of the nature of the legal process and of the crucial distinctions that can be made on the basis of a single fact, I caution readers to use extreme care in using information contained herein as the basis for deciding on an appropriate course of behavior.

While this book is not meant to be a political analysis or a critique of the law, I think my bias is obvious. I am partisan toward unions because of my life experience, because of my professional role, and because of my ideology. I have presented the law and the rules as the lawmakers and judges have declared them to be. I have sometimes commented on the impact of these laws and rules on unions. Generally, however, I believe that editorializing is unnecessary. The law usually speaks for itself, eloquently justifying or indicting the policies behind it. Whether it is a justification or an indictment depends, of course, on one's point of reference, and I suggest that we each have one. I make mine obvious. I think it more insidious to hide under a veneer of academic neutrality and, thereby, disarm the reader on the importance of critically analyzing the material presented. I do not ask that readers be won over to my conclusions, but rather that they think for themselves.

BETTY W. JUSTICE
January 1983

Acknowledgments

Writing a book is in an immediate sense an individual experience, and authorship is reserved to named individuals. Even though those who have made specific and concrete contributions to this book can be named, scores of people who have participated in shaping my understanding of the law in the employment context go unnamed. In my role as an instructor in the labor education program at the Institute for Labor Studies at West Virginia University, I have "taught" thousands of workers and union members. But these students have also been my teachers, because they have required me to think clearly on issues that emerge from their practical experience on the job. I am grateful to these men and women for sharing their experience and their knowledge and for their desire to learn about the law. No less important has been their patience, and affection, and the example they set by their dedication and vision of a more just society for all of us, as workers and as citizens. I also acknowledge warm regards for my formal teacher of Labor Law, David Scribner.

This book was initiated by the George Meany Center for Labor Studies through its Tripartite Program for Apprenticeship and Associate Degree in Labor Studies. The staff of that project conceived the idea of an undergraduate labor studies curriculum with a complete series of texts and has guided the production of this book from beginning to end. Richard Hindle and David Alexander of the project staff also commented on the draft, as did Jacqueline Brophy of the Meany Center faculty. Fred K. Hoehler, director of the Meany Center, and Russell Allen, deputy director, also provided important support.

Patricia Eames's reading of the original draft for accuracy and Emily Spieler's suggestions on the organization and the presentation were enormously helpful. In one of its several former lives, the draft was used by students at West Virginia State College, West Virginia Institute of Technology, Des Moines Community College, and Rhode Island Junior College. I appreciate the opportunity for a trial run and

xvi / *Unions, Workers, and the Law*

the helpful comments on the draft's usability. Thanks go to Dutch Kleywegt, Grant Crandall, and John David.

Others who have provided comments, assistance, and encouragement are Kathleen Abate, Paul Becker, Lee Balliet, Steve Early, Robert Pleasure, James Weeks, John Wernet, Janice Xaver, and Wilbur Yahnke. Richard Humphreys, director of the Institute for Labor Studies at West Virginia University, provided both institutional and personal support.

Numerous people have been responsible for the production of an intelligible manuscript derived from my original scribblings and several revisions. In particular, Hazel Gibson, Irene Kirk, Susie Ross and Stephanie Pauley brought skill, dedication, and good humor to the task, and to them, I give thanks and respect.

Portions of the chapter on "Law and the Employment Relationship" appeared in Lee Balliet's *Survey of Labor Relations,* published by the Bureau of National Affairs in 1981.

1

Law and the
Employment Relationship

Labor law is a recent historical phenomenon. Prior to industrialization, there existed little basis for collective action by workers, since economic organization was characterized by various forms of unfree labor, such as slavery, feudalism, and indentured servitude. The first free labor primarily involved self-employed workers in subsistence-type enterprises in both agriculture and the crafts, wherein the participants bartered their own product or services for others that they needed. Money played only a rudimentary role in the society.

Trade unions, in the modern sense of concerted action by workers to improve their wages and working conditions, could develop only under a wage-labor system, wherein workers sell their labor power to employers. In this context, workers discovered that they could most effectively improve their wages and working conditions by dealing collectively with employers. Individually, they found themselves powerless, forced by economic reality to compete with each other in terms of the wages and conditions they would accept.

Collective action by workers in the United States has, from its earliest manifestation, engendered a public response via the law, particularly as developed and applied by the courts. Until the 1930s, the law generally was unfavorable toward workers who combined to protect their self-interest. Application of restrictive theories of law reflected the political assumptions that competition, the right of individuals to enter contracts without any outside interference, and the property rights of individuals were fundamental and supreme values of society. This law reflected classic economic theory in which the free operation of the law of supply and demand was considered fundamental. According to this theory, control of wage rates by workers artificially inflated prices, ultimately harming commerce, the com-

1

munity, and even workers themselves, because higher prices discouraged consumption and created unemployment. Therefore the only prescription for a healthy economy was one free of either government regulation or private regulation via collective action of workers. Since 1935 labor-management relations in the United States have been subject to direct government regulation and to regulation by workers through a legally recognized right to join unions and to engage in collective bargaining. Although this regulation initially helped unions to flourish, it has since 1947 served to channel disputes into narrow legalistic categories, undercutting efforts of workers and unions to become more conscious of their interests as a group vis-à-vis employers as a group.

What Is Law?

Law is made when a society, acting through government, formally adopts rules governing particular activities of its members. These rules are enforced by persons officially delegated the responsibility to implement the rules. The rules that become law reflect the attitudes and needs of the society, or at least that portion of the society that controls the law-making processes. Because attitudes and needs are ever changing, the law is also ever changing. Behavior acceptable today may be considered a crime next year.

For example, until less than a century ago, the decision on whether a child was to receive any formal schooling was left entirely to the parents. Now the prevailing view is that society has a right to require parents to send their children to school in order that they may acquire knowledge and skills necessary for them to be useful members of the society. Acting through government, society has passed laws requiring school attendance. A once private matter has become a public concern, dealt with not in the home but by law enforcement officials, social workers, and courts. This change in the law reflects changing social attitudes as to the needs of the society and the appropriate role government should play in meeting those needs.

All law, including labor law, is the result of this kind of process—the contention of differing social forces over the relationship of individual citizens to their government and to each other. Labor law is society's notion of the socially desirable relationship between people who work for wages and those for whom they work.

Types of Law

Customs, attitudes, and beliefs become law in different ways.

Constitutional Law. The constitutions of the United States and of the states are the fundamental source of all law in the United States. A constitution establishes a government, contains the basic principles on which it is based, and organizes the government by defining the powers that each branch of government is to exercise. Because the United States has a government in which power is shared between a central government and individual states, the U.S. Constitution also delineates the powers reserved to the states and those delegated to the federal government. The Bill of Rights and other later amendments to the U.S. Constitution restrict all levels of government (not private parties) from interfering with certain rights of citizens. For instance, the First Amendment limits the ability of government to interfere with the right of citizens to express themselves; this is usually called the right to free speech. Other than outlawing slavery, the U.S. Constitution does not regulate the relations of private citizens to each other. For instance, the First Amendment does not limit the ability of a private employer to take action against an employee based on that employee's expression of views. Other forms of law may regulate this relationship. Because the U.S. Constitution limits governmental action, it does have significant impact on the manner in which the government as an employer must relate to its own employees.

Because a constitution is to endure over time and preserve fundamental values and concepts, it is purposely difficult to change. In theory this prevents changes from being made impulsively, without sufficient regard to their long-range impact on the very nature of the form of government. The recurring debate on whether to add an amendment to the U.S. Constitution to require a balanced federal budget illustrates this point. The essential dispute is not the merits of a balanced budget but whether the fundamental instrument of government ought to be used to establish a specific rule on a particular issue, since a balanced budget could be mandated by statute. Opponents argue that substitution of a constitutional amendment for the legislative process will make the Constitution too rigid and deprive the government of the ability to meet changing societal circumstances.

The highest court acting under a constitution is the final authority for interpreting what a constitutional provision means. In the case of the U.S. Constitution, that court is the Supreme Court of the United States. No legislative act, administrative rule, or judicial decision of a lower court can conflict with the constitution under which it is adopted. The U.S. Constitution is supreme to any state constitution, and if a state constitution or law conflicts with it, the U.S. Constitution prevails.

Common Law. Until this century, almost all law prescribing the manner in which society required citizens to act toward each other was made by courts. This kind of law, sometimes called judicial law, is ordinarily referred to as common law. Judges formulated the law because disputes arose on matters to which no formally legislated rules applied. Typically, two persons would have a dispute, and a court would become involved for the purpose of settling it. With no established rules defining the respective rights and obligations of the parties in a specific situation, the judge, acting on behalf of the public, had to make the law—to decide whether and in what way a party's rights had been violated. The judge would look at the facts and order a resolution based on the prevailing notions of fairness and justice. This decision, called a "precedent" because it preceded other similar situations, would then be applied to future similar disputes. Some of the law under which we live today is common law—for example, the law of negligence and much of property law. Until 1935 nearly all law governing the employer-employee relationship was common law.

Statutory Law. Rules that are formally adopted by a lawmaking body, such as the U.S. Congress, state legislatures, or a city council, are statutory law. The amount of statutory law continues to increase as legislative bodies in the several different tiers of government adopt new laws pertaining to matters not previously regulated by government. For example, most states now, by statue, require that motor vehicles be periodically inspected. This is a rule of recent origin based on the belief that emerged during the past two decades that public safety can be promoted through requiring inspections that will eliminate unsafe vehicles from the roads. Much of the law that today governs the employment relationship is statutory law. Some examples are the National Labor Relations Act, the Social Security Act, and the Davis-Bacon Act.

Administrative Law. This type of law is quite recent in origin and derives from statutory law in the following typical manner. Congress passes a law such as the National Labor Relations Act (NLRA), written in broad and general language to cover many situations, the details of which are hard to predict in advance. Congress simultaneously creates an enforcement agency, the National Labor Relations Board (NLRB), and delegates to it the power to develop rules and apply them to specific situations as long as they do not conflict with or exceed the purposes of the statute or the U.S. Constitution. For example, in the NLRA Congress made it an unfair labor practice for an employer to interfere with rights of its employees to engage in union organizing activities. The NLRB has the authority to decide just what employer conduct constitutes interference and is therefore forbidden.

Administrative rules may be adopted by an agency in a formal rule-making procedure, or they may be developed in individual cases raising a particular issue. Many agencies at all levels of government have the power to make administrative law. Examples of other federal administrative agencies are the Occupational Safety and Health Administration, the Food and Drug Administration, and the Federal Aviation Administration.

Kinds of Cases

The law is an enforceable standard of conduct established by the government which describes the rights and duties of parties in particular situations. The task of resolving disputes among parties as to their rights and duties in any given situation belongs to the courts—the judicial branch of government.

A case is a dispute between parties over their respective rights and duties in a certain situation. There are two basic types of cases—civil cases and criminal cases. A civil case involves one private party suing another private party or private parties suing or being sued by the government, so long as no crime is involved. Some examples of civil cases are divorces, bankruptcy proceedings, and land condemnation actions by the government. A criminal case is one in which individuals are accused by the government of engaging in prohibited conduct, such as littering or kidnapping. A prosecutor, who represents the public's interest in seeing that its laws are obeyed, brings an action seeking to have the accused found guilty and punished for violating the governmentally, or publicly, established standard of conduct.

Both a civil and a criminal case may arise out of the same situation. For instance, one person attacks another person, seriously injuring the second person. The injured party may seek to have the aggressor arrested and charged with the crime of aggravated assault. The charges issued will be in the name of the government, because the public at large has an interest in seeing that the law against physical attacks on people is upheld. The case becomes the government's or the public's case. The public, as well as the victim, is wronged when its law is violated. Therefore the public can seek to have the aggressor punished for the wrong to the public regardless of the desires of the victimized individual.

Apart from any criminal action that may take place against the aggressor, the victim may also sue the aggressor in a civil action for damages resulting from the assault. Control of a civil case remains entirely in the hands of the plaintiff, the person bringing it to court. The basis of this case is a violation of socially recognized rights for which the wronged is entitled to seek redress.

The Judicial System

In the system of government in the United States, the Constitution defines the powers of each of the three branches of government. The legislative branch, Congress, makes policy when it enacts laws. The task of implementing and enforcing the laws belongs to the executive branch, headed by the President. The resolution of disputes as to the interpretation and application of laws and the right to decide whether a law is a permissible act of government under the Constitution is reserved to the judicial or court system. State government systems generally parallel that of the federal government. The judicial system, in its role of deciding disputes as to the meaning and application of law, has a huge impact on the administration of labor and employment laws. Although organizationally in the executive branch of government, many administrative agencies, such as the NLRB, have also been delegated power to adjudicate, or to judge, particular disputes, subject to court review. The decision reached through such agencies is called an administrative remedy, and under many laws, one must exhaust, or go through, the administrative process before seeking a judicial remedy.

Courts are defined by their jurisdiction. Each court has at least two types of jurisdiction. First, jurisdiction refers to the geographic area over which a court has authority. Second, the word "jurisdiction" refers to the types of disputes a court has the power to adjudicate.

Most employment-related law described in this book is federal law. Although state courts may sometimes act under these laws, enforcement is primarily through the federal system. The federal judicial system is structured in the following manner:

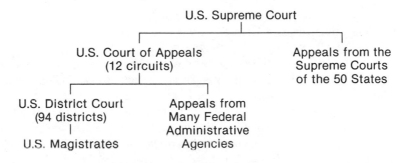

Federal Trial Courts. The basic federal trial court is the U.S. district court. There is at least one federal district for each state. These courts handle most litigation arising under federal laws, including federal criminal charges, and actions arising under state law when the parties are residents of different states and the amount in controversy is $10,000 or more. Trial courts initially hear a dispute, determine the facts, and make the initial ruling.

U.S. Court of Appeals. The federal court system has an intermediate level of appeal, the U.S. Court of Appeals. Divided into 12 geographic areas, these courts review decisions of U.S. district courts and the decisions of some federal administrative agencies, including the NLRB. The basic function of an appeal court is to review decisions made by trial courts, or administrative agencies, to make sure that the law has been correctly interpreted and applied to the facts of a particular case. Appeals courts do not accept new evidence, nor do they make new findings of facts. Their decisions generally are limited to interpreting and applying the law to the facts as the trial court found them to be.

The U.S. Supreme Court. The court of final appeal is the U.S. Supreme Court. This court reviews decisions of the U.S. courts of appeal, some few decisions of the U.S. district courts, and opinions of state supreme courts that raise questions involving the U.S. Constitution or a federal statute.

Chronology of Labor Law

Labor law in the United States has developed and changed in accordance with the changes in the nature and organization of economic activity in the nation. Several distinct periods of labor law can be identified.

Union Membership as a Crime

Prior to 1850, employers sought with the aid of the courts to suppress unions entirely. At this time, much work, aside from agriculture, was craft work. A tight labor market combined with the fact that few people possessed the requisite skills meant that craft workers could not easily be replaced. Consequently, employers had to resort to public authority to keep their workers in line. Suppression was accomplished primarily through application of the common law doctrine of criminal conspiracy. A conspiracy is a combination of two or more persons who join together to harm the rights of society or of other citizens. The mere act of joining together to affect working conditions was considered to be a criminal conspiracy for which workers could be prosecuted in the same manner as those accused, for example, of robbery.

The law viewed the employment relationship as a contract between the employer and the individual worker. In its most basic sense, a contract is simply an agreement between two parties. Each promises to do or to refrain from doing a certain thing. Typically, an employment contract was oral; the employee promising to work and the employer promising to pay a prescribed amount for the completed work. Legally, this constituted a contract even though it lacked the formalities ordinarily associated with contracts.

The freedom to contract was a fundamental principle of the social and the legal system. Collective action by workers was considered to interfere with both an employer's and the individual employee's right to freely make a bargain and to violate society's interest in preserving the right to contract for its members. For example, an employer in dealing with individual workers might be able to secure the services of one worker only by paying 60¢ per day but obtain the same services from another worker for 50¢ because the second worker needed the money more. If workers joined together and demanded 75¢ per day, then the employee could no longer play upon their individual weaknesses for its own advantage. The employer maintained that such collective activity interfered with its freedom to contract in the marketplace for the best bargain possible and ought therefore to be outlawed. It was further argued that such collective action often intimidated and coerced individual workers in the exercise of their freedom of contract because it deprived them of their opportunity to work under different terms if they chose to do so. The courts agreed that combinations of workers to improve their working lot were injurious to society and therefore illegal. As the Court observed in *Commonwealth v. Pullis (The Boot and Shoemakers of Philadelphia)* (1806), an early conspiracy trial, "A combination of workmen to raise their wages may be considered in a two-fold point of view: one is to benefit themselves ... the other is to injure those who do not join their society. The rule of law condemns both."

As the economy became industrialized, greater numbers of workers went to work in the mines and the mills, where they experienced long hours, low wages, and dangerous conditions. Despite the fact that such an act was considered a crime, workers joined together in organized efforts to improve their work lives. It soon became evident that if workers were to have any respect for the law, their organizations could not be totally suppressed. A major break in the conspiracy doctrine occurred when the Supreme Court of Massachusetts in *Commonwealth v. Hunt* (1842) held that the simple act of joining a union was not a crime. However, the same court enunciated the "end/means" test, under which the courts continued to scrutinize the ends a union sought and the methods it used to achieve those ends in deciding whether concerted worker activity was legal. Using this test, courts continued to cripple workers' efforts to further their interests collectively.

Use of the Injunction

The criminal law was increasingly replaced by the use of the civil law, and by the 1880s, the civil injunction became the preferred legal method of combating labor organizations. An injunction is a court order which requires a person to perform some specified act or to refrain from or desist from certain activity. An injunction, known in the law as an "equitable remedy," is based on a concept in early English law in which the Chancellor of Equity was empowered to make orders to achieve fairness regardless of the legalities of a situation. An injunction is issued to maintain the status quo until legal issues can be decided and to prevent irreparable harm to another party's rights. An injunction must be obeyed as long as it is in effect, regardless of the circumstances under which it was granted. In labor disputes, it matters little what the merits of a situation are, since the mere granting of the injunction is usually sufficient to chill the activity enjoined.

By the late 1800s, injunctions became routinely available against any combined worker activity allegedly carried out by illegal methods or seeking to achieve illegal goals. The illegality of both methods and goals was determined by reference to existing law, all of which was based on the sanctity of property and the right to contract. This was highly unfavorable to workers, whose essential purpose in organizing was to diminish the absolute power employers possessed under the existing system. The reach of the injunction was virtually unlimited in terms of the conduct that could be enjoined and, with its advantages of speed and flexibility, was less cumbersome than criminal prosecution and consequently more effective in stifling the efforts of workers to organize themselves into unions.

The full force of the injunction was felt in its use to enforce "yellow-dog contracts," wherein a worker, as a condition of employment, promised that he/she was not and would not become a member of a union while in the employ of the employer. Whenever a union attempted to organize workers who had signed yellow-dog agreements, the employer would seek an order enjoining the union organizers from interfering with these "contracts." The Supreme Court approved the propriety of injunctions in such situations in *Hitchman Coal & Coke v. Mitchell* (1917) and overturned state laws outlawing yellow-dog contracts. This judicial reverence for the "freedom to contract" encouraged employers to use yellow-dog agreements as a very effective way of preventing worker organization. The yellow-dog contract used by the Hitchman Coal and Coke Company read in part:

> I am employed by and work for the Hitchman Coal and Coke Company with the express understanding that I am not a member of the United Mine Workers of America, and will not become a member of the United Mine Workers of America so long as I am in the employ of the Hitchman Coal and Coke Company . . . and that the Hitchman Coal and Coke Company is run nonunion and agrees with me that it will run nonunion so long as I am in its employ. I have either read the above or heard same read.

Judicial Hostility

During the 1880s, the United States entered a period of dramatic social upheaval, signaling the transition of the nation from an agrarian economy and culture to an industrialized society. The growing concentration of economic power in large corporations was accompanied by an unstable economy, agrarian discontent, and the development of a militant labor movement. The character of the social unrest of the period was primarily economic and class-oriented. Workers and farmers alike were upset by the favoritism of the government, particularly the courts, toward business interests. The violent and bitter strikes during this period, such as the Haymarket episode in 1886, the Homestead strike in 1892, and the Pullman strike of 1894, indicate the intensity of the conflict between labor and management.

Threatened by the growing militancy of workers who, through the vote, could have a more direct impact on legislative bodies, industrialists came to regard the federal courts as the most reliable protector of economic and social stability. In restraining organized labor and serving as guardians of corporate property interests, the courts repeatedly placed the property rights of the corporations ahead of the human rights of workers seeking to improve the quality of their work lives. For example, the Sherman Anti-Trust Act was passed by the U.S. Congress in 1890 to limit the ability of companies to engage in price fixing and other concerted acts that lessened competition. Ironically, the law as interpreted was more severe in its impact on unions than on monopolies. The Supreme Court approved the application of the Sherman Act to union activity in *Loewe v. Lawlor* (*Danbury Hatters*) (1913) when it upheld a finding of liability for damages against a union and its individual members for losses resulting from a boycott of stores selling hats produced by a nonunion hatmaker. By outlawing one of its most effective organizing weapons, this ruling was a crushing blow to labor.

In 1914, after intensive lobbying efforts by organized labor, Congress passed the Clayton Anti-Trust Act, which labor believed would exempt its organizations from the anti-trust laws (Section 6) and limit the right of federal courts to issue injunctions in labor disputes (Section 20). However, the Clayton Act was vaguely written and did not in plain language provide what labor hoped for—that is, an outright exemption. The Supreme Court proved unwilling to allow Congress to legislate away its role as the protector of the status quo. In interpreting the Clayton Act it concluded in *Duplex Printing Co. v. Deering* (1921) that by the use of the terms "lawful," "lawfully," "peaceful," and "peacefully" in reference to union activities, Congress had intended to confer immunity only to activity permitted under the law at the time of the Clayton Act's passage.

This meant that anything violative of the Sherman Act could not be protected under the Clayton Act. By providing that private parties could seek injunctions in anti-trust cases, the Clayton Act actually increased the power of employers to further handicap union organizing efforts. Before, only the government had the power to do so under the Sherman Act.

Furthermore, the Supreme Court employed a double standard in its application of anti-trust law. The Court, in reviewing business combinations, distinguished between "reasonable" and "unreasonable" restraint of trade, finding only the latter unlawful. Although its express purpose was to acquire the stock of independent companies, the organization of the United States Steel Corporation, which by 1920 controlled 50 percent of the nation's steel industry, was found not to be a violation in *U.S. v. United States Steel Corp.* (1920). In contrast, the Supreme Court found in *Coronado Coal Co. v. Mine Workers* (1925) that the union was guilty of violating the anti-trust act when it struck a mine which the company was attempting to run on a nonunion basis despite a current valid contract with the UMWA. The union's strike was found to unlawfully restrict the movement of coal in interstate commerce. The significance of *Coronado Coal* was that the union activity was directed at the employer immediately involved rather than at secondary parties, as in the Danbury hatters case. Since all strikes have the effect of reducing the amount of products in commerce, this decision cast doubt on the legality of any strike. The Court seemed to be saying that monopoly restraint of trade was "reasonable" but that workers' attempts to protect themselves from monopoly abuses were "unreasonable."

Social Recognition

The continuing class hostilities and economic disruption during the early years of the twentieth century indicated that industrial stability could be obtained only by legally permitting workers to form unions and bargain collectively. As long as workers could make gains solely through the use of their economic power, economic disruption would continue. Because of the impact of railroad transportation on the public welfare, it is not surprising that the first efforts in developing a national labor policy focused on that industry. Several serious strikes in the late nineteenth century brought the western rail industry to a virtual standstill. This history provided the incentive for congressional action to bring order to the chaotic labor relations of the industry. Beginning with the Arbitration Act of 1888, federal legislation over the next few decades firmly established a government role in the labor-management relations of the railroad industry. This legislation culminated in the Railway Labor Act of 1926, incorporating the more progressive aspects of earlier legislation and clearly establishing the right of railroad workers to join unions and to select representatives for the purposes of collective bargaining. The constitutionality of the Railway Labor Act was upheld by the Supreme Court in *Texas & New Orleans Railroad v. Railway & Steamship Clerks* (1930) when it expressly approved collective bargaining in the industry as in the public interest. The Railway Labor Act as amended currently covers employees in the railroad and airlines industries.

Norris-LaGuardia Act. Recognizing that the development of large corporations had inevitably caused the organization of workers to defend themselves, the U.S. Congress adopted the Norris-LaGuardia Act in 1932. Admitting that government had in the past cooperated with employers to thwart the efforts of workers to protect and further their interests, Congress delineated a role of government neutrality with respect to labor-management relations. In direct and clear language, the Norris-LaGuardia Act denied federal courts the right to issue injunctions in ordinary labor disputes. It also removed most labor activities from the sanction of anti-trust laws and outlawed the yellow-dog contract.

In enacting the Norris-LaGuardia Act, Congress noted for the first time the general imbalance of power that had long existed between individual workers and their employers. The preamble of the Norris-LaGuardia Act stated that the law had long recognized and aided the right of capital to consolidate itself. This consolidation had rendered individual, unorganized workers helpless to effectively exercise their freedom of labor and liberty of contract to obain acceptable terms and conditions of employment. To remedy this imbalance, the law now recognized the right of employees to associate and self-organize freely and to designate representatives to negotiate terms and conditions of employment free from the interference, restraint, or coercion of employers.

The philosophical underpinning of the Norris-LaGuardia Act was the belief that government should not resolve labor disputes or substitute its determination for private contracts in a free market. This policy of allowing labor and management to resolve their disputes free of governmental intervention lasted only a short time before the United States initiated the policy of comprehensive regulation that characterizes labor-management relations today.

The National Industrial Recovery Act. The New Deal's general plan to promote economic improvement was contained in the National Industrial Recovery Act (NIRA), adopted by Congress in 1933. It provided for the regulation of prices and production by the operators in an industry. This industrial self-regulation was an effort to rationalize the economy and represented an express departure from the anti-trust laws. The NIRA further required that each covered industry establish a minimum wage for its workers. Section 7(a) of the act protected the right of workers to organize and bargain collectively.

President Franklin Roosevelt created the National Labor Board to administer the labor policy of the NIRA. But because it lacked enforcement powers, the Board was successful only when employers did not challenge its authority. Consequently, in 1934, Congress passed Joint Resolution 44, creating a National Labor Relations Board to enforce Section 7(a). Questions of enforcement soon became moot. In *Schecter Poultry Corp. v. U.S.* (1935), the Supreme Court declared the NIRA unconstitutional, not because of Section 7, but because other sections attempted to regulate business transactions not part of interstate commerce.

The National Labor Relations Act. Following the demise of the NIRA, Congress again acted to adopt legislation pertaining specifically to labor-management relations in private industry. Sponsored by Senator Robert Wagner of New York and formally entitled the National Labor Relations Act (NLRA), the law was adopted in response to the deteriorating stability of the nation's industrial and commercial life. Signed into law on July 5, 1935, the NLRA represented the government's major legislative step into an arena previously regulated by the organized economic strength of the two parties. (Actually, government had long been involved via the courts, maintaining all the while that the judiciary was not regulating labor-management relations but was simply enforcing other legally protected rights.) Abandoning altogether the remnants of the laissez-faire philosophy calling for government neutrality with respect to economic enterprise, Congress declared that the policy of the United States was to encourage the practice of collective bargaining and full freedom of worker self-organization. The law placed the power of the federal government behind trade unionism.

A common misconception is that Congress passed the Wagner Act solely because workers needed unions. Probably a more important stimulus, Congress was prompted by the need for industrial stability to recognize the legitimacy of unions. Congress hoped that unions, by countering the power of employers, could bring order and stability to the otherwise unrestrained and chaotic practices of businesses. That Congress chose to empower unions with this responsibility rather than imposing industrial order by direct governmental action reflected the prevailing ideology abhoring government intrusion into business. The vitality of that notion has persisted even to the present day in the debates over the appropriateness of government regulation of such substantive aspects of employment as health and safety and government-imposed wage and price ceilings.

Employees covered by the NLRA were guaranteed in Section 7 the right to organize through secret ballot elections and to bargain collectively. To assure realization of these rights, Section 8 of the act defined as "unfair labor practices" five types of employer conduct and prohibited the following activities:

- Interference with employee rights of self-organization
- Domination and/or interference with the formation and administration of unions
- Discrimination to encourage or discourage union membership
- Employer discrimination or discharge for filing unfair labor practice charges or giving testimony under the act
- Refusal to bargain with the duly chosen representatives of employees.

The responsibility for the enforcement of the law and for overseeing the process by which employees were to select their collective bargaining representatives was vested in a newly created federal agency, the National Labor Realtions Board (NLRB). The NLRA survived the challenge to its existence when the Supreme Court ruled in *NLRB v. Jones & Laughlin Steel Corp.* (1937) that the power of Congress to regulate "commerce" included the power to regulate labor-management activity in the public interest.

The Taft-Hartley Act. In one sense, the NLRA was highly partisan in that it imposed restraints on employers but not on employees or unions. The deferential treatment was based in part on the fact that despite a high level of individual worker militance, unions as institutions were in 1935 still relatively weak. The NLRA was designed to be conducive to the organizing of unions and to the establishing of stable collective bargaining relationships and to allowing unions to flourish thereby.

The process of converting to a peacetime economy after World War II was accompanied by strikes in most major industries. This activity formed the backdrop against which Congress acted in passing the Taft-Hartley Act in 1947—actually a series of amendments to the Wagner Act. The Taft-Hartley Act, formally known as the Labor Management Relations Act (LMRA), represented a basic shift in the regulatory scheme from protecting unions to restraining them. It initiated a period of restrictive regulation that continues to the present day. The LMRA was premised on the belief that unions were no longer fragile institutions that needed special protection. In fact, proponents of the Taft-Hartley law argued that overprotection had resulted in unions becoming so strong that they exercised a stranglehold over the economic life of the nation and tyrannical control over their members.

Section 7 of the NLRA was amended to include the right of employees to refrain from engaging in union activities. Closed shops were outlawed; states were empowered to enact so-called "right-to-work" laws restricting the application of union security agreements. Various union practices were prohibited as secondary boycotts, and the NLRB was directed to summarily seek injunctions against such activity. Unions were made subject to unfair labor practice charges paralleling those applying to employers. Additionally, the LMRA guaranteed employers a "free speech" right to express their opinions concerning unions, provided for national emergency injunctions against otherwise legal contract strikes, and made labor contracts enforceable in federal court.

Landrum-Griffin Act. During the 1950s, much public attention was focused on the corruption and the lack of democracy in the internal operations of several unions, particularly the Teamsters. The abuses by unions of their power over members were well documented, but probably not coincidentially, the Teamsters had been very successful in securing wage and benefits gains for their members and were a natural target of those who wanted to keep labor in line. The result was the adoption of the Labor Management Reporting and Disclosure Act (LMRDA) of 1959 to regulate internal union affairs. Popularly known as the Landrum-Griffin Act, the LMRDA contains elaborate reporting requirements for unions, particularly on the handling of money. The law also created a union member's "bill of rights" to apply in matters such as union meetings, elections, eligibility for office, and union disciplinary proceedings. It also amended the Taft-Hartley Act to clarify and close loopholes in the secondary boycott provisions, further restricting the range of legal union activity in the area of labor-management relations.

The only major recent attempt to revise statutorily the federal labor law was the proposed Labor Law Reform Act of 1977. Because of the ineffectiveness of existing labor law in dealing with employers who flagrantly violated its requirements, organized labor sought amendments designed to bolster enforcement. The proposed changes were primarily of two types. One type would have eliminated the delays that attend NLRB elections to choose bargaining representatives. These delays aid employers in eroding a union's majority and are a significant factor in union losses in representation elections. Another set of changes would have made penalities for violating the law more severe, thereby providing a greater incentive for employers to comply with the law.

The proposed reform contained no major structural changes in labor relations law and did not address the anti-labor provisions contained in the Taft-Hartley Act. Rather, it was geared toward achieving the basic promises of a law enacted more than 40 years earlier. Nonetheless it prompted frenzied opposition from employers and their organizations and, after passing the House of Representatives, was shelved because procedural maneuvering prevented its consideration by the Senate.

With minor changes, the statutory law governing labor-management relations in the private sector has been the same for 30 years. However, unions function in an ever changing or evolving legal environment. The NLRB, in its role of interpreter and enforcer of the law, continues to refine and sometimes reverse the meaning of the law. The courts likewise continue to engage in law-making activity which, particularly in the 1970s, has imposed significant restraints on the range of "legal" activity permitted to unions. These restrictions continue to erode union gains and undermine the fragile labor peace that has existed since 1935.

Key Words and Phrases

administrative agency	Landrum-Griffin Act
administrative law	law
civil law	legislative branch
common law	*Loewe v. Lawlor*
Commonwealth v. Hunt	National Labor Relations Act
conspiracy	*NLRB v. Jones & Laughlin*
constitutional law	*Steel Corp.*
contract	Norris-LaGuardia Act
criminal law	precedent
executive branch	Railway Labor Act
injunction	Section 7 rights
judicial system	Sherman Anti-Trust Act
jurisdiction	statutory law
labor law	unfair labor practices
labor law reform	"yellow-dog" contract
Labor Management	
Relations Act	

Review and Discussion Questions

1. Evaluate the statement, "We live in a society based on law, not on men."

2. Is there a significant difference between enjoying a right based on statutory law and enjoying the same right based on a constitutional interpretation?

3. Consider this quote:

> Unrest, to my mind, never can be removed—and fortunately never can be removed—by mere improvement of the physical and material condition of the workingman. If it were possible, we should run the risk of improving their material condition and reducing their manhood.

> Louis D. Brandeis, attorney and, later, Justice of the Supreme Court, before the U.S. Commission on Industrial Relations, 1915.

From this statement, what do you expect would be Justice Brandeis' view of the greatest contribution unions can make to working people? Otherwise stated, toward what end do workers continue to struggle even if material comfort is achieved? To what extent is present U.S. labor law based on this view?

4. Why are unions a recent historical phenomenon?

5. What is the significance of the shift from the use of the criminal law to the use of the civil law to suppress unions?

6. What was the philosophical underpinning of the Norris-LaGuardia Act? What do you think of that view of the role of government?

7. Do you think that it is appropriate for nonelected governmental bodies, such as the National Labor Relations Board, to have the power to "make" law? Explain.

8. What is the basic difference between the Wagner Act and the Taft-Hartley Act? What is the underlying view of the role of unions incorporated into each?

9. What reasons explain the historically deep and persistent hostility of the courts to unions?

10. Why is the term "evolving" frequently used to describe the state of the law applying to labor?

11. Had it passed, what effect would the Labor Law Reform Act have had on the basic legal framework within which present-day labor relations take place?

12. Does the present role of unions as defined and embodied in the law permit them to deal with the basic problems facing workers today?

2

The LMRA and Its Enforcement

In enacting the National Labor Relations Act in 1935, Congress relied on its constitutional power to regulate interstate commerce. The term "interstate" describes activity carried on between points located in two or more states. The Supreme Court's approval of the congressional ban of certain activity by private employers was a momentous departure from most previous constitutional interpretation. Until this time, the Supreme Court had believed that government ought not, and in its view of the Constitution could not, regulate business activity. This interpretation of the Constitution as giving government narrowly limited power over private parties led the Court to invalidate even state laws attempting to regulate business activity within particular states. Some standards legislation, such as workers' compensation, received earlier approval (1917) by the Supreme Court. The hostility to federal regulation was even greater than that accorded to state laws. This view is demonstrated, for example, in the Supreme Court's repeated overriding of congressional efforts to eliminate exploitive child labor. In *Hammer v. Dagenhart* (1918), the Court said:

> The far reaching result of upholding the act cannot be more plainly indicated than by pointing out that if Congress can thus regulate matters entrusted to local authority by prohibition of the movement of commodities in interstate commerce all freedom of commerce will be at end, and the power of the States over local matters may be eliminated, and thus our system of government be practically destroyed.

It was not the prevailing belief that government affirmatively gave an employer a right to use child labor. Rather, the Supreme Court believed that the Constitution specifically restricted the ability of government to prohibit such a practice. To governmentally prescribe a standard of conduct for an employer was considered to de-

20

prive the employer of its Fifth Amendment right to contract without affording it due process of law.

After a public clash with President Franklin Roosevelt over its decision to invalidate various New Deal legislation, the Supreme Court finally relented in its view. In *NLRB v. Jones & Laughlin Steel* (1937), a landmark decision in constitutional interpretation, the Supreme Court upheld the National Labor Relations Act as a legitimate exercise of congressional authority, signaling a new era of government regulation of business. The decision affirmed that the Constitution's general grant of authority to Congress to act in the public good through the regulation of interstate commerce could override some conflicting claims of constitutional rights by individuals, such as employers. This notion has its positive and its negative aspects, depending on one's view of the appropriate or desirable exercise of governmental power. Consider the current debate over the use of laetrile, believed by some to be an effective treatment for cancer. The Food and Drug Administration, acting pursuant to congressionally delegated authority to protect the public health, has banned the substance, believing its reputed powers to be a hoax on desperate people unable to weigh the risks inherent in their decision. This government policy overrides any individual right to acquire the substance. Today's arena of conflict centers more in efforts to persuade Congress to use its power in a particular manner or to decline to use it altogether—the deregulation mania. Since 1937, the Supreme Court has routinely approved legislation regulating business activity.

However, with the advent of the Burger Court in the 1970s, developments indicate an emerging willingness of the Court to restrict the range of the congressional power over commerce. (The Supreme Court is commonly identified by a reference to the person serving as its Chief Justice. The present Supreme Court is headed by Chief Justice Warren Burger, appointed to his position by President Richard Nixon.) For instance, in 1977 the Supreme Court found in *Marshall v. Barlow's* (1978) that the Occupational Safety and Health Act's authorization of inspection of workplaces by federal enforcement officials could not override an employer's constitutional right under the Fourth Amendment to be free of governmental searches without a warrant. Another decision involved the extent to which Congress may legislate on matters concerning state and local employment. In *National League of Cities v. Usery* (1976) the Court rejected the extension of the federal minimum wage and overtime protection to nonfederal public employees, and found that Congress was exercising "power in a fashion that impair[ed] the States' integrity or their ability to function effectively in a federal system."

The NLRB's Jurisdiction

The Labor Management Relations Act, by its own terms, applies to "labor disputes" affecting "commerce." Historically, commerce signified an exchange of goods. In modern usage, labor, transportation, communication, intelligence, and the media of exchange are considered objects of commerce and are thus subject to congressional regulation.

The Supreme Court in *NLRB v. Jones & Laughlin Steel Corp.* (1937) construed the National Labor Relations Act as giving the NLRB jurisdiction over all commerce subject to the congressional power. In describing the extent of this power, the Court noted that

> It is the effect on commerce, not the source of the injury, which is the criterion. . . . Although activities may be intrastate in character when separately considered, if they have such a close and substantial relation to interstate commerce that their control is essential or appropriate to protect that commerce from burdens and obstructions, Congress cannot be denied the power to exercise that control.

In addition to limiting NLRA coverage to labor disputes affecting commerce, Congress imposed a second limitation on the law's coverage, defining "employer" and "employees" so as to exclude certain workers.

Employers. The term "employer" is defined in Section 2(2) of the LMRA as including:

> . . . any person acting as an agent of an employer, directly or indirectly, but shall not include the United States or any wholly owned Government corporation, or any Federal Reserve Bank, or any State or political subdivision thereof, or any person subject to the Railway Labor Act, . . .

This definition encompasses nearly all private employers so long as the employer is engaged in "commerce." When the Post Office was reorganized as a public corporation in 1970, postal workers became subject to the LMRA in all respects except that strikes and union security clauses were prohibited and compulsory arbitration was substituted to determine contract terms unsettled by negotiation. Private nonprofit hospitals, specifically excluded from the definition of "employer" until a congressional amendment deleted the exemption, became covered employers in 1974. Railway and airline employees are subject to the Railway Labor Act, which has comparable provisions to those in the LMRA but has an entirely different enforcement scheme. The Supreme Court judicially created another exception to the definition of "employer" in *NLRB v. Catholic Bishop of Chicago* (1979), when it decided that Congress did not intend NLRB jurisdiction to extend to church-operated schools.

Employees. The term "employee" is defined in Section 2(3) of the LMRA as

> Any employee . . . but shall not include any individual employed as an agricultural laborer, or in the domestic service of any family or person at his home, or any individual employed by his parent or spouse, or any individual having the status of an independent contractor or any individual employed as a supervisor, or any individual employed by an employer subject to the Railway Labor Act, . . .

The NLRB has the task of deciding the scope of each of these excluded classes of employees. For instance, in deciding whether a worker is a covered employee or an exempted agricultural employee, the NLRB looks at the nature of the job and distinguishes between agricultural and commercial activity. In deciding whether a person is an independent contractor or an employee, the NRLB considers the following factors: (1) the entrepreneurial aspects of the operation; (2) the risk of loss and opportunity for profit; and (3) the person's proprietary interest in the enterprise. One of the more significant decisions of the 1970s was the Supreme Court's ruling in *Chemical Workers v. Pittsburgh Plate Glass Co.* (1971) that retired persons are not employees within the meaning of the LMRA. By excluding retirees from employee status, employers were relieved of the duty to bargain concerning their rights and benefits.

Supervisory and Managerial Employees. Supervisors are specifically exempted from the status of "employee" and therefore enjoy no rights under the LMRA. (Many other laws, such as workers' compensation statutes and the Social Security Act, define "employee" more broadly and include supervisors.) The law makes it clear that actual duties and the exercise of independent judgment are the key factors in determining supervisory status. The NLRB may not classify supervisors in units for collective bargaining purposes, nor does an employer have a legal obligation to recognize and bargain with a union composed of supervisors. Although supervisors' organizations are not illegal, the lack of any protection under the law effectively prevents most efforts by supervisors to organize and bargain.

Managerial employees, other than supervisors or foremen, are not expressly excluded by statutory language from the protections of the LMRA. Until 1970, the NLRB excluded all managerial employees from the scope of coverage. In 1970, it changed its policy to one excluding only managerial employees who deal with labor relations. However, the Supreme Court concluded in *NLRB v. Bell Aerospace Co.* (1974) that Congress implicitly intended that all managerial employees be excluded from the reach of the LMRA and rejected the policy. The NLRB does retain the authority to determine who is in fact a managerial employee. The standard for making this determination is whether an employee has the authority to "formulate and effectuate management policies by expressing and making operative the decisions of the employer."

In *NLRB v. Hendricks County Rural Electric Membership Corp.* (1981), the Supreme Court also excluded support personnel who act in a confidential capacity to management persons involved in the employer's labor relations from coverage under the law. Such employees are considered to have access to information that potentially could result in a conflict of interest if the person is allied with other employees or a union seeking to deal with management.

Jurisdictional Standards. A further restriction of the LMRA's coverage is found in the NLRB's jurisdictional standards. Although its jurisdiction over labor disputes affecting commerce is plenary (unlimited), the NLRB has by choice declined to exercise its power to the fullest extent granted by Congress. This discretionary denial of coverage has included the refusal of jurisdiction in some industries altogether. In others, the NLRB has set a dollar standard in the annual volume of business that an enterprise must exceed before it will assume jurisdiction. The primary justification for this policy is that it conserves and maximizes NLRB resources by focusing only on those enterprises which have a substantial effect on interstate commerce. In the 1959 Landrum-Griffin amendments to the LMRA, Congress approved this NLRB policy but prohibited it from making the standards more restrictive than those prevailing at that time.

In determining whether an enterprise meets its dollar standard in volume of business, the NLRB adds the direct and indirect inflow of goods and services to the employer and the direct and indirect outflow of goods and services from the employer. In computing the amount of business, all of an employer's operations are considered regardless of their location. Jurisdictional standards for the main categories of enterprises are set out in Table 1.

Table 1. NLRB Standards for Asserting Jurisdiction

1. Nonretail business: Direct sales of goods to customers in other States, or indirect sales through others (called *outflow*), of at least $50,000 a year; or direct purchases of goods from suppliers in other States, or indirect purchases through others (called *inflow*), of at least $50,000 a year.
2. Office buildings: Total annual revenue of $100,000 of which $25,000 or more is derived from organizations which meet any of the standards except the indirect outflow and indirect inflow standards established for nonretail enterprises.
3. Retail enterprises: At least $500,000 total annual volume of business.
4. Public utilities: At least $250,000 total annual volume of business, or $50,000 direct or indirect outflow or inflow.
5. Newspapers: At least $200,000 total annual volume of business.
6. Radio, telegraph, television, and telephone enterprises: At least $100,000 total annual volume of business.
7. Hotels, motels, and residential apartment houses: At least $500,000 total annual volume of business.
8. Privately owned hospitals and nursing homes operated for profit: At least $250,000 total annual volume of business for hospitals; at least $100,000 for nursing homes.
9. Transportation enterprises, links and channels of interstate commerce: At least $50,000 total annual income from furnishing interstate passenger and freight transportation services; also performing services valued at $50,000 or more for businesses which meet any of the jurisdictional standards except the indirect outflow and indirect inflow standards established for nonretail enterprises.
10. Transit systems: At least $250,000 total annual volume of business.
11. Taxicab companies: At least $500,000 total annual volume of business.
12. Associations: These are regarded as a single employer in that the annual business of all association members is totaled to determine whether any of the standards apply.
13. Enterprises in the Territories and the District of Columbia: The jurisdictional standards apply in the Territories; all businesses in the District of Columbia come under NLRB jurisdiction.
14. National defense: Jurisdiction is asserted over all enterprises affecting commerce when their operations have a substantial impact on national defense, whether or not their enterprises satisfy any other standard.
15. Private nonprofit universities and colleges: At least $1,000,000 gross annual revenue from all sources (excluding contributions not available for operating expenses because of limitations imposed by the grantor).

Through enactment of the Postal Reorganization Act in 1970, jurisdiction of the NLRB was extended to the United States Postal Service, effective July 1, 1971.

Source: National Labor Relations Board, *Summary of the National Labor Relations Act* (Washington, D.C.: Government Printing Office, 1971).

Until recently, the NLRB declined to exert jurisdiction over charitable, educational, and other nonprofit enterprises as well as proprietary hospitals and private universities. As the size and nature of these institutions changed, the NLRB decided that the potential impact of disruption at such facilities required it to assume jurisdiction over them. Other areas in which the NLRB has recently assumed jurisdiction are symphony orchestras that have a gross annual revenue from all sources of $1 million or more (except for grants not available for operating expenses) and law firms having a gross annual revenue of at least $250,000. The NLRB continues to refuse jurisdiction over dog racing and horse racing, although it has assumed jurisdiction over casino gambling enterprises.

Section 10(a) of the LMRA permits the NLRB to give its authority to a state or territorial agency operating under a statute not inconsistent with the LMRA. The NLRB has never ceded any of its authority pursuant to this section. The Supreme Court held in *Guss v. Utah* (1957) that Section 10(a) was the only means by which states could act on matters covered by the LMRA. This rule was held to apply even to those cases on which the NLRB declined to assert jurisdiction. This decision created a situation where the NLRB refused to extend its jurisdiction over some types of cases while the parties involved were denied coverage elsewhere.

Congress closed this gap when it recognized the NLRB's discretion to decline jurisdiction over certain categories of cases in Section 14(c)(1) of the 1959 Landrum-Griffin Act. But Congress prohibited the NLRB from narrowing its jurisdiction to a level less than that existing on August 1, 1959, and Section 14(c)(2) empowered states and territories to act on any matter over which the NLRB declines to assert jurisdiction. Acting under Section 14(c)(2), states apply their own law rather than the LMRA and the interpretations developed under it. The states also have complete authority to regulate labor-management relations of employees (except for federal government employees) who are by statutory language exempt from coverage under the LMRA. For example, many states have their own laws pertaining to public-sector labor relations covering employees who work for state or local governments. California has also adopted a comprehensive law governing labor relations in its agricultural industry.

Federal Preemption of State Regulation

Apart from the basic regulatory framework for labor-management relations, a matter of continuing controversy is the relationship of federal law to state law governing the same substantive conduct. Prior to 1935, almost all governmental regulation of labor-management relations was conducted in state court proceedings applying state law. In creating a body of federal law to apply to the field, the Wagner Act raised questions about the effect of its provisions on state law and about the right of the individual states to continue to act on conduct arising in a labor-management context.

The LMRA does not deprive the states of their jurisdiction over labor relations matters specifically. Under the act, the states retain the power and the right to act in certain areas, particularly under Section 14(b), which permits the individual states to enact laws prohibiting the application of union security clauses. The lack of a clear statutory division of power has meant that the Supreme Court has been called upon to delineate the respective authority of the NLRB, the federal courts, and state legislatures, courts, and administrative bodies in regulating labor relations.

The general rule as developed in numerous cases on the issue has two aspects. First, on those matters in which the NLRB has authority to act, the states are preempted, or deprived, of all authority except in limited situations (preemption as to forum). Second, federal law governs all situations where the application of state law would lead to a different result, even when the case is one which can be processed in a state court or agency (preemption as to the law). This assures uniform standards uniformly applied.

The legal basis for federal preemption of state authority to regulate labor-management relations is the supremacy clause in Article VI of the U.S. Constitution, which provides that:

> This Constitution and the Laws of the United States which shall be made in Pursuance thereof . . . shall be the supreme Law of the Land; and the Judges in every State shall be bound thereby, any Thing in the Constitution or Laws of any State to the Contrary notwithstanding.

The practical basis for federal preemption is: (1) the potential for conflict between the substantive provisions of the federal labor law and those contained in state laws; and (2) the potential conflict between the NLRB—the specialized and expert enforcement agency established to administer the federal law—and state enforcement bodies, even if they were to administer the same substantive law.

A 1953 decision articulates most clearly the principles underlying federal preemption of state regulation in labor disputes. In the case, a state court had enjoined picketing by a minority union because it sought to coerce the employer into influencing its employees to join the union. A minority union is one which seeks to act on behalf of a group of employees even though it has not been authorized to do so by the majority of the affected employees. The Supreme Court noted in *Garner v. Teamsters, Local 776* (1953) that the NLRB could entertain an action challenging the legality of the union's conduct and ruled that the State of Pennsylvania, therefore, lacked authority to adjudge the same controversy and extend its own form of relief. In the Supreme Court's words:

> Congress did not merely lay down a substantive rule of law to be enforced by any tribunal competent to apply law generally to the parties. It went on to confide primary interpretation and application of its rules to a specific and specially constituted tribunal and prescribed a particular procedure for investigation, complaint and notice, and hearing and decision, including judicial relief pending a final administrative order. Congress evidently considered that centralized administration of specially designed procedures was necessary to obtain uniform application of its substantive rules and to avoid these diversities and conflicts likely to result from a variety of local procedures and attitudes toward labor controversies.

The other major case establishing the rule of preemption was *San Diego Building Trades Council v. Garmon* (1959). The Court declared that state regulation is preempted when the activities in question are either protected by Section 7 of the LMRA or prohibited as an unfair labor practice under Section 8. Even when a matter is merely "arguably subject" to Section 7 or Section 8, the states as well as the federal courts must defer to the exclusive competence of the NLRB. The NLRB's right to decide the status of particular conduct under the LMRA can be preserved only by prohibiting the states as well as other federal bodies from taking action in such matters, since to allow them to do so would in many instances foreclose the opportunity for the NLRB to consider the activity in question.

Although state regulation of conduct subject to the NLRB's jurisdiction is generally prohibited, the *Garmon* case articulated two exceptions to this rule. One exception applies to conduct that is only a peripheral concern of the LMRA, such as certain disputes arising out of the internal operations of the union. The other applies to conduct touching interests deeply rooted in local responsibilities. As to the latter, the Supreme Court felt that there was no basis to infer that the LMRA stripped the states of their power to preserve law and order. The exercise of a state's constitutionally reserved "police power" and the application of criminal laws are common examples of state regulation of labor-management relations. For instance, state courts may issue injunctions specifying the manner of picketing and the permissible number of otherwise legal pickets to protect both the public and the other employees against violence. And murder or destruction of property is no less a state crime punishable by the state because it occurs in the context of a protected strike. Although the principle of preemption has been affirmed in numerous subsequent cases, others have opened the possibility of states assuming a greater role in regulating labor-management relations, particularly in their incidental aspects.

Structure of the National Labor Relations Board

The present structure of the National Labor Relations Board—fundamentally different from the original one—was adopted as part of the Taft-Hartley amendments to the National Labor Relations Act. The NLRB was initially composed of three members. This body was delegated responsibility for all aspects of representation elections and unfair labor practice proceedings under the Wagner Act. Since 1947, however, the NLRB has been composed of two independent branches, the Board and the General Counsel.

The Board consists of five members appointed by the President of the United States for staggered five-year terms. Any three Board members may act as a panel to make decisions on behalf of the entire Board. The Board is based in Washington, D.C., and its primary function is comparable to that of a judge in the legal system. The Board has final authority to establish the requirements pertaining to NLRB-conducted elections. It also has the responsibility of determining whether particular conduct by an employer or a union violates the law.

A separate and arguably more important office in the NLRB is that of the General Counsel. This officer is also appointed by the President for a term of four years and therefore, in carrying out the responsibilities of the office, is shielded from pressure by the Board. Under Section 3(d) of the LMRA, the General Counsel has final authority over the investigation and prosecution of unfair labor practices. The Board or the courts cannot review a decision of the General Counsel to accept or reject an unfair labor practice complaint. This in effect means that the General Counsel controls the keys to the door of justice. Once a charge is issued, the General Counsel, through a representative, prosecutes the case on behalf of the public against the accused violator of the law.

The General Counsel also supervises the 31 regional offices of the NLRB located throughout the United States. Each of these offices is headed by a regional director and includes attorneys and field examiners. These offices perform the vast bulk of the day-to-day enforcement of the law. Although the five-member Board has ultimate authority in deciding representation issues, it has delegated this responsibility to the regional offices, whose decisions are subject to Board review.

The NLRB also maintains a staff of administrative law judges—formerly called trial examiners—who conduct hearings on unfair labor practice charges. Although initially selected by the Board, these judges are independent officers and cannot be removed except for cause after a Civil Service Commission hearing. Administrative law judges conduct hearings on unfair labor practice cases intitated by the regional offices.

No office within the National Labor Relations Board has the authority to seek out violations of the law on its own. The NLRB becomes involved only when a matter is initiated by some affected private party. This is true of both election and unfair labor practice cases. The procedures are discussed in later chapters.

Key Words and Phrases

commerce	interstate
confidential employee	intrastate
employee	jurisdictional standard
employer	no-man's land
independent contractor	supervisor

Review and Discussion Questions

1. Discuss the source of the congressional power to adopt the National Labor Relations Act and later legislation regulating labor-management relations. Explain the relationship of this power to the individual rights of citizens, including employers, under the Constitution.

2. What reasons might justify the Supreme Court's decision in *Chemical Workers v. Pittsburgh Plate Glass Co.*, ruling that retirees are not employees within the meaning of the Labor Management Relations Act?

3. What effect does the exclusion of supervisors from coverage under the Labor Management Relations Act have on the employees whom they supervise?

4. Discuss the National Labor Relations Board policy establishing dollar standards in volume of business which an employer must exceed before

the National Labor Relations Board will apply the Labor Management Relations Act to that employer.

5. How could the Supreme Court's decision that Congress did not intend the term "employer" to include church-operated schools be changed?

6. Explain both the legal basis and the practical reasons for federal authority to preempt state authority to regulate labor-management relations.

7. Differentiate between preemption as to forum and preemption as to law.

8. What was the doctrine of preemption as developed in the *San Diego Building Trades v. Garmon* case?

3

The Concept of Employee Rights

All of labor management law—the Labor Management Relations Act—in the most basic sense deals with employees' rights. The rights provided in the LMRA are primarily procedural rights—a guarantee by the public that employees have the right to join a union, to collectively bargain about wages, hours, and working conditions, and to engage in concerted activity. The LMRA does not entitle workers to substantive rights in the workplace, *i.e.*, it does not guarantee that any desired levels of actual job conditions and benefits are due a worker who exercises the right to join a union. The legal rights provided in the LMRA are most significant in the context of organizing a union. Although unionized employees have many of the same rights, for them the law is often only a backdrop for rights won and enforced through collective bargaining.

Section 7 of the LMRA is the fountainhead of employees' rights under the law. This provision guarantees:

> Employees shall have the right to self-organization, to form, join, or assist labor organizations, to bargain collectively through representatives of their own choosing, and to engage in other concerted activities for the purpose of collective bargaining or other mutual aid or protection, and shall also have the right to refrain from any or all of such activities except to the extent that such right may be affected by an agreement requiring membership in a labor organization as a condition of employment as authorized in section 8(a)(3).

Fundamentally, the LMRA creates rights for "employees" rather than rights for unions, whose rights derive from those of employees. The enforcement of the rights guaranteed in this section is secured by making it an unfair labor practice for an employer "to interfere with, restrain, or coerce employees in the exercise of the rights guaranteed in Section 7" and by prohibiting several specific

32

forms of employer and union conduct. This chapter focuses on the meaning of the concept "employee rights" and the NLRB's role in securing those rights through its power over unfair labor practices.

The Right To Communicate

One of the most important factors in organizing a union is the ability of those workers who support a union to communicate with co-workers. The right of employees to freely choose or reject a union depends in part on their access to information concerning the union. Generally, the right of employees to communicate with each other and with a union, as guaranteed by Section 7, is balanced against an employer's need for order and for safe and efficient production.

Solicitation. Employers sometimes attempt to prevent all forms of solicitation, including that by unions, on their premises by broad no-solicitation rules. The Supreme Court has found no-solicitation rules to be impermissible, even if the rules have no anti-union purpose and do not actually impair the ability of employees to communicate with each other concerning unionism. In *Republic Aviation Co. v. NLRB* (1945), the Supreme Court found a long-standing rule which applied equally to all forms of solicitation, including that for charitable purposes, to be unlawful because the rule barred employee solicitation on behalf of the union during non-working time. In effect, this decision created a privileged status for communication and oral solicitation concerning unions, including the seeking of signatures on union authorization cards.

Distribution. Rules prohibiting the distribution of literature in work areas even during nonworking time are valid if non-discriminatorily applied. Rules against distribution are justified both on safety reasons—preventing litter in the work areas—and on the basis that distribution of physical materials essentially is different from oral communication. In the opinion of the NLRB, distribution requires only limited contact and can be accomplished outside the work area. Effective solicitation requires more than a momentary contact and cannot as easily be achieved elsewhere. However, rules against distribution which may be valid when applied to work areas ordinarily cannot regulate distribution of materials in nonwork areas, such as the lunchroom.

The Supreme Court recently approved the NLRB's application of the *Republic Aviation* rule to hospitals. The Court found in *Beth Israel Hospital v. NLRB* (1978) that employee solicitation and distribution of union literature must be permitted during nonworking time in nonworking areas unless it can be shown that such activity disrupts health care operations. The hospital had maintained that its ban on solicitation in the hospital cafeteria ought to be upheld because such activity might alarm patients who also had access to the area.

Solicitation by Nonemployees. The legal right of an employee to communicate with other employees concerning a union is greater than that of a union staff representative who does not have employee status. An employer may lawfully restrict the right of a nonemployee to come onto the premises and to engage in solicitation of employees unless such restriction can be shown to interfere with the Section 7 rights of the employees involved. This restriction is partially justified by the fact that nonemployees are unfamiliar with the employer's operations and rules; thus nonemployees are capable of creating problems of security and safety that otherwise are absent when solicitation is conducted by the employees.

The Supreme Court's clearest statement on the range of permissible nonemployee union activity on an employer's premises was made in *NLRB v. Babcock & Wilcox Co.* (1956) in which the Court approved a broad nondiscriminatory rule against nonemployee distribution of literature anywhere on the employer's premises. The Court concluded:

> . . . that an employer may validly post his property against nonemployee distribution of union literature if reasonable efforts by the union through other available channels of communication will enable it to reach employees with its message. . . .

The NLRB has strictly interpreted this standard to allow employers to forbid nonemployee representatives on their premises almost entirely. Employers are required to permit the presence of nonemployee organizers only when circumstances preclude solicitation through other means. Examples are employees who both work and live on the premises or workers on ships.

Wearing Union Buttons. The advertising of union sympathies by wearing a union button is a protected activity. Wearing pins can be restricted only when an employer can demonstrate special adverse circumstances, such as the effect they could have on an employer's business or their interference with the ability of employees to perform their jobs. A rule banning only union buttons is especially suspect but not categorically invalid. The right to wear union buttons is a Section 7 statutory right. It is not based on the right to free speech under the U.S. Constitution, which restricts only governmental regulation of speech.

The Right To Engage in "Concerted" Activities

Section 7 provides that employees have the right to engage in *concerted* activities. Concerted activity clearly includes efforts toward securing union representation or a collective bargaining agreement, signing a union card, promoting the union, participating in many forms of collective action, including strikes, and respecting picket lines. However, the meaning of concerted and the distinction between "protected" and "unprotected" concerted activity have been the basis of numerous cases brought to the NLRB. These cases generally involve an action by the employer taken in response to employee activities. The employer defends its conduct on the grounds that the employee conduct in question was: (1) not concerted and therefore not protected or (2) if concerted, should not be protected because its nature undermines other rights and policies protected by law.

Collective, or concerted, activities lose their protected status if accompanied by serious violence. A strike in violation of a contractual no-strike promise renders participants subject to discipline, since the violation is not considered a protected activity. Slowdowns and quickie strikes are unprotected on the theory that employees should not be paid while depriving an employer of their services. Disparagement of the employer's product or disloyalty toward the employer, even in conjunction with otherwise legal activity, is also unprotected activity. Concerted activity is not protected if it is in conflict with the union's right to act solely and exclusively as the bargaining agent for employees in a unit.

The term concerted implies participation in an activity by two or more employees. However, activity by a single individual is protected even if the employee acts solely on his/her own behalf as long as the goal sought is one shared by fellow employees. For instance, in *Alleluia Cushion Co.* (1975) an employee who was not covered by a contract or represented by a union wrote a letter to a state agency complaining of health and safety conditions at an employer's facility. The employee had not at any time discussed the matter with any fellow employee, but the NLRB found the employee to have engaged in protected concerted activity. The Supreme Court found in *NLRB v. J. Weingarten, Inc.* (1975) that under Section 7 an individual employee also has the right to request union representation during an interview with management which the employee believes might result in disciplinary action.

A union may through collective bargaining lawfully waive the right of its members to exercise certain Section 7 rights. The inclusion of a no-strike promise in a contract, for example, waives the rights of covered employees to strike in regard to matters covered by the contract. However, in *NLRB v. Magnavox Co.* (1974) the Supreme Court distinguished between a waiver of Section 7 rights related to obtaining economic goals and other Section 7 rights going to the very heart of organizing rights. At issue was a contract provision imposing limitations on the rights of employees opposed to the union to engage in the distribution of literature and solicitation activities. The Supreme Court ruled that a union cannot waive these "organizing" rights through collective bargaining. In the same vein, the Supreme Court in *Eastex, Inc. v. NLRB* (1978) approved the NLRB's extension of Section 7 to include union members' right to distribute leaflets at the workplace pertaining to relevant political issues, such as "right-to-work" laws and minimum wage legislation, as well as issues arising directly out of the employer-union relationship.

A union need not be involved in order for employee activity to be protected under the law. In *NLRB v. Washington Aluminum* (1962), the Supreme Court upheld the NLRB's order of reinstatement of seven workers who were fired for leaving their work to protest cold temperatures in their workplace. The workers were not represented by a union and were not involved in any effort to organize one. If the workers had been covered by a contract, their protest might have been considered unprotected activity for failure to follow contract procedure, thereby subjecting them to employer discipline.

The Right To Be Free of Employer Interference, Restraint, and Coercion

The broadest of the prohibitions on employer conduct is that contained in Section 8(a)(1), which forbids an employer "to interfere with, restrain, or coerce employees in the exercise of the rights guaranteed in Section 7." A violation of any other Section 8(a) provision is also a violation of Section 8(a)(1).

A Section 8(a)(1) violation may occur without one of the specific violations. In most cases where an employer is accused of interfering with Section 7 rights of employees, the employer's motive or purpose is irrelevant to the determination of whether the law has been violated. Instead, the NLRB looks to see whether the employer engaged in conduct which tended to interfere with the free exercise of employee rights under the act. The question is not whether the employer intended the result. Moreover, it is not whether the employer's conduct in a particular situation actually interfered with the exercise of rights by particular employees. The Court decided in *Republic Aviation Co. v. NLRB* (1945) that the test is rather whether certain conduct would *tend* to interfere. However, even Section 7 rights of employees are not absolute. Consequently, employer conduct that does interfere with the exercise of those rights is permissible if the employer can show that it is related to a substantial and legitimate interest in the safety and efficiency of its operation.

Surveillance. Free discussion among employees concerning unionism is fundamental to the exercise of Section 7 rights. From its earliest days the NLRB has held both actual or threatened spying on union activities by employers or their agents to be unlawful. The underlying premise is that employees are deterred from free discussion if they know or are led to believe by employer actions that their activity is being reported to the employer. Therefore, both open and secret surveillance, whether isolated instances or part of a larger pattern, is prohibited.

Interrogation. Systematic questioning, or polling, of employees concerning their attitudes toward unions is a violation of employees' Section 7 rights. In *Strucksnes Construction Co.* (1967), the Board established the following safeguards which must be observed:

(1) the purpose of the poll is to determine the truth of a union's claim of majority (not simple curiosity);
(2) that purpose is communicated to the employees;
(3) assurances against reprisals are given;
(4) the employees are polled by secret ballot; and
(5) the employer has not engaged in unfair labor practices or otherwise created a coercive atmosphere.

When departures from these rules are isolated and relatively insignificant given all of the circumstances of the situation, the NLRB will usually not find unlawful interrogation. Courts of appeals, in reviewing the application of the *Struksnes* standard, have often required more—either a showing of anti-union purpose or a showing that questioning was coercive in nature. If an election is pending, the NLRB believes the employer to have no legitimate interest in questioning employees. An election is thought to be a more accurate measure of employee support of the union than is the questioning, where some creation of fear, and therefore interference with free choice, is probably unavoidable.

While systematic questioning is fairly strictly defined, the legality of the interrogation of particular individuals depends on all of the circumstances surrounding the questioning. Relevant factors include the identity of the interrogator, the time and place of questioning, whether the questioning was specific or incidental to a larger conversation, and whether the atmosphere was colored by other unlawful employer activity. It is the employee's perception and not the intent of the employer in the questioning that is decisive. The NLRB more carefully scrutinizes the questioning of job applicants about union sympathies. The Board finds such questioning to be inherently coercive without regard to any other circumstance. An employer also has a limited right to question employees in preparation for a pending unfair labor practice hearing against itself.

The Employer's Right to Free Speech

The LMRA, by statutory language, protects one form of employer conduct that may have a substantial effect on employees in the exercise of Section 7 rights. When confronted with a union organizing campaign, an employer naturally can be expected to make some statement concerning its view of the campaign. Under the Wagner Act, the NLRB interpreted any anti-union communications by an employer to be inherently destructive of employee's rights and imposed a strict requirement of employer neutrality during an election campaign. However, the Supreme Court rejected this absolute view in *NLRB v. Virginia Electric and Power* (1941), because the Court believed a total ban on speech deprived an employer of rights under the First Amendment to the U.S. Constitution.

In the Taft-Hartley Act, Congress included a section guaranteeing the right of employer speech, thereby eliminating the notion that employers ought to be neutral. Section 8(c) protects a wide range of employer speech. For instance, an employer is free to make predictions about the likely effect of unionization on the enterprise, to appeal to employees to vote against a strike, and to ask them to work in spite of a strike. But this section does not protect all employer speech. Employer threats or promises are specifically denied protection, while other speech may be part of a larger pattern of coercive conduct and can therefore form the basis for an unfair labor practice charge against the employer.

Threats of Reprisals or Promises of Benefits. When an employer makes threats of reprisals or promises of benefits based on the outcome of an election, the NLRB will frequently find that the employer has interfered with its employees' exercise of the right to freely choose or reject a union. Such activity also may destroy the "laboratory conditions" which the NLRB requires for conducting a valid election and may be the basis for setting aside election results.

The Board basically prohibits employers from using any economic leverage in the belief that such action is inherently coercive and it is thereby destructive of free choice. The Supreme Court has described an employer's ability to promise or to give economic benefits as the "fist inside a velvet glove." The Court decided in *NLRB v. Exchange Parts* (1964) that such actions of generosity could be interpreted by employees as a demonstration of economic power that could just as easily be used in reprisals. Thus the actual or even promised exercise of economic power can intimidate employees in the exercise of legal rights.

The law does permit an employer to grant a legitimate increase in benefits during an election campaign. In fact, it requires the granting of any benefit that employees have a reasonable right to expect, such as an annual readjustment of wages. The NLRB looks at all factors in a given situation to determine if an increase is legitimate or if it is given to induce employees to vote against the union. In essence, the employer is required to act as it would have acted if no union activity were taking place.

Often there is a fine distinction between a forbidden threat and a lawful prediction of the consequences of unionization. The Supreme Court described the employer's right in *NLRB v. Gissel Packing* (1969) as follows:

> Thus, an employer is free to communicate to his employees any of his general views about unionism or any of his specific views about a particular union, so long as the communications do not contain a "threat of reprisal or force or promise of benefit." He may even make a prediction as to the precise effects he believes unionization will have

on his company. In such a case, however, the prediction must be carefully phrased on the basis of objective fact to convey an employer's belief as to demonstrably probable consequences beyond his control.... If there is any implication that an employer may or may not take action solely on his own initiative for reasons unrelated to economic necessities and known only to him, the statement is no longer a reasonable prediction based on available facts but a threat of retaliation based on misrepresentation and coercion....

It is not possible to compile a list of "permissible predictions," because employer communications may only be illegal in certain situations. The same speech which is in one case a prediction may be considered a threat under different circumstances. Some examples of employer speech which may or may not be considered a violation are statements about

- the impact which unionization will have on a firm's customers.
- the impact on its competitive position in the market.
- the ill effects of strikes on employees.
- the costs of being a union member.
- the loss of existing rights and benefits through collective bargaining.

Employer Liability for Conduct of Others. Only employers can commit unfair labor practices under Section 8(a) prohibitions. The question of what conduct can be attributed to the employer is therefore important, particularly in Section 8(a)(1) cases where a wide range of employer conduct can possibly interfere with employees' Section 7 rights. The law attributes to an employer any acts of an agent who acts under actual formal authority or in a manner creating the appearance of authority. In determining employer liability for the acts of others, the appearance of the conduct in the eyes of the employees is the most significant factor. Supervisory personnel are normally presumed to be acting on behalf of the employer. If supervisors engage in illegal conduct, it is reasonable for employees to assume that they are acting in their role as management representatives. The apparent authority of supervisors to act and speak for the employer can be countered only by an explicit employer statement to the contrary communicated to the affected employees. For instance, a foreman engaging in surveillance is presumed to be acting on behalf of the employer unless the employer clearly disassociates itself from the unlawful activity. In contrast, the employer is not liable for acts of rank-and-file employees unless such activity is authorized or instigated or otherwise ratified by the employer. In some circumstances, the employer may also be held liable for activities of outsiders—such as newspapers and civic leaders who denounce unions. If the employer instigates or cooperates in prohibited activities by outsiders or fails to disavow their efforts adequately, it is considered a party to them.

Curtailment or Shutdown of Operations. Apart from the illegality of threats of shutdown or relocation that accompany many union organizing campaigns, the actual shutdown or relocation to avoid or to escape a union also raises legal issues. The issue was addressed by the Supreme Court in a case involving Deering Milliken, a textile distributor that owned controlling shares in 17 different textile manufacturers operating 27 different mills, including the Darlington Company. After threats that a union victory would result in Darlington's closing, the board of directors voted to sell the company's assets and to go out of business when the union won the election. The NLRB concluded that the entire operation—the distributor and the 17 companies—was really one operation and that the shutdown of Darlington violated the LMRA, even if the company had economic reasons for going out of business.

In its review of *Textile Workers v. Darlington Mfg. Co.* (1965), the Supreme Court held that the legality of the employer's decision turned upon whether the shutdown was a complete or a partial one. The Court held as follows:

> ... that when an employer closes his entire business even if the liquidation is motivated by vindictiveness toward the union, such action is not an unfair labor practice.
> ... (A) partial closing is an unfair labor practice under 8(a)(3) if motivated by a purpose to chill unionism in any of the remaining plants of the single employer and if the employer may reasonably have foreseen that such closing will likely have that effect.

Although the Darlington mill was closed in 1956, the back pay due the 525 terminated workers and their heirs for the employer's unlawful activity was not accomplished until late in 1981. This quarter-century turn of the wheels of justice is a startling illustration of the difference between legal rights and their actual enforcement.

Right To Be Free of Discrimination or Retaliation

The freedom of employees to choose or reject a union requires that employees be protected from discrimination that would encourage them to either support or oppose a union. The LMRA specifically protects employees against employer discrimination and retaliation for the exercise of their Section 7 rights in Section 8(a)(3). These prohibitions against discrimination are limited. They do not protect employees against general forms of discrimination by an employer which may be unlawful under some other law or may simply be unfair in a moral sense. Only when discrimination interferes with the rights protected by the LMRA, will the NLRB consider it a violation of the LMRA. In the words of one court, an employee "may be discharged by the employer for a good reason, a poor reason, or no reason at all, so long as the terms of the statute are not violated." (*NLRB v. Condensor Corp.* (1942)). Section 8(a)(3) protections also apply to applicants for employment and probationary employees, *i.e.,* employees not covered under any applicable collective bargaining agreement.

Discharge of union adherents is the most frequently occurring basis of Section 8(a)(3) charges. But the section covers other forms of differential treatment or employer actions that would not have occurred but for the employee's actual or suspected union activity. The key to proving a Section 8(a)(3) violation is to show anti-union purpose. This differs greatly from Section 8(a)(1) charges, where the resulting effect or the likely effect of employer action is the criterion for finding particular conduct unlawful. Since motive is a central aspect of a violation, an employer must be shown to know of an employee's union activities before it can be found to have the requisite intent to discriminate because of those activities.

When charged with discrimination in violation of the LMRA, an employer often maintains that changes in the employee's status were made for a job-related purpose, such as job performance or attendance, and were therefore permissible. The NLRB has used various tests to determine unlawful conduct if an employer had two motives—a justifiable one and a discriminatory one—in taking action against an employee. One formulation has been whether the employee would have been fired but for the union activity. Another has been that anti-union purpose be the dominant motive, while still others have required only that it contribute to the employer's decision. The Board's present standard in dual-motive discharges requires a showing of evidence sufficient to support an inference that an employee's participation in protected conduct was the motivating factor in the employer's action. The Board found in its *Wright Line* (1980) decision that this showing then shifts the burden to the employer to demonstrate that it would have taken the same action even in the absence of such participation.

Persons found to be discriminatorily discharged or demoted are entitled to lost pay, including all benefits plus interest less any earnings during the period covered. Back pay is computed on a quarterly basis so as not to penalize employees who might have high earnings elsewhere for some part of the period. This system is supposed to prevent an unwarranted bonus to the employer who has engaged in unlawful activity. Nevertheless, employers have little financial incentive to comply with the law. Since economic necessity generally dictates that an unfairly discharged worker seek other employment, the subtraction of other earnings means that even if the employer is found guilty, it may be liable for little or no back pay.

The Right To Be Free of Union Restraint and Coercion

Employees are free to exercise Section 7 rights without interference or coercion by unions as well as by employers. Union restraint or coercion is an unfair labor practice under Section 8(b)(1)(A) of the LMRA. Because a union in an organizing situation has little formal power over employees it is trying to organize and lacks any substantial means of inducing particular employee behavior, the prohibition against union restraint and coercion is less meaningful than that against the employer.

However, the limitation on union conduct does have some applicability to organizing situations and strikes. Since Section 7 includes the right of an employee to decline to exercise any of the rights granted in Section 7, unions sometimes run afoul of Section 8(b)(1)(A) in trying to pressure employees to join a union and support its cause. Thus, for example, the NLRB ruled in its *Carey Corp.* (1949) decision that mass picketing, although entirely peaceful, is unlawful, since it discourages employees who might choose to enter picketed premises from doing so.

Like employer threats, union threats are an unfair labor practice. Promises made by a union, however, are in a different category from those made by employers. The Board believes that employees view union promises as "puffing" and are not induced to vote a certain way because of such promises. Furthermore, the union does not possess any independent ability comparable to the employer's economic power to take action against employees because of the way they voted. Since they cannot be implemented unilaterally and no threats can be implied from them, a wide range of union promises are considered lawful.

The Right To Be Free of an Employer-Dominated or Employer-Supported Union

At the time the Wagner Act was passed in 1935, company unions purposefully created and controlled by the employer to avoid dealing with a legitimate union frustrated employees in the exercise of a free choice in selecting a union. This type of employer conduct is largely a thing of the past. However, Section 8(a)(2), which makes employer domination or interference with the formation or administration of a union unlawful, does have some continued application to modern employer-employee relations. Cases today usually involve the extent to which an employer can lawfully support the legitimate union which represents its employees or employer dealings with a union which has not established that it represents a majority of the employer's employees.

Questions of unlawful assistance have been raised on matters such as permitting the union the profits on vending machines; allowing union use of company telephones, office supplies, and secretarial help; and permitting union representatives to draw their usual pay for time spent in contract negotiations and enforcement. In the past, the NLRB carefully scrutinized such employer conduct. However, today such assistance resulting from an arm's-length relationship is generally considered as desirable employer-union cooperation. For instance, both contract negotiations and contract enforcement by the union are often conducted on employer time. An interesting question on the reach of Section 8(a)(2) is presented by the flourishing growth of employer-initiated worker-participation schemes, such as quality circles.

An employer may lawfully state a preference that its employees join a particular union. Otherwise, an employer is required to maintain strict neutrality as between two or more unions during the process in which employees select one as their representative. This issue particularly arises when competing unions seek to acquire bargaining rights already held by an incumbent union. The NLRB decided in *Midwest Piping and Supply Co., Inc.* (1945) that an employer rendered unlawful assistance when it recognized and bargained with one union after another union had claimed majority support and had filed for a representation election. The Board rejected the employer's defense that it had recognized the union after it had proved majority status by presenting signed authorization cards. The NLRB noted that signatures obtained during the intensity of an organizing campaign—particularly since some employees had signed cards for both unions—were less than a reliable measure of employees' reasoned choice of a representative. In the NLRB's view, this choice can best be made by the conduct of a secret ballot election. The employer's act of recognition of one of two or more competing unions appropriates to the employer a task that the NLRB believes Congress delegated to it.

Union Members as Supervisors. Employer influence in the formulation of union policy is unlawful interference. Although supervisors may retain their union membership for job security or the protection of accrued benefits, their participation in the union's activities is strictly circumscribed by the law. It is unlawful for supervisory members to serve as union officials, to serve on union bargaining and grievance adjustment panels, to vote in union elections, or to vote for convention delegates. That such activities are considered interference is based merely on the supervisor's status and not on the intentions of the supervisor, the knowledge of his/her superiors, or the degree of impact such activity may actually have had.

Unfair Labor Practice Cases

Section 7 of the LMRA is enforced by a set of provisions in the law denoting certain employer and union conduct as unfair labor practices. An unfair labor practice case begins when any person notifies a regional office of the NLRB that he/she desires to file a charge against either a union or an employer. The law contains a six-month statute of limitations—the charge must be filed within six months of the date on which the alleged unlawful conduct took place. Conduct that is of a continuing nature may be the basis of a charge even though more than six months have elapsed.

The case then is assigned to a field examiner or field attorney, whose role is to gather all of the evidence pertinent to the case. Based on the investigation, the field examiner or attorney prepares a report with recommendations. The decision on how to proceed on the charge is made by the regional director. At this point, four different actions may occur: withdrawal, dismissal, settlement, or the issuance of a formal complaint.

The regional office may ask the charging party to withdraw the charge if investigation reveals that the charge lacks merit. The charging party may also initiate a withdrawal request. The regional director must approve any withdrawal. Such approval is customary as long as the regional director feels that the action is not in conflict with the purposes of the law. Once a charge is filed, it officially becomes the property of the NLRB, and no action can be taken on the charge without its permission.

The regional director will dismiss a charge when investigation fails to find sufficient evidence of a violation of the law. Dismissal often results when the complaining party refuses voluntarily to withdraw a charge. A dismissal decision may be appealed within 10 days to the General Counsel. The General Counsel's decision whether to institutue an action against the accused cannot be reviewed. If dismissal is upheld, the case ends. If dismissal is rejected, the regional director must proceed on the charge.

Settlement is attempted on all cases where the investigation shows the charge to have merit. It allows the accused party voluntarily to remedy conduct which appears to be a violation of the law. The majority of unfair labor practice charges are settled on an informal basis. Settlements may be made with the participation and agreement of all parties—the charging party, the charged party, and the regional director. Or the settlement may be a unilateral one—a settlement made without the consent of the charging party if the regional director feels that the settlement corrects the violation or is all that can be obtained given the evidence. If dissatisfied with a settlement, the charging party can appeal the settlement decision within 10 days to the General Counsel of the NLRB. If the complaining party and the accused reach a private settlement of their differences, the settlement must be presented to the NLRB for approval. The regional director is not obligated to approve the settlement but will routinely do so.

If a charge is not disposed of through withdrawal, dismissal, or settlement, then the regional director issues a formal complaint against the accused violator of the law. This complaint is quite similar to an indictment against a person accused of committing a crime. The complaint lists the violations of law which the regional director believes the accused to have committed. The accused must answer the complaint, admitting, denying, or explaining the allegations contained in the complaint within 10 days.

The hearing on the complaint somewhat resembles a criminal trial, with an administrative law judge sitting as a representative of the NLRB. The regional director, represented by an attorney, attempts to prove that the accused has in fact violated the law, as charged in the complaint. The accused has an opportunity to show why he/she is not guilty. The person who filed the charge, or a union representing a worker, or the employer, if the complaint is against the union, will ordinarily be present to give testimony and may even participate in the formal presentation of the case. However, the regional director has the burden of proving the accused guilty. After the hearing, the judge will make a decision, usually several months later, whether the allegations of wrongdoing by the accused have been proved. This decision will state findings of fact, conclusions on the law pertaining to the situation, and a recommended order. If no party files objections to this report, the Board will adopt it as its decision.

The accused, the charging party, and the regional director each may file exceptions to the decision of an administrative law judge with a request for the members of the NLRB to review the decision. If there are objections, the NLRB will review the case. Unless the issues presented are either complex or novel, a three-member panel instead of the entire five-member board will conduct the review. The reviewing panel does not conduct a new hearing or accept new evidence, although by law it could do so. In most cases, there is no an oral argument on the case. Ordinarily, the review is based on written arguments, or briefs, submitted by the parties. This is done basically to conserve time and to enable review of a greater number of cases.

A decision of the NLRB may be appealed to a U.S. circuit court of appeals. In extremely rare cases, the Supreme Court of the United States will agree to review a decision by a court of appeals in an unfair labor practice case. At the point at which no further appeals are made, an order of the NLRB becomes final. However, the NLRB has no enforcement power. If a party fails to comply with an order of the Board, then the NLRB must seek enforcement by asking a U.S. court of appeals to issue an injunction. In this context, the guilty party may challenge the appropriateness of the NLRB order. Generally, reviewing courts respect NLRB decisions and therefore have been willing to grant injunctions. But these courts have in recent years substituted their judgment, particularly in interpreting the law, and have denied enforcement to an increasing number of NLRB orders. Normally, a court order will be obeyed, since the court can compel compliance through its power to hold in contempt, or punish, anyone who violates its orders.

Key Words and Phrases

administrative law judge
Babcock & Wilcox rule
charge
company union
complaint
concerted activities
Darlington Mfg. case
discrimination under the LMRA
dismissal
General Counsel
interrogation
no-distribution rule

no-solicitation rule
Republic Aviation rule
Section 7 rights
Section 8(a)(1)
Section 8(b)(1)
settlement
statute of limitations
Struksnes standard
surveillance
unfair labor practice
withdrawal

Review and Discussion Questions

1. A recent case before the National Labor Relations Board involved an employer who refused to allow the union representing its employees to distribute leaflets supporting candidates for the U.S. Senate and other public offices in nonworking areas during nonworking time. Identify the issues in the case. Predict the NLRB decision as to whether the employer's action was unlawful. State your reasoning.

2. What kinds of discriminatory employer (or union) conduct does the Labor Management Relations Act prohibit? Do you think that the Board's narrow view of discrimination prohibited by the Labor Management Relations Act is correct or reasonable? Why or why not?

3. Do you think that the Labor Management Relations Act provides sufficient financial incentive to deter employers from discriminating against workers on account of their union activities?

4. What is the law concerning the ability of an employer to shut down or cut back operations in order to avoid a union? Do you think that the government should have the power to compel an employer to remain in business? If so, under what circumstances?

5. Do you think it is appropriate for the law to hold an employer accountable for, and even guilty of, unlawful activity even though the employer did not intend to violate the law?

6. Is it possible for one person to engage in protected "concerted" activities? Explain.

7. Why should a union have the right to distribute in the workplace information concerning proposed changes in the minimum wage law, since the employer has no control over whether such changes take place?

8. What is the law concerning the right of a worker to wear a union button on the job?

9. Do you agree that the law should hold an employer responsible for the conduct of third parties, such as newspapers?

10. Do you believe that an employer should have the right to express its views concerning unions? Why or why not?

11. Within what period of time must an unfair labor practice charge be filed? What are some reasons for and against a longer period of time for filing a charge?

12. Do you agree with the policy that an unfair labor practice charge, once filed, becomes the "property" of the National Labor Relations Board, so that the charging party cannot withdraw the charge without the NLRB's permission?

13. Discuss the statutorily defined roles of the National Labor Relations Board and the General Counsel relative to the handling of unfair labor practice charges. Do you think that the General Counsel has too much authority? Why or why not?

14. What kind of enforcement powers does the National Labor Relations Board have? Stated otherwise, what can the Board do to a party found guilty of violating the law? Does this prevent or advance the accomplishment of justice? What other powers might it have?

15. May the employer under any circumstances grant improvements in wages and benefits while a Board representation is pending? Explain.

4

Selecting a Bargaining Representative

One of the major functions of the National Labor Relations Board is to oversee the process by which employees exercise their right to choose or reject a union to represent them. The Labor Management Relations Act delegates authority over representation proceedings to the five-member NLRB, which has in turn delegated the responsibility for day-to-day supervision to the regional directors of the NLRB.

Unions are sometimes organized and accorded representation status, or recognition, without any involvement by the NLRB. However, the overwhelming majority of efforts to organize a union result in a petition for an election. The NLRB is directed to conduct an election whenever presented with a petition raising a question concerning representation. The petition for a representation election may be filed by employees, by a union acting on their behalf, or by an employer. The "question concerning representation" is generally raised when an employer refuses to recognize a union which maintains that a majority of the affected employees have authorized it to act on their behalf. An employer is entitled to file an election petition whenever there has been a demand by a union for recognition.

When a petition for an election is filed either by a union or by employees, a determination of a "showing of interest" is the first step in the regional director's consideration of the petition. The NLRB has a rule requiring that the petition be supported by evidence that at least 30 percent of the employees in the proposed bargaining unit desire the union as their representative. This showing of interest is usually accomplished by cards—called authorization cards—signed by individual workers, empowering the union to act as their collective bargaining representative. (A card cannot be counted in the 30

50

percent if it merely requests the conduct of an election.) In addition to establishing that a question of representation exists, a representative of the regional director investigates the petition to determine whether the NLRB has jurisdiction over the case in terms of the kind of employees or employer involved and in terms of the volume of business of the operation. The investigator must also decide whether the petition meets certain time limit requirements and must determine the acceptability of the scope of the unit for which the union desires representation rights.

Jurisdictional Time Limits

In some circumstances, the NLRB will refuse to conduct elections despite the extent of the interest shown by the affected employees. This policy is based on a belief that too frequent elections could unnecessarily disrupt the employer's business, prevent the maturing of solid collective bargaining relationships, and interfere with stable relationships once they are achieved.

Election Bar Rule. Section 9(c)(3) of the LMRA states:

> ... no election shall be directed in any bargaining unit or any subdivision within which, in the preceding twelve-month period, a valid election shall have been held.

The previous election must have been valid in order to bar a later election. This provision does not bar a new election if the previous election results have been set aside or necessitate a runoff election because no choice received a majority in the first election. It also does not bar an election in a unit larger than the one in which the first election occurred. It does mean that if any union has been unsuccessful in an election, no union can obtain another election for one year. Nor can an employer or employees seek an election within the year.

Certification Bar Rule. Once a union has been certified as a bargaining representative by the NLRB, no challenge to that status can take place within 12 months after the certification. The NLRB developed this rule to allow a union to consolidate its position and to seek to develop a mature collective bargaining relationship with the employer without doubt of its status. This discourages the employer from seeking to erode the union's majority, prevents a raid or takeover attempt by another union, and shields the union from the pressure and frustrations of employees who may expect too much too soon. The certification rule applies regardless of the desires of the affected employees. If an employer refuses to engage in good-faith bargaining, the certification year will not begin to run until good-faith bargaining begins.

Contract Bar Rule. The NLRB has also developed a rule restricting the right to file election petitions during the term of an existing collective bargaining agreement. The purpose of the rule is to minimize the disruption in an ongoing collective bargaining relationship caused by the filing of an election petition by a competing union or by employees seeking to remove the union's bargaining authority. The major aspects of the rule are as follows:

(1) An election petition is untimely if filed during the term of an existing agreement having a definite termination date and covering a period of three years or less.

(2) Contracts of longer, but definite, duration of more than three years will bar elections only during the first three years of the contract if the election is sought by a competing union or by employees wishing to decertify but will bar any election sought by the parties to the agreement for the entire life of the agreement.

(3) If a contract bar applies, a petition can be filed only during an "open period" beginning 90 days prior to and ending 60 days before the contract expires. (Because of the different time periods specified in the statute which apply to health care institutions, the open period is that period between 120 days and 90 days before contract expiration.) The final 60 days prior to expiration are an "insulated period," which allows the parties to engage in collective bargaining free of external pressures. If no new agreement has been concluded after the contract expires, than an election petition is timely. The contract bar rule will again become effective as soon as a new agreement is executed.

There are some special circumstances in which an election petition is timely even though a valid contract is in effect. These include contracts of indefinite duration, since these do not assure the stability that the contract bar rule is designed to protect. To bar an election a contract must be a written one and must cover substantially all aspects of the employees' relationship to their employer—wages, hours, and conditions. Another situation in which elections are not barred is when the nature and the size of the employer have changed. Schisms within a union or the failure of a union to engage in any normal union activities may also be the basis for an election petition despite an existing contract.

Blocking. The NLRB, as a general rule, also declines to direct elections in a situation where unfair labor practice charges are pending unless the charging party requests the NLRB to proceed with the election. This rule is a discretionary one on the part of the NLRB and derives from its concept that laboratory conditions are necessary for the exercise of free choice. The theory is that if the unfair labor practice charges are later proved to be true, the illegal conduct on which they are based might interfere with the laboratory conditions. The NLRB's declining to proceed is called "blocking." The charging party's request to proceed is referred to as a request to "unblock." The NLRB may direct an election without a request to unblock where particular circumstances outweigh the need to resolve the pending charges.

Defining the Appropriate Bargaining Unit

Another of the decisions made by the NLRB in considering a petition for an election is the makeup of the unit for which the election is proposed. The LMRA provides for collective bargaining in a unit "appropriate for such purposes." An employer and a union that has organized a majority of a particular group of the employer's employees may voluntarily agree on the contours of the unit which the union is to represent. If there is a dispute, however, as to which employees should be included, the NLRB by statute has the authority to decide the appropriateness of a unit.

The definition of the unit is frequently a critical factor in the success of a union organizing campaign. For instance, a large unit comprised of geographically separated workers of varying skills and conditions and differing levels of interest in a union may be very difficult to organize. Smaller segments of the unit which do desire a union may thereby be denied the opportunity to organize because they are not a majority of the entire unit.

The Wagner Act empowered the NLRB with unrestricted discretion to determine the appropriateness of a bargaining unit. However, the Taft-Hartley Act directs the NLRB to establish units in such a manner as "to assure the fullest freedom in exercising the rights guaranteed by this Act." In addition, Taft-Hartley includes some specific restrictions on the NLRB's authority to define bargaining units. These restrictions, contained in Sections 9(b) and 9(c)(5), deny the NLRB authority to decide:

(1) That a unit containing both professional employees and other employees is appropriate unless a majority of the professionals vote for inclusion in such a unit.

(2) That a craft unit is inappropriate on the ground that a different unit has been established by a prior NLRB determination.

(3) That a unit containing both guards and other employees is appropriate. Furthermore, a union representing guards cannot admit to membership other employees, nor can it be affiliated with an organization which directly or indirectly admits other employees to membership.

(4) That in deciding whether a unit is appropriate, the extent to which employees have been organized shall not be controlling.

Outside of these statutory restrictions, the Board has the authority to establish general rules defining the appropriate unit for certain categories of cases. In deciding "appropriateness," it uses several tests and makes the determination on a case-by-case basis. In deciding whether a particular unit is appropriate, the NLRB ordinarily applies a "community of interest" standard. The basis of this standard is to group together workers who share a unity of economic interests and to exclude those with a conflicting economic interest. Using this standard, the NLRB decides, for instance, whether craft, technical, maintenance, semi-skilled, unskilled, and clerical workers belong in the same or separate units or whether a unit ought to include only workers in a single facility, or other, or all employees of the particular employer. A bargaining unit is made up of jobs rather than particular individuals who hold certain jobs.

In deciding whether there is a community of interest among a group of employees, the NLRB considers the following factors:

(1) Similarity of kind of work performed;

(2) Similarity in the qualifications, skills, and training of the employees;

(3) Continuity and integration of the production process;

(4) Common supervision and determination of labor relations policy;

(5) Geographical proximity;

(6) Desires of the affected employees;

(7) Extent of union organization; and

(8) History of collective bargaining.

The Board may use any or all of these as well as others in making a determination of unit boundaries. By statute the Board is forbidden, however, to rely exclusively on the extent of union organization. Using these guidelines, the NLRB could analyze a group of employees and delineate several different appropriate units. However, the NLRB is directed merely to determine an "appropriate" unit. This does not require it to decide the *most* appropriate of several acceptable alternatives. Thus its decision is binding despite preferences by the parties for alternative, appropriate units.

Upon petition, the NLRB through its regional offices will conduct unit clarification proceedings. Such proceedings can take place both for units initially established by the NLRB and for units informally agreed upon by the union and the employer. Either an employer or a union may file petitions for clarification. These become necessary when disputes arise as to whether an existing unit includes certain employees. This problem may arise when new jobs are created or when the employer acquires other operations. The criteria used in unit clarification are the same as those used in deciding the appropriateness of units in the first instance.

Craft Units. A craftworker is one who performs specialized work usually requiring a high level of skill and who may be employed in a variety of employment situations. For example, an electrician may work in construction, in a manufacturing plant, in a hospital, or even in public employment. Under the Wagner Act, the NLRB had unrestricted discretion to establish bargaining units along lines that would best effectuate the process of collective bargaining. During the period the Wagner Act was in effect, conflict between craft unions and industrial unions was a continuing source of controversy. The American Federation of Labor (AFL), consisting primarily of craft-based unions, regularly accused the NLRB of showing favoritism to industrial units proposed by unions in the Congress of Industrial Organizations (CIO).

The Taft-Hartley Act included the restriction that the NLRB may not:

> ... decide that any craft unit is inappropriate for such purposes on the ground that a different unit has been established by a prior Board determination, unless a majority of the employees in the proposed craft unit vote against separate representation.

This provision as presently interpreted by the NLRB does not give craft workers an absolute right to vote in a self-determination election to decide whether to separate themselves from an industrial unit. In its decision regarding *Mallinckrodt Chemical Works* (1966), the NLRB listed some factors it considers in each case brought before it on this issue. These are as follows:

(1) The status of the employees as craftspeople working at their craft or of employees in a traditionally distinct department;
(2) The existing patterns of bargaining relationships, their stabilizing effects, and the possible effect of altering them;
(3) The separate identity of the employees within the unit;
(4) The history and pattern of bargaining within the industry;
(5) The degree of integration and interdependence of the production system; and
(6) The qualification and experience of the union seeking to represent the employees.

In a recent case on the issue of separate craft units within industrial workplaces, craftworkers in the rubber industry attempted to leave the industrial unit and form their own unit. The NLRB refused to approve a separate craft unit in *Firestone Tire and Rubber Co.* (1976) because of the highly integrated nature of the employer's operation and the likely disruptive effect of a severance on the employer's operation. Severance has been permitted, however, when the interests of craftworkers are likely to be more effectively served to a degree that justifies the resulting disruption for the industrial unit and the employer.

Plant Guards. Under the Wagner Act, plant guards enjoyed the full protection of the law. Other than a requirement that guards be organized into a separate unit, guards were free to select any union they desired to represent them, including one which held bargaining rights for other employees. A provision of the Taft-Hartley Act restricted this right. Although guards still enjoy the protection of the law, the NLRB may certify a guard union only if it has no affiliation or connection with any union which represents any nonguard employees anywhere. Even affiliation with the AFL-CIO is denied to guard unions, since the federation's members include unions which represent workers other than guards. The NLRB decides whether a worker is a guard based on whether he/she enforces rules against other employees and the public to protect the employer's property or premises.

Multi-Employer Units. Multi-employer collective bargaining occurs when employers in the same industry join together and bargain as a group with a union or a group of unions that represent employees of each of the employers. For instance, the dominant pattern in the steel, trucking, and coal industries is one of national multi-employer bargaining. The pattern in construction is one of area multi-employer bargaining. Such bargaining is less expensive for all parties and promotes uniform standards and stability within an industry. In the construction industry where employment of any particular group of employees is not of long duration, multi-employer bargaining eliminates the necessity of frequent bargaining.

Multi-employer collective bargaining is not explicitly authorized by the LMRA. Lacking explicit authority to define larger than employer-wide units, the Board approves multi-employer units only if all parties consent to bargain on a multi-employer basis. A substantial history of bargaining on a multi-employer basis is considered as evidence of consent. An employer who has not participated in the bargaining process cannot by merely adopting a group contract be considered to belong to a multi-employer group.

To prevent disruptions to the bargaining process, the NLRB has developed the following guidelines governing the withdrawal of both employers and unions from multi-employer bargaining units:

- A withdrawal must be complete and must be announced prior to the beginning of contract negotiations.
- Before bargaining begins, a union may withdraw with respect to one or more employers in a multiemployer unit while continuing to bargain with other employers in the multi-employer unit.
- An employer can withdraw even after bargaining begins if both the union and the employer association consent thereto.
- A party is not in any way required to justify a decision to withdraw—it is an absolute right as long as it is unequivocal and is made before bargaining begins.
- An untimely withdrawal is basis for a refusal to bargain charge regardless of the intent in withdrawing.

Companywide Bargaining. A union which has not been certified or recognized in a companywide unit cannot insist on companywide bargaining. A union lawfully can insist, however, that contracts covering different units manufacturing the same product have a common expiration date. Such a demand is ultimately related to a union's ability to protect the interests of its members, since it prevents an employer's shuffling struck work to other units to avoid the impact of a strike. A union can even base its demands on a contract already concluded elsewhere. What must be avoided is the appearance or inference that a union representing one particular group of employees is trying to bargain on behalf of other employees at the same time.

Coordinated or Coalition Bargaining. An employer may have employees represented by several different unions. Different unions may even coexist within the same facility. Because of the ability of employers—particularly large scale enterprises that have operations in various parts of the country—to play unions off against each other, unions have sought to coordinate their bargaining efforts with such employers. Since its decision in *General Electric Co.* (1968), the NLRB has permitted a union to include as observers representatives of other unions on its contract negotiations committee.

As employers consolidate themselves into larger enterprises having virtual control of an entire or even several industries, the necessity for unions to find new methods of bargaining increases. Coalitions of all unions representing an employer's employees is one method. This is presently taking place among unions in the United States, and the increasingly multi-national character of many employers has created an incentive for unions to more closely work with unions in other countries which represent employees of the same employer. Coordinated bargaining—unlike multi-employer bargaining—does not mean unit consolidation.

Voter Eligibility

After determining the appropriateness of a bargaining unit in terms of the jobs it includes, the Board must decide which employees can vote in an NLRB-conducted election. Generally, any employee who holds a full-time position in the bargaining unit and who is on the employer's payroll both at the end of the payroll period preceding the election and on the date of the election is eligible to vote in a representation election. Additionally, employees who have a "reasonable expectation of reemployment or continued employment," such as those on temporary layoff, sick leave, leave of absence, or probationary status, are ordinarily eligible to vote.

A special rule applies to economic strikers who at the time of an election have been permanently replaced. This issue will arise only where a union has already established bargaining rights for a unit but is experiencing a challenge to its status. Section 9(c)(3) of the LMRA provides:

> . . . employees engaged in an economic strike who are not entitled to reinstatement shall be eligible to vote under such regulations as the Board shall find are consistent with the purposes and provisions of this Act in any election conducted within twelve months after the commencement of the strike. . . .

The present NLRB rule permits voting by permanently replaced employees who on the date of the election have been engaged in an economic strike for not more than 12 months. (The law does not permit permanent replacement of employees striking in protest of an employer's unfair labor practices. Such strikers are entitled to vote without regard to the length of a strike, and their replacements are not at any time entitled to vote.) If an employer has for legitimate business reasons discharged an economic striker or terminated that employee's position or if the striking employee has accepted other employment under conditions that tend to show abandonment of any interest in the struck job, that employee will not be permitted to vote even within the 12-month period. Strikers who have not been permanently replaced and who have not abandoned their interest in their job and whose work has not been permanently abolished can vote in any election regardless of the date held. Any employee hired as a permanent replacement for an economic striker has immediate voting rights, provided the other eligibility requirements are met and irrespective of whether the replaced striker can vote. Since economic strikers lose voting rights after 12 months, employers sometimes use long economic strikes to unload the union representing the striking employees by hiring replacements and forcing an election in which only the replacements can vote.

Excelsior List. A list of names and addresses of all employees in a bargaining unit who are eligible to vote in any NLRB election is called an *Excelsior* list. The employer must submit the list to the regional director within seven days after an election is ordered. The NLRB then makes the list available to all parties in the case. The Board ruled in *Excelsior Underwear Co.* (1966) that an employer's failure to supply the list is a sufficient basis for setting aside an election.

The purpose of an *Excelsior* list is to facilitate communication between the union and the employees, since the union has less opportunity to provide information to employees than does the employer.

The list also permits an opportunity for disputes about the eligibility of particular employees to be resolved prior to the election, thereby averting some challenges to the election's validity.

The Election Procedure

If a petition meets the NLRB's jurisdictional requirements, the regional office encourages the parties to make a *consent election* agreement in which they agree to the date, place, and eligibility of voters. If agreement cannot be achieved, a formal hearing is conducted by a member of the regional office staff. (These hearing officers should not be confused with administrative law judges, who sit in place of the NLRB on unfair labor practice charges.) In this hearing, evidence on the disputed matters, such as jurisdiction or the appropriateness of the proposed bargaining unit, is presented. A member of the regional office then analyzes the issues and the evidence presented in the hearing and makes a report to the regional director, who decides whether and on what basis an election is to be held. One of the more serious flaws in the LMRA is the extent to which an employer may delay the scheduling of an election by forcing a hearing on numerous points.

In cases raising new issues, the regional director may decline to make the decision and may transmit the case to the Board for a decision. If the regional director makes the decision, any party may request that the NLRB review it. Review is granted only under the following limited circumstances:

(1) That a substantial question of law or policy is raised because of the absence of, or a departure from, officially reported NLRB precedent.
(2) That the regional director's decision on a substantial factual issue is clearly erroneous on the record, and such error prejudicially affects the rights of the parties.
(3) That the conduct of the hearing or any ruling made in connection with the proceeding has resulted in prejudicial error.
(4) That there are compelling reasons for reconsideration of an important NLRB rule or policy.

It is virtually impossible for a union to obtain a judicial review of NLRB decisions on pre-election questions. However, after a union has won an election, an employer can challenge the NLRB's decision on pre-election issues by refusing to bargain with the union. If charged with an unfair labor practice, the employer then asserts the error of the NLRB as a defense. An unfair labor practice finding by the NLRB can then be reviewed by the courts, and thereby the underlying election issue can be presented for review.

Representation elections are conducted by secret ballot under the supervision of regional office agents. Elections usually take place at the employer's premises but may be held elsewhere and in some cases may be accomplished by a mail ballot. Each party may designate an equal number of observers to oversee the conduct of the election and may challenge the vote of any person whose eligibility is in question. The observer is also to note any conduct which is in conflict with NLRB rules or which might interfere with the exercise of free choice by the voters. No promotional activities are permitted at the site of the election.

Challenges to a voter's eligibility must be made before a ballot is marked. A challenge may be made by either the NLRB agent or an official observer. A challenged ballot is placed in an envelope on which the reason for the challenge is specified. Challenged ballots are not counted until all other ballots are counted. If the challenged ballots are too few to change the outcome, they are discarded. But if they could affect the outcome, the regional director must determine the validity of each challenged ballot.

At the conclusion of the voting, the NLRB agent, in the presence of the observers, counts the ballots and serves a tally on each of the parties. Any party may, within five days of the service of the vote tally, file objections to the manner in which the election was conducted or to campaign conduct which destroyed the "laboratory conditions" that the Board requires.

The regional director investigates objections to determine if they are supported by evidence and if they raise substantial and material issues. A formal hearing to develop evidence supporting the objections may be conducted. A decision is then made by the regional director whether to certify the results or to set aside the election. This decision is in some, but not all, circumstances appealable to the NLRB.

If there are no objections or if objections are found to be without merit, a union which receives the majority of the *votes cast* will be certified as the bargaining representative of the unit covered by the election. If more than one union is involved in an election and there is no majority for either union nor for no representation, then a runoff election will be conducted, allowing employees to choose between the two choices receiving the highest number of votes in the first election.

Challenges to a Union's Status

Sometimes a union which has won a representation election will have its right to be certified under the law challenged because of its past activities, such as corruption. Generally, the NLRB, in a certification proceeding, will not entertain charges made against the character and the policies of the union seeking certification. The Board believes that should wrongdoing occur ample remedies exist—such as decertification and unfair labor practice proceedings—to deal with the union that abuses its responsibilities to a particular unit of members. To investigate such charges based on a union's past record would likely delay the certification process in many cases while seldom resulting in any change in the union's status in the particular case.

A short-term departure from this policy in the NLRB's decision regarding *Bekins Moving & Storage Co.* (1974) involved denial of certification to a union that engaged in discrimination on the basis of race, citizenship, or national origin. After a change in the Board's makeup, this policy was overruled in *Handy Andy, Inc.* (1977).

Decertification Elections. A decertification election is conducted by the NLRB when at least 30 percent of the employees in the bargaining unit petition for such an election. An employer is not permitted to file or even to instigate a decertification petition. To remove a union's bargaining rights, a decertification election is required whether the union initially won bargaining rights through NLRB processes or was voluntarily recognized by the employer. Both the certification bar rule and the contract bar rule apply to decertification elections, as do other rules pertaining to the conduct of representation elections.

Deauthorization Elections. Deauthorization elections are conducted by the NLRB to ascertain whether employees desire to revoke a union security agreement that requires membership in the union or the payment of money to the union as a condition of continued employment. By statutory language, petitions for deauthorization must be supported by a showing of interest of at least 30 percent of the employees in a unit. Deauthorization is achieved only if a majority of those in the unit eligible to vote actually vote to rescind the union's authority.

Assuring "Free Choice"

In conducting an election, the NLRB seeks to insulate the voting employee from conduct of the employer and/or union that would interfere with the employee's right to freely choose or reject representation by a union. To protect an employee's free choice, the Board requires "laboratory conditions" from the time an election is scheduled until it is concluded. This concept was announced in *General Shoe Corp.* (1948), a case which involved (1) an anti-union speech delivered to groups of employees in the office of the company president and (2) supervisors who visited employees in their homes to dissuade them from voting for the union. In finding that this speech went beyond acceptable campaign conduct, the NLRB declared:

> In election proceedings, it is the board's function to provide a laboratory in which an experiment may be conducted, under conditions as nearly ideal as possible to determine the uninhibited desires of the employees.... When, in the rare extreme case, the standard drops too low, because of our fault or that of others, the requisite laboratory conditions are not present and the experiment must be conducted over again.

This principle was affirmed and strengthened by the NLRB when it ruled in *Dal-Tex Optical Co.* (1962) that any pre-election conduct that is an unfair labor practice under 8(a)(1) necessarily interferes with the "laboratory conditions" and is a basis for setting aside election results. Speech that cannot be used as grounds for an unfair labor practice charge may still interfere with the free choice of the employees and thus be the basis for setting aside election results.

Captive Audiences. Pursuant to the "free speech" right provided in Section 8(c), an employer has a right to gather employees together to discuss its views concerning unions. The ability of an employer to use clock time for such purposes ensures an audience for its views and guarantees employee access to this viewpoint. A union has no equivalent right or ability to assemble employees and present its story, and in fact may be denied effective access to employees by a valid no-solicitation/no-distribution rule that prevents organizational activity on company property by anyone except employees. In *NLRB v. United Steelworkers of America* (1957), the Supreme Court found that it is not an unfair labor practice for an employer to apply a solicitation ban to a union but not to itself.

A union is permitted equal time only where (1) the NLRB approves an employer rule against any solicitation on behalf of the union, even by employees during their working time (such as in a retail store) *and* (2) where an employer has made its views known to a captive audience. In the face of massive employer unfair labor practices, the NLRB on occasion has ordered an employer to permit the union to address all of the employer's employees as a way of remedying the employer's unlawful activity.

The *Peerless Plywood Co.* (1953) decision formulated the single restriction applying to captive audience speech. The 24-hour rule prohibits both employers and unions from making captive audience speeches on company time and premises within the 24-hour period preceding an election. A violation of this rule is a sufficient basis to set aside an election victory by the party that violated the rule. This rule does not prohibit other forms of speech, such as the distribution of literature or communications in which an employee voluntarily participates, during the 24-hour period.

Misrepresentations. The intensity of election campaigns frequently leads to statements by employers and unions that contain factually inaccurate information. An example might be a statement by the union on the extent of an employer's profits or a statement by the employer concerning how much it costs to be a union member. This kind of conduct could be an unfair labor practice if it misleads or confuses employees, or it could merely destroy the laboratory conditions without qualifying as an unfair labor practice. The NLRB does not automatically set aside any election in which misrepresentation of facts occurs. Some exaggeration and overstatement is considered a normal incident to the election process. Objections to elections which allege misrepresentation by the winning party are considered on a case-by-case basis.

For many years, the NLRB followed the rule developed in *Hollywood Ceramics Co.* (1962) to set aside an election if the prevailing party misrepresented a material fact within its special knowledge so shortly before an election that the other party did not have time to verify it and the employees were not in a position to know the truth or the falsity of the fact asserted. Other aspects of the rule were that the statement had to substantially depart from the truth, that no intent to deceive need be shown, and that actual special knowledge was unnecessary as long as the employees perceived a matter to be within the purview of the person making the statement. The actual impact on employee choice was irrelevant.

This strict regulation of campaign speech was criticized as unnecessarily increasing the NLRB's workload with little evidence that such misrepresentations affected the outcome of elections. In 1977, the NLRB discarded the rule in *Shopping Kart Food Market* (1977), announcing that it would no longer probe into the truth or falsity of parties' campaign statements. The case involved an election eve speech by a union representative stating that the employer had enjoyed profits of $500,000 during the past year when, in fact, the employer had profits of approximately $50,000. The NLRB explained that while its previous regulation had sought to ensure employee free choice, it had in fact impeded the attainment of that goal (1) by requiring extensive analysis of campaign propaganda, (2) by restricting free speech, (3) by the varying applications of the rule by the NLRB and the reviewing courts, (4) by increasing litigation, and (5) by decreasing finality in election results. Despite all of these administrative problems, the NLRB asserted that it would have retained the rule if there had been any evidence that employees actually needed "protection" against misrepresentation. The NLRB declared that it refused to assume that employees are naive and unworldly enough to permit their choice on an issue as critical as that of union representation to be altered by the obviously self-serving campaign statements of the parties.

The policy change was a controversial one, however, and was not supported by the entire NLRB. Subsequently, the NLRB in a 1978 decision, *General Knit of California, Inc.*, readopted the *Hollywood Ceramics* rule. More recently, a new Board majority ruled in *Midland National Life Insurance Co.* (1982) that deceptive tactics will not invalidate an election even if the other side has no opportunity to set the record straight. The only exception that will be recognized to this rule is forgery of a document. The flip-flop on this rule and the rationale behind the competing views is an excellent illustration of differing views of the role of the NLRB in representation proceedings.

Appeals to Racial Hostilities. Electioneering conducted by either an employer or a union that appeals to the racial hostilities of employees is in some circumstances considered an interference with the requisite laboratory conditions. The NLRB set aside an election in *Sewell Mfg. Co.* (1962) without finding any unfair labor practice where an employer in rural Georgia distributed copies of newspaper stories and pictures emphasizing the pro-black activities of some unions and asserting that unionization would require race-mixing.

The NLRB admitted that accurate statements about a union's position on race issues might be relevant to employees' choice and ought to be lawful speech. However, it ruled that appeals seeking to exacerbate racial feelings by irrelevant and inflammatory statements that displace the ability to reason should be grounds for setting aside an election. The NLRB occasionally continues to apply this decision to overturn election results, but a wide range of election speech focusing on race is tolerated. A specific example is an appeal to racial pride based on the assertion that unionism can bring economic benefits and security to black workers. Some racial appeals continue to be grounds for an unfair labor practice charge; for example, those accompanied by threats or promises. Such situations should not be confused with the conduct in *Sewell* and like cases that merely interferes with the laboratory conditions the NLRB believes necessary for free choice.

Union Interference. The Board views any form of payment to employees by a union before an election or a promise of special treatment to employees who join the union before the election as an unlawful attempt to buy loyalty and votes. Waivers of initiation fees to employees who join the union prior to the election while charging those who join afterward is also a violation. The Supreme Court has compared such a waiver to a grant of benefits by an employer. The Court found in *NLRB v. Savair Mfg. Co.* (1973) that a waiver interfered with employee free choice since taking advantage of the waiver would make employees feel obligated to support the union when they voted. The court did not decide whether the union's activity constituted an unfair labor practice. A union may waive or reduce initiation fees for all employees who join the union before the first contract is negotiated. The Board believes this eliminates the pressure to join a union before an election and therefore does not interfere with free choice.

Recognition Without an Election

An employer may, when presented with proof that a union represents a majority of its employees, voluntarily recognize the union and negotiate a contract without an election. In a 1969 case, *NLRB v. Gissel Packing Co.*, the Supreme Court considered whether an employer can be compelled by law to bargain with a union that has established a majority status by authorization cards but has not won a representation election. In *Gissel*, the union had demanded recognition based on authorization cards from a majority of the employees in the unit. The employer refused on the ground that authorization cards were inherently unreliable. At the same time the employer conducted a vigorous antiunion campaign. The union did not ask for an election but instead filed unfair labor practice charges including a refusal to bargain with the union. The NLRB ordered the employer to bargain with the union based on the card majority because the employer's own conduct interfered with election processes and tended to preclude a fair election. The Supreme Court approved this imposition of a bargaining order on an employer who refuses to give union recognition based on card majority while simultaneously committing serious or extensive unfair labor practices that undermine the union's majority status and impede the election process. This principle was later applied to cases where the union had actually lost an election after establishing its majority status via authorization cards. However, the *Gissel* remedy is not available in every case where organizational efforts are thwarted by an employer's unfair labor practices. It applies only in cases where the employer's conduct makes the holding of any election, including a rerun, an inadequate measure of true employee sentiment free of the taint of illegal conduct.

To support the issuance of a bargaining order, the employer's unfair labor practices must be more than a simple refusal to bargain. The Supreme Court ruled in *Linden Lumber v. NLRB* (1974) that it is not unlawful for an employer to refuse recognition to a union claiming a card majority even if the employer refuses to petition for an election to determine the union's representative status. On the other hand, in *Steel-Fab, Inc.* (1974) the Board decided that a refusal-to-bargain violation is unnecessary to secure a *Gissel* order, if

---

Key Words and Phrases

authorization card	employer speech right
bargaining unit	*Excelsior* list
blocking	*Gissel* order
captive audience	*Hollywood Ceramics* rule
certification bar rule	"laboratory conditions"
consent election	*Mallinckrodt* decision
contract bar rule	*Peerless Plywood* rule
craft employee	professional employee
deauthorization election	representation election
decertification election	self-determination election
election bar rule	30 percent showing

the order is required to remedy other unfair labor practices by the employer that are so serious as to make a fair election an unlikely possibility. However, an employer who rejects bargaining based on a card majority but commits itself to be bound by a process other than an election—polling, for example—cannot later disavow that process if it produces an unfavorable result. Such a disavowal would be an appropriate reason for the NLRB to issue an order to bargain.

Review and Discussion Questions

1. Defend the National Labor Relations Board's policy of conducting an election when only 30 percent—substantially less than a majority—of affected employees have indicated a desire to be represented by a union.

2. Explain why Board elections are unavailable at certain times even though most affected employees desire to vote in such an election.

3. What is the significance of the NLRB's authority to define "units" appropriate for the purpose of bargaining?

4. Do you agree with the National Labor Relations Board's decision in *Firestone Tire and Rubber Co.* (1976) refusing to sever craftworkers in the rubber industry from the general unit and permit them to establish their own unit? What do you think of the argument of the craftworkers that they would be able to secure a better contract for themselves, since their interests as a small group would not be traded off in the interests of the majority of the larger unit?

5. What reasons might be offered to justify the Labor Management Relations Act statutorily giving "professional" workers the right to be excluded from a general bargaining unit? Are those reasons as compelling in 1979 as they were in 1947, when the Labor Management Relations Act was adopted?

6. Why should economic strikers who have been permanently replaced not be permitted to vote in an election occurring more than 12 months after the strike began?

7. Do you believe that misrepresentation of the facts by either an employer or a union should be the basis for setting aside a Board election? Why or why not?

8. Should the National Labor Relations Board have the authority to order an employer to recognize and bargain with a union if the union has not established its majority status in a representation election? Explain.

5

The Nature of Collective Bargaining

Collective bargaining is the process by which workers participate in making the decisions that affect their work lives. Through collective bargaining, workers, represented by their union, are able to impose restraints upon the otherwise largely unrestrained authority of management to make decisions regarding conditions of work. The very obligation to recognize a union and to bargain is in an absolute sense a restriction on the employer's "management rights." Public law has imposed this limitation. Furthermore, the heart of collective bargaining is that management must share some of its previously exclusive decision-making authority and must participate in a joint determination of "wages, hours, and other conditions" of employment.

The collective bargaining process typically results in a collective bargaining agreement, generally referred to as a "contract." The contract, almost always a written document, binds both parties to specified rules on which they have mutually agreed for a set period of time. These rules cover a wide variety of issues, such as rates of pay, pension benefits, procedures for layoffs, rights of the union and management, and methods for resolving disputes over the meaning of contract language. In a sense, collective bargaining is a form of lawmaking, wherein the rules embodied in the contract are the laws that govern the workplace.

Prior to the Wagner Act, workers could participate in this decisionmaking concerning their work lives only through the threat or the use of economic action, such as a strike, against an employer. The Wagner Act imposed a legal obligation to bargain on the employer and thereby substituted, or at least added, legal compulsion to the resources of workers seeking to bargain with their employer.

The bargaining duty of employers and unions is described in Section 8(d) of the Labor Management Relations Act (LMRA):

> ... to bargain collectively is the performance of the mutual obligation of the employer and the representatives of the employees to meet at reasonable times and *confer in good faith* with respect to wages, hours and other terms and conditions of employment, on the negotiation of an agreement, on any question arising thereunder, ... but such obligation *does not compel either party to agree to a proposal or to require the making of a concession* ... (Emphasis added.)

In addition to defining the duty to bargain, Section 8(d) also contains detailed procedural notice requirements that must be met when a party seeks to "terminate or modify" a contract. Failure to abide by these requirements is not a basis for a refusal-to-bargain charge, but employees who engage in a strike in violation of these requirements lose their status as employees under the law and therefore all of their protection and rights under the LMRA.

One of the employer practices defined as an unfair labor practice by the Wagner Act in Section 8(a)(5) was "to refuse to bargain collectively with the representatives of his employees with respect to rates of pay, wages, hours of employment or other conditions of employment." This provision imposed upon an employer the obligation to bargain and made failure to do so a violation of the law. It did not, however, impose a reciprocal obligation on unions. The Taft-Hartley Act shifted the emphasis of federal labor policy from one of protecting the rights of employees to organize unions to one of umpiring disputes between two competing forces assumed to be of relatively stable and equal strength. Consequently, it imposed upon a union an obligation to bargain collectively with an employer whose employees it represents. The failure to do so was defined as a union unfair labor practice in Section 8(b)(3): "It shall be an unfair labor practice for a union ... to refuse to bargain collectively with an employer, provided it is the representative of his employees subject to the provisions of section 9(a). ..."

The duty to bargain applies to every decision that affects "wages, hours, [and] terms and conditions" of employment. This means that the duty to bargain applies not just to negotiations for a contract but continues throughout the term of the contract. For example, if an employer wants to change the work schedule during the term of a contract, then the duty to bargain applies. If the employer makes a unilateral decision—a decision made without bargaining—in changing the schedule, the union can file an unfair labor practice charge. Such a change would ordinarily be a violation of a substantive contract provision as well as of the procedural right to bargain. A union would typically seek correction of the violation through the contract procedure instead of going to the National Labor Relations Board (NLRB) with an unfair labor practice charge. This course would be followed because the NLRB does not as a rule have the authority to condemn the substantive decision of the employer, whereas the decisionmaker under the contract does have such power. The duty to bargain also requires compliance with the grievance/arbitration procedure or any contractually established method for dispute settlement.

In enacting the Wagner and Taft-Hartley Acts, Congress did no more than erect a skeleton—a bare framework of the manner in which it believed collective bargaining ought to take place. During the more than 45 years since collective bargaining became subject to governmental regulation, there have been thousands of NLRB and court decisions which have spelled out just what the duty of collective bargaining entails.

The Union as Exclusive Representative

A primary feature of U.S. labor law as it applies to collective bargaining is the principle of exclusive representation by a majority union. This principle is specifically declared in Section 9 of the LMRA:

> Representatives designated or selected for the purposes of collective bargaining by the majority of the employees in a unit appropriate for such purposes, shall be the exclusive representative of all the employees in the unit for the purpose of collective bargaining in respect to rates of pay, wages, hours of employment, or other conditions of employment....

This provision means that once a union is selected as the collective bargaining representative, by law it acquires the right and the responsibility to deal with the employer on behalf of all employees in the unit. Philosophically, this derives from the notion of "one for all, all for one" that historically underpins organized labor. Practically, it recognizes that the individual worker possesses little meaningful power to deal with an employer. The union which holds bargaining rights for a unit of employees is entitled to represent all of the employees in that unit regardless of the desires of individual employees to represent themselves and regardless of whether or not employees are union members.

The LMRA makes it an unfair labor practice for an employer to refuse to bargain collectively with the representative of his employees. An employer is obligated to deal with a designated majority union and is forbidden to deal individually with employees or with a competing organization about any matter subject to collective bargaining. In *J. I. Case v. NLRB* (1944), a case which involved the impact of a collective agreement on existing individual contracts, the Supreme Court stated:

> The practice and philosophy of collective bargaining looks with suspicion on such individual advantages. . . . They are a fruitful way of interfering with organization and choice of representatives . . . often earned at the cost of breaking down some other standard thought to be for the welfare of the group and . . . paid at the long-range expense of the group as a whole.

The basis for exclusive representation is a belief that any form of plural representation would permit an employer to grant favor to certain individuals or groups and thereby foster rivalries that would erode the strength of the union, ultimately resulting in disadvantages for all.

In *Emporium Capwell v. WACO* (1975), the Supreme Court clarified the extent to which public policy exalts the principle of exclusive representation by a majority union under the LMRA. Through contractually specified procedures, a union was pursuing charges of racial discrimination against an employer, a department store, which was forbidden by contract to engage in racial discrimination. Several employees felt that the contract grievance procedure focusing on individual grievances was inadequate to correct a problem as deep-rooted and widespread as racial discrimination. These employees unsuccessfully urged direct economic action by the union against the employer and refused to participate in meetings concerning the grievance.

After failing in their attempts to meet with company officials to discuss the problem as they saw it (companywide, or systematic, discrimination), the dissident employees themselves instituted the direct action which the union had refused to take. They held a press conference, denounced the store's policy as racist, reiterated their desire to deal directly with top management over minority employment, and subsequently on their own time picketed the store, urging customers not to patronize it.

Two of the dissident employees, after being warned by the employer that a repetition of the picketing would subject them to discharge, were fired following a second day of picketing. The General Counsel of the NLRB charged the employer with an unfair labor practice, maintaining that the discharges violated the right of employees to engage in concerted activity under Section 7 of the LMRA. The NLRB dismissed the complaint, however, concluding that protection of such activity would undermine the principle of exclusive representation mandated by the statute. To pemit workers to make direct demands on the employer would diminish the effectiveness of the union's efforts. The Board believed that an employer would be unreasonably burdened if legally required to bargain with the union but economically forced to deal with a competing group concerning issues lawfully subject to bargaining.

An appeals court reversed the NLRB decision, holding that the principle of exclusive representation must be subordinated to the strong national policy requiring the elimination of racial discrimination in employment. The Supreme Court reversed the court of appeals, however, and adopted the NLRB's reasoning that the right and responsibility to bargain belong exclusively to the majority union. In rejecting the premise that the employees' efforts complemented rather than clashed with those of the union, the Supreme Court declared:

> This argument confuses the employees' substantive right to be free of racial discrimination with the procedures available under the NLRA for securing these rights. Whether they are thought to depend upon Title VII [of the Civil Rights Act of 1964] or have an independent source in the NLRA, they cannot be pursued at the expense of the orderly collective bargaining process contemplated by the NLRA. The elimination of discrimination and its vestiges is an appropriate subject for bargaining, and an employer may have no objection to incorporating into a collective agreement the substance of his obligation not to discriminate in personnel decisions.... But that does not mean that he may not have strong and legitimate objections to bargaining on several fronts over the implementation of the right to be free of discrimination.... Similarly, while a union cannot lawfully bargain for the establishment or continuation of discriminatory practices, it has a legitimate interest in presenting a united front on this and on other issues and in not seeing its strength dissipated and its stature denigrated by subgroups within the unit separately pursuing what they see as separate interests.

The reaffirmation of the primacy of the exclusive representation principle rejects any form of plural representation—either by individuals or by organizations. It clears the way for a union to speak with a united voice in asserting workers' interests. However, another aspect of exclusive representation is the channeling of all disputes into narrowly defined procedures, thereby insulating the employer from more basic challenges to its authority. This relieves the employer of the burden of dealing with individual employees who are sometimes more militant in their demands than their union—often severely constrained both by the law and by the contract in its ability to assert employee interests.

The Role of the Government in Collective Bargaining

An oft repeated description of industrial relations in the United States is that "free" collective bargaining is the basic feature of the country's labor policy. A fundamental policy articulated in the LMRA is to promote private bargaining without governmental interference into the substantive terms of collective bargaining agreements. (One of the provisions contained in the proposed Labor Law Reform Act of 1977 would have granted the NLRB some of the authority it lacks under the present system. In cases where the parties are negotiating their first contract and where an employer was found by the NLRB to have unlawfully refused to bargain, the provision would have authorized the NLRB to order compensation lost because of the delay. In essence, it would have permitted the NLRB to write the economic terms of a contract to cover the period of time between the time the bargaining obligation arose and the time the employer actually began to bargain in good faith. The current trend for many employers to invest substantial effort and resources into resisting unionization, including systematic violations of the law, means that this issue is likely to emerge in the future.) However, both in statutory language and in decisions by the NLRB and the courts, the government has carved out a significant role for itself in shaping collective bargaining. Some types of contract provisions are forbidden by statute as contrary to public policy without regard to the willingness or desire of the parties to collective bargaining to bind themselves to such provisions. Two examples of these forbidden practices are closed shops, and hot cargo agreements. The NLRB, with the statutory authority to decide "appropriateness" of bargaining units and a court-approved arrogation of the power to decide what subjects are covered by collective bargaining, also exercises substantial control on the structure of collective bargaining.

Despite these intrusions by government into collective bargaining, the clearest statement in the LMRA concerning the role of the government in labor-management relations is the declaration that the law does not "compel either party to agree to a proposal or require the making of a concession." A significant exception to this concept of "free" collective bargaining is government-imposed wage ceilings, a subject of great controversy during the 1970s.

The high regard for this view of collective bargaining free of governmental interference into the actual outcome is demonstrated by Supreme Court decisions rebuking intrusions by the NLRB into this forbidden territory of the substantive terms of a contract. The NLRB cannot force the making of a concession; the right to use economic weapons allows either party to attempt to force concessions that the opposing party is otherwise unwilling to make.

In *H. K. Porter Co. v. NLRB* (1970), a major case on the issue, the Supreme Court was asked to decide whether the NLRB might require the inclusion of a checkoff provision in a contract as a remedy for the employer's unlawful refusal to bargain in good faith on that subject. A checkoff clause requires the employer, upon authorization from the employee, to automatically deduct union dues from the employee's paycheck and transmit them to the union. Finding that the policy of neutrality expressed in Section 8(d) applied to Section 10(c), which describes the Board's remedial powers, the Supreme Court declared:

> ... allowing the Board to compel agreement when the parties themselves are unable to do so would violate the fundamental premise on which the Act is based—private bargaining under governmental supervision of the procedure alone, without any official compulsion over the actual terms of the contract.

Bargaining in Good Faith

To promote collective bargaining, Section 8(d) requires a standard of conduct demonstrating good faith—an open mind and a willingness to try to find common ground. Good faith is the standard of conduct which a party must bring to bargaining in order to protect itself against a charge of refusal to bargain by the other party to the negotiations.

However, some kinds of conduct are considered to be so destructive of bargaining that the NLRB has decided that such conduct is a *per se violation* of the duty to bargain. The Supreme Court expressed approval of the Board's position in *NLRB v. Katz* (1962). "Per se" literally means "in and of itself." If a party engages in this kind of conduct, it is subject to a refusal-to-bargain charge regardless of its intent and regardless of the good faith its other conduct may have shown. Only a few types of conduct are grounds for a *per se* bargaining charge. Some of these are (1) a refusal to meet for the purposes of collective bargaining, (2) a refusal to execute a written agreement, (3) a refusal to discuss mandatory subjects (discussed at length in the next chapter), and (4) a change in a condition subject to bargaining without consulting the union. Despite what appears to be a clear-cut rule, its application is sometimes fuzzy. Cases may have elements of objectionable conduct of the *per se* variety and other conduct tending to show bad faith.

Measuring Good Faith. Other than *per se* cases in which the conduct alone is sufficient to support a refusal-to-bargain charge, the question is whether a party has shown good faith in its bargaining conduct. Since good faith describes a party's state of mind, it cannot be precisely measured. The NLRB, in considering charges of bad-faith bargaining, has adopted a case-by-case approach. In making a determination, the Board looks at the *totality* or the *entire course of that party's bargaining conduct*. (*NLRB v. Virginia Electric & Power Co.* (1941) and *General Electric Co.* (1964)) The NLRB attempts to deduce the state of mind or attitudes that the party has brought to the bargaining process from a party's actual behavior. While no single element of a party's behavior may be sufficient to constitute a breach of good faith, its overall conduct may be such as to support a charge of refusing to bargain in good faith.

The NLRB utilizes several tests in determining a party's good faith. Even though the law does not compel agreement, it does require that parties meet and sincerely attempt to reach agreement. Meeting together for the purpose of bargaining contemplates more than merely "going through the motions." Consequently, many bad-faith bargaining cases involve types of conduct that the NLRB has concluded demonstrate an absence of any sincere desire to reach agreement. The NLRB has identified several of these types of conduct that may but do not necessarily support a charge of bad-faith bargaining. *Surface Bargaining* is one type: Even though a party is willing to meet, inflexible adherence to its own demands and the total rejection of those of the other party are considered an indication of a "closed mind." Surface bargaining refers to the nature or the quality of bargaining and not to the frequency of bargaining.

The law clearly states that bargaining does not require the making of a concession. However, the *willingness of a party to compromise*—to engage in give-and-take—is frequently looked to as evidence of a party's good faith. The NLRB found in *NLRB v. Reed & Prince Mfg. Co.* (1953) that while the Board itself cannot require specific concessions, the Board can look at the making of some concessions in the overall context of bargaining as highly relevant to a determination of a party's desire to reach agreement. The *willingness of a party to make proposals, demands, and counterproposals* is also a measure of its good faith. Withdrawal of proposals after their prior acceptance has been considered evidence of bad faith, as has the introduction of new issues after an agreement has been substantially concluded. Proposals that are so unreasonable that their predictable effect would be to frustrate further negotiations and agreement may also be considered evidence of bad faith.

An outright refusal to meet at all is a *per se* bargaining violation. Lesser forms of similar conduct, such as repeated *delays* in scheduling or other evasions of the responsibility to meet and seek agreement, are indications of a party's bad faith. For instance, failure to invest the bargaining representative with any significant authority to conclude an agreement is a sign that a party is not taking negotiations seriously.

Stipulating that an agreement must include acceptance of prescribed conditions may be considered to show a closed mind. The *preconditions* may relate to matters subject to bargaining, such as the settling of certain contract terms before negotiating on others. Such barriers are thought to interfere with a give-and-take atmosphere. Or preconditions may relate to external issues, such as an insistence on bargaining about voluntary subjects (discussed in the next chapter) or the relinquishment of certain rights, like the dropping of pending unfair labor practice charges. A refusal to negotiate for the duration of a legal economic strike is an unacceptable condition that could predictably frustrate agreement and is generally the basis for a refusal-to-bargain charge.

Employer conduct occurring contemporaneously to bargaining that discriminates against union members, or undermines the union, or promotes the decertification of the union as bargaining representative raises questions as to the employer's sincerity and genuine participation in the bargaining process. Such conduct then—in addition to being independent unfair labor practices—may also be considered as evidence of bad-faith bargaining.

Boulwarism. "Boulwarism" is the popular name of a bargaining technique pioneered by the General Electric Company and named after the GE vice-president who developed the strategy in the 1950s. Based on its own research of the employees' needs, the company formulated a set of proposals. It presented this package as a "firm and fair offer" with nothing held back for later trading and subject to change only if new facts were shown to require it. The company then conducted an extensive advertising campaign designed to convince both its employees and the public that it was doing the best possible for its employees. It asserted that it was doing so voluntarily, without the need for any union pressure or a strike.

Along with several specific refusal-to-bargain findings, the NLRB found GE guilty of refusing to bargain based on the totality of its conduct. In affirming this NLRB finding, the U.S. court of appeals emphasized in *NLRB v. General Electric Co.* (1969) that

> . . . an employer may not so combine "take-it-or-leave-it" bargaining methods with a widely publicized stance of unbending firmness that he is himself unable to alter a position once taken.

In effect, the employer had attempted by its action to preempt entirely the bilateral decisionmaking which the LMRA requires. Central to the court's condemnation of GE's approach was the company's attempt to deal directly with employees. Through the use of the publicity campaign and direct communications, the employer sought to bypass the union altogether and convince employees that the company could be relied on to look after their best interests without any need for the union. According to the court, the company desired "to deal with the union through the employees, rather than with the employees through the union," as the law requires.

Boulwarism, as revealed in later cases, exists *only* if it features a combination of "firm offers" and communication of this to employees. The law does not prohibit either hard bargaining or all communications to employees. At some point in the negotiations, an employer may make a firm and final offer. The NLRB in *Philip Carey Mfg. Co.* (1963) held that an employer did not violate Section 8(a)(5) when it made a final offer in the eleventh session of a series of "give-and-take" sessions.

Unilateral Actions. The essence of collective bargaining is the mutual obligation of an employer and a union to "bargain" concerning the wages, hours, terms, and conditions of employment of those employees whom the union represents. Bargaining implies that joint determination or bilateral decisionmaking is to be substituted for unilateral, or one-sided, decisions by an employer regarding those matters subject to bargaining. For example, during the term of an existing contract, an employer that unilaterally granted merit increases, changed the sick leave policy, and instituted a new system of automatic wage increases was subsequently charged with a refusal to bargain. The employer contended that unilateral actions alone were insufficient to support a refusal-to-bargain charge. It argued that the NLRB must make a finding of bad faith—of which unilateral changes might be evidence—in order to find it guilty of refusing to bargain. The Supreme Court noted in *NLRB v. Katz* (1962) that when a party has refused to negotiate or has circumvented negotiations by instituting changes, then the opportunity to consider the issue of good faith is foreclosed. Bargaining is preempted by the actual making of changes and in effect bypasses the union. In finding that unilateral action by an employer obstructs bargaining, the Supreme Court approved the use of the *per se* refusal-to-bargain concept with respect to this type of conduct but declined to announce an absolute rule pertaining to such changes. Thus, the NLRB may occasionally consider a unilateral change merely as evidence of bad faith rather than as an outright violation of the duty to bargain.

In thinking about unilateral changes, it should be remembered that what the law requires is bargaining. If bargaining possibilities have been exhausted so that an impasse exists, then an employer is free to make changes. A unilateral action consistent with past practice, or which maintains the status quo, is lawful despite the fact that a union is not afforded an opportunity to bargain. However, any past practice can be made the subject of future contract negotiations, and contract language can change the application of the practice.

Use of Economic Weapons During Bargaining

A major case on the issue of good faith involved bargaining in which the union, during contract negotiations, simultaneously engaged in economic activity designed to further its position. The question for the NLRB was whether economic pressure used to support union demands during negotiations with an employer was equivalent to an unlawful refusal to bargain. The NLRB ruled that the union's reliance upon harassing tactics during the course of negotiations, for the avowed purpose of compelling the company to capitulate, was the antithesis of reasoned discussion which the union was duty-bound to follow. In *NLRB v. Insurance Agents Int'l Union* (1960), the Supreme Court disagreed, finding that apart from a requirement that parties confer in good faith, "Congress intended that the parties should have wide latitude in their negotiations, unrestricted by any governmental power to regulate the substantive solution of their differences." The Supreme Court condemned what it perceived as NLRB intrusion into the substantive aspects of bargaining and discussed at length the concept of collective bargaining premised on government neutrality. The Supreme Court declared:

> It must be realized that collective bargaining, under a system where the government does not attempt to control the results of negotiations, cannot be equated with an academic collective search for truth—or even what might be thought to be the ideal of one. The parties—even granting the modification of views that may come from a realization of economic interdependence—still proceed from contrary and, to an extent, antagonistic viewpoints and concepts of self-interest. The system has not reached the ideal of the philosophic notion that perfect understanding among people would lead to perfect agreement among them on values. The presence of economic weapons in reserve, and their actual exercise on occasion by the parties, is part and parcel of the system that the Wagner and Taft-Hartley Acts have recognized. ... At the present statutory stage of our national labor relations policy, the two factors—necessity for good faith bargaining between parties and the availability of economic pressure devices to each to make the other party incline to agree on one's terms—exist side by side.

Employers too are permitted to use economic weapons, such as a lockout, in furtherance of a bargaining position.

Since the right to use economic weapons is independent of the duty to bargain, their use does not suspend the duty to bargain. An employer still has a duty to bargain even when the union is engaged in a lawful economic strike, and the employer cannot in any way make cessation of the strike a condition for further bargaining. The employer is free to use certain countermeasures to employees' concerted activity without consulting the union. For instance, the employer is not required to subsidize a strike and can therefore terminate wages and economic benefits, such as payment of insurance premiums, to striking employees. An employer is also free to replace strikers and to temporarily subcontract out the struck work in order to maintain business operations. However, an employer has no obligation to bargain with a union engaging in unlawful strike activity, such as strikes characterized by violence and strikes in violation of the union's contract obligations.

Impasse

The duty to bargain does not require the parties to actually conclude an agreement. After good-faith bargaining possibilities have been exhausted and there remain irreconcilable differences in the parties' positions, the law recognizes an impasse. An impasse may occur either in negotiations for a new contract or during the term of an agreement when an employer proposes to make a change in a condition of employment subject to bargaining. There is, however, no litmus test to distinguish between a legal impasse and a stalemate caused by unlawful bargaining conduct. Whether the NLRB will find that a legal impasse has occurred depends on all of the facts in each case. If a party takes an action based on a belief that a lawful impasse exists, it risks the NLRB later finding that no "legal" impasse existed.

Generally an impasse occurs at that point when further discussions would be fruitless. This determination, like that relative to other aspects of collective bargaining, depends upon all of the circumstances peculiar to each situation. In *Taft Broadcasting Co.* (1967), the Board described it in the following manner:

> Whether a bargaining impasse exists is a matter of judgment. The bargaining history, the good faith of the parties in negotiations, the length of the negotiations, the importance of the issue or issues as to which there is disagreement, the contemporaneous understanding of the parties as to the state of negotiations, are all relevant factors to be considered in deciding whether an impasse in bargaining existed.

During the period of an impasse, the duty to bargain on those subjects on which impasse has been reached is suspended. Typically, an impasse applies to all bargaining and not to particular subjects, since bargaining is usually aimed at securing a total "package" or contract. Once impasse is reached, an employer is free to make unilateral changes in wages and conditions consistent with but no more favorable than those which have been rejected by the union. However, an employer may not take any action on any other matter subject to bargaining that is not covered by the impasse.

The end of an impasse is as imprecise as its beginning. Any circumstance which changes the relative bargaining position of the parties will terminate an impasse. Examples of such changes are strikes, lockouts, changes in the business environment, or any development which indicates that a party might now be willing to depart from its previous position and that bargaining would no longer be futile.

Waiver of Bargaining Rights

A frequent employer defense to a refusal-to-bargain charge is that the union has waived its right to bargain on the matter in dispute. The waiver argument often arises out of a unilateral action taken by an employer during the term of an agreement.

Several types of waivers are recognized by the NLRB. Since the obligation to bargain arises only when bargaining is requested, the failure to ask for bargaining, acquiescence, is a basis for assuming that a party is waiving its bargaining rights with respect to a particular change. A waiver of the right to bargain over certain issues may also be expressed in the contract. However, the NLRB is reluctant to recognize such waivers and will usually do so only when a waiver is supported by "clear and unmistakable" language in the contract. A broadly stated management rights clause is, as a rule, not sufficient reason to infer that a union has waived its right to bargain on changes in working conditions during the term of the contract. But management rights clauses with specific reservations of authority to management do permit an employer to make unilateral decisions with regard to the matters such reservations cover. For instance, a clause reserving to the employer the sole right to determine employee qualifications was found by the NLRB in *Le Roy Machine Co.* (1964) to constitute a waiver by the union of its right to bargain over the use of physical examinations. The Supreme Court in *NLRB v. C & C Plywood* (1967) upheld the authority of the NLRB to review and construe contract language for the purpose of determining whether a union has by contract waived its statutory right to bargain. However, the NLRB cannot determine the extent of contract rights but only whether the union by agreement has ceded its right to bargain.

Waivers can also be based on the bargaining history of a subject if the issue was fully discussed and if the union consciously yielded its position. The mere discussion and discarding of a demand does not constitute a waiver. To find that all issues put on the table and then abandoned constitute a waiver would discourage the give-and-take that is integral to collective bargaining. When a contract is in effect, it usually contains language that binds both parties on all subjects covered in the agreement. Neither side can compel bargaining on the subjects covered in the contract during the term of the agreement, although the two parties may voluntarily reconsider and amend contract language.

The Right to Information

The LMRA does not specifically establish a right of access to information for unions nor does it create an obligation for the employer to supply requested information. However, the right of the union to relevant information within the possession of the employer has become firmly grafted onto the law as a corollary of the duty to bargain. The failure to supply requested information is an unlawful refusal to bargain. A contract may also create a union's right to information. This right is independent of the statutory right.

The Supreme Court first had occasion to review this concept in *NLRB v. Truitt Manufacturing Co.* (1956) when the NLRB upheld a charge of refusal to bargain against an employer claiming that it could not afford the wage level the union demanded while at the same time refusing to supply any information to substantiate its claim. In upholding the NLRB, the Supreme Court noted:

> Good faith bargaining necessarily requires that claims made by either bargainer should be honest claims.... If an argument is important enough to present in the give and take of bargaining, it is important enough to require some sort of proof of its accuracy.

Subsequent cases have made it clear that this right to information applies to all aspects of collective bargaining performed by a union on behalf of its members. The justification is that the lack of adequate and accurate information prevents the occurrence of effective bargaining and denies the union the opportunity to properly perform its bargaining responsibilities. The right to information pertains to contract negotiations, grievance adjustments, the policing of a contract, and preparing for future bargaining. It is not clear under what circumstances a union might be required to supply information to an employer.

Examples of information which the NLRB has required an employer to share with the union are wages paid to individual employees and groups of employees, compensation of employees outside the bargaining unit, wage rates paid at other plants of the employer, costs of an insurance plan, information on job classifications, time study materials, employees' ages, and productivity information. This list illustrates but does not exhaust the types of information covered.

A union is entitled to information only if it requests it. A request must be fairly specific about what information the union requires. The information a union can obtain must pertain to matters of negotiation with the employer. Both the NLRB and the courts use a liberal definition in deciding "relevance," saying that information is relevant if it is reasonably necessary for the union to perform its bargaining representative function. Some categories of information are presumed relevant, which means that the union does not have to show why it desires or needs the information. For instance, in connection with wage negotiations, an employer is required to supply wage data upon request in a form that allows the union to determine exactly what each person is being paid. Financial information on the employer's operation is relevant any time an employer asserts that it cannot afford to meet a union's demand for wages or benefits. This requirement is based on the notion that parties to negotiations should make "honest" claims which they should be willing to prove. An employer's claim that it is financially unable to meet a union's demand is usually called a "plea of poverty." It includes not only outright inability to pay but also includes claims that meeting the union's demands would make it uncompetitive or erode its profit margin.

The NLRB and the courts must evaluate the confidentiality of requested information before requiring an employer to disclose such information to a union. Recently, the Supreme Court concluded in *Detroit Edison v. NLRB* (1979) that an employer lawfully refused to disclose aptitude test scores of individual employees who had not consented to disclosure even though the scores might have been relevant to the processing of promotion grievances. The Board had ordered the release of both the test itself and the individual answer sheets to the union. The employer had offered to submit the test and the answer sheets to an industrial psychologist selected by the union and to disclose to the union the score of any employee who consented thereto. The Supreme Court held that the "arguably relevant" nature of information does not always predominate over all other interests. In this case, the employer's interest in protecting the integrity of the test for future use plus the privacy of the tested employees were sufficient to offset even the legitimate interests the union had in the information.

The Board has subsequently ruled in *Minnesota Mining and Manufacturing Co.* (1982) that employers must give unions access to worker health and safety records with names and identifiers deleted. The Board also ordered the employers—three chemical companies—to provide a listing of substances used and produced at the plants in question. As to substances on which the employers claimed a trade secret, the Board suggested that the parties negotiate a method under which the unions could receive the information while maintaining safeguards for the employers' interests. If such efforts fail to reach a mutually satisfactory result, then the Board will engage in a balancing of the competing rights of the unions and the employers.

Bargaining With Successor Employers

With the current growth in the number of mergers, sales, and consolidations of business operations, the effect of a change in the employer on collective bargaining agreements is a concern for unionized workers. The LMRA does not require an employer to assume the preceding employer's collective bargaining agreement, since to do so would compel the employer to accept the previous employer's concessions and would therefore conflict with Section 8(d). Nor does a succeeding employer have to hire the predecessor's employees. Contracts generally provide greater protection in this area.

The Supreme Court ruled in *NLRB v. Burns International Security Services* (1972) that a successor employer does have an obligation to recognize and bargain with the union which represented its predecessor's employees if it retains those employees. But not every employer that takes over another employer's operations is a "successor" employer. The finding as to whether a new employer is a "successor" employer within the meaning of the law involves several inquiries, all focusing on the continuity between the old and new employer's enterprise. Some of these are:

- Is there continuity in the work force?
- Is there continuity in the employing industry? (Does it produce the same product or service?)
- Is the bargaining unit still an appropriate one?
- What was the impact of any shutdown before the new employer began operations?

If it is clear that the new employer intends to retain the employees in the unit with no indication that they are expected to work under new or different terms, then the obligation to bargain arises. But if the offer to hire is conditioned upon acceptance of different terms of employment, then the new employer is not required to consult with the union over those changes. NLRB policy generally favors allowing the new employer to establish its own initial terms and conditions of employment on the theory that to do otherwise would discourage new employers from even considering the continued employment of original employees.

However, the Board determined in *Mason City Dressed Beef, Inc.* (1977) that an employer cannot intentionally refuse to hire employees of the former employer simply as a way to avoid dealing with the union. The NLRB soundly condemned such discrimination in *Potter's Drug Enterprises* (1977) by finding an employer to be a successor even though holdover employees were not a majority of the new work force.

Where a successor employer not only applies the substantive terms of a predecessor's agreement but consults and negotiates with the union as well, the NLRB has held that the employer has by its actions assumed the contract. But the continuation of economic benefits provided in the contract is not considered sufficient evidence to support a charge that the new employer has adopted the contract. The Supreme Court held in *Golden State Bottling Co. v. NLRB* (1973) that a purchaser of a business with notice of pending unfair labor practice proceeedings against the predecessor may have a duty to remedy those practices including reinstatement and back pay. However, this rule applies only if there is continued operation of the business without interruption or changes in method of operation or personnel.

Key Words and Phrases

Boulwarism	refusal-to-bargain charge
collective bargaining	right to information
duty to bargain	Section 8(d)
good-faith bargaining	successor employers
impasse	surface bargaining
"notice" requirement	unilateral change
per se violation	waiver

Review and Discussion Questions

1. Discuss the present role of government in collective bargaining as developed in the *H. K. Porter* case.

2. Does collective bargaining as practiced in the United States permit workers a sufficiently strong voice in decisionmaking concerning their work lives? Explain.

3. Do you agree that certain bargaining conduct ought to be considered an unlawful refusal to bargain, or a *per se* violation, regardless of the intent of the party engaging in the conduct? Why or why not?

4. A provision of the proposed Labor Law Reform Act of 1977 would have permitted the National Labor Relations Board to write wage terms of a first contract in order to remedy an employer's refusal to bargain. Is such a provision consistent with the concept of collective bargaining as practiced since 1935?

5. What effect do you think that the increasing number of governmentally imposed standards on the employment relationship, such as health and safety, wage standards, etc., will have on the vitality of collective bargaining?

6. Why does a unilateral change in working conditions by an employer conflict with the principle of collective bargaining?

7. Do you think that the Boulware method of employee relations ought to be permitted in those circumstances where workers are offered more than their union might obtain for them through collective bargaining?

8. In defending a worker discharged for absenteeism, why should the employer be required to give the union the absentee record of the discharged worker as well as those of other workers? What should happen if other workers are opposed to a union having access to their records?

9. Should a discharged worker who is represented by a union be permitted to retain an attorney in an effort to regain his job instead of having to rely on the union?

10. Should an employer who takes over another employer's business be required to assume the existing collective bargaining agreement? Why?

6

Subjects of Bargaining

As noted in the previous chapter, the Labor Management Relations Act requires the parties to the collective bargaining process to confer on "wages, hours, and other terms and conditions of employment" subject to specific restrictions contained in the act. The LMRA does not give any further direction as to the reach of the phrase "wages, hours, and other terms and conditions" and does not assign authority for deciding whether a particular issue qualifies as a subject for bargaining. Nor does it specify the procedures that are to apply to subjects outside these categories about which one or both of the parties might want to bargain.

Subjects of Bargaining Defined

The questions "what is an appropriate subject for bargaining, who has the authority to make that decision, and what is the decision's implication on other rights" were resolved by the Supreme Court in its *NLRB v. Borg-Warner Corp.* (1958) decision. As part of the employer's conditions for settlement of a contract, the employer demanded a provision requiring a prestrike secret vote of employees on the employer's last offer. Additionally, the employer demanded a recognition clause in which the local union would be recognized as the exclusive bargaining agent, excluding the international union which had been certified by the NLRB.

Although both clauses were contained in the final agreement, the international union filed a refusal-to-bargain charge against the employer for its insistence in bargaining on the two subjects. In its consideration of the issue, the NLRB found that the employer had violated its duty to bargain by insisting upon bargaining about a subject outside the category of "wages, hours, and other terms and conditions of employment." The *Borg-Warner* decision divided bargaining proposals into the following three categories: mandatory subjects, permissive or voluntary subjects, and illegal subjects.

Mandatory Subjects are those pertaining to wages, hours, and terms and conditions of employment. Each party must bargain in good faith on these subjects when either party offers a proposal to bargain on such a subject. Either side may insist to the point of impasse on its position and may back up its position through the use of economic weapons. This is not a finite category, and the NLRB and the courts have over time significantly expanded its scope.

Permissive or *Voluntary Subjects* deal with matters outside the Section 8(d) category—wages, hours, and other terms and conditions—but are lawful contract provisions if voluntarily incorporated into a collective bargaining agreement. Either party may propose a voluntary subject for consideration, but the other party is not obligated to bargain on it. A party cannot insist to the point of impasse on its inclusion in a contract nor use economic weapons to secure its inclusion.

Illegal Subjects are those which are forbidden under the law and over which bargaining cannot be required and which may not be incorporated into a contract even if both parties voluntarily agree to their inclusion.

These classifications were approved by the Supreme Court and are still the basis for determining the extent of the bargaining obligation. The *Borg-Warner* decision permits the NLRB, through its classification authority, to have great impact on the substance of bargaining. By deciding that a subject is a mandatory one, the NLRB increases the likelihood that the subject will be included in a contract. Should either party refuse to bargain on the issue, the Board would consider its refusal to be a *per se* bargaining violation. Furthermore, by inserting itself into the bargaining relationship in this manner, the Board can blunt the economic strength of either party by declaring an issue to be a voluntary subject of bargaining thereby prohibiting the use of economic leverage to win concessions on that issue.

Management Rights

From a union's point of view, probably no contract clause is as important or as serious in its implications as the management rights clause. Virtually every collective bargaining agreement contains such a clause, reserving to management the exclusive right to make certain decisions. The inclusion of a broad management rights clause allows an employer to evade joint determination of many important aspects of employment. Thus a perennial struggle of any union is to restrict the reach of the management rights clause and to thereby protect the union's right to engage in joint decisionmaking.

The law permits an employer to seek and to use economic strength to secure a management rights clause that all but eliminates any obligation on the part of the employer to bargain. Such a clause can relieve an employer from the obligation to bargain over substantive aspects of employment during the contract negotiations as well as limit the right of the union to request bargaining during the term of the contract. In *NLRB v. American National Insurance Co.* (1952), the Supreme Court upheld the right of an employer, otherwise engaged in good-faith bargaining, to insist to the point of impasse on a broad management rights clause. The clause granted the employer the unrestricted ability to make decisions on selection and hiring, work scheduling, and discipline and discharge of employees—subjects which are themselves mandatory subjects of bargaining. The clause further rendered employer decisions concerning these matters to be nonarbitrable under the contract's grievance procedure. Nonarbitrable means that disputes cannot be submitted to a third-party neutral for a binding decision on the employer's right under the contract to follow a particular course of action. The Supreme Court rejected the NLRB's view that to insist on a management rights clause covering mandatory subjects was in effect to refuse to bargain concerning those subjects. The Court emphasized:

> Congress provided expressly that the Board should not pass upon the desirability of the substantive terms of labor agreements. Whether a contract should contain a clause fixing standards for such matters as work scheduling or should provide for more flexible treatment of such matters is an issue for determination across the bargaining table, not by the Board. If the latter approach is agreed upon, the extent of union and management participation in the administration of such matters is itself a condition of employment to be settled by bargaining.

Translated, this language means that a union has a right to joint determination only if it is strong enough to secure and preserve it in the collective bargaining process. However, insistence on a broad management rights clause when coupled with other unlawful conduct or with other proposed contract terms that strip the union of all authority may well be evidence of bad-faith bargaining.

Mandatory Subjects

In determining what constitutes wages, hours, terms, and conditions, the NLRB analyzes changing economic conditions and social needs to decide whether a concern is one that employees might reasonably expect to be relevant to their employment. "Wages" is broadly construed to mean any form of compensation for services. Some examples of wages in addition to actual rates of pay are overtime rates, pension plans, profit-sharing schemes, shift differentials, incentive plans, and merit pay. There are no absolute rules covering bonuses, *e.g.*, cash, food items, Christmas parties, etc. Employers often maintain that bonuses are gifts—acts of generosity on their part—and that the frequency and amount are therefore discretionary and not subject to bargaining. However, the NLRB maintains that bonuses are subject to bargaining if they are remuneration which employees have come to believe is incidental to the job. The most important factor in determining the nature of a bonus appears to be the regularity with which it is paid. Other factors, such as the relation of the bonus amount to the employee's earnings and the taxability of the bonus, may also be considered.

"Terms and conditions" embraces a wide range of relationships between the employer and the employee as well as between the employer and the union. A partial listing of mandatory subjects of bargaining illustrates the breadth of interests which fall within the category of other terms and conditions of employment. Included are such things as sick leave, vacations and holidays, job classifications, work rules, scheduling, seniority, layoffs, the grievance procedure, safety, pensions, child care facilities, management rights, the use of lie detector tests, and union security.

A recent Supreme Court case illustrates the elasticity of the "terms and conditions" provision and ends a 30-year controversy over whether in-plant cafeteria and vending machine prices are subject to bargaining. In *Ford Motor Co. v. NLRB* (1979), the food service was operated by a caterer, but the employer retained the right to review the prices established by the caterer. Previously the appeals courts had been hostile to a flat-out rule, preferring to decide on a case-by-case basis whether "under the facts and circumstances" of each case the prices in canteens were subject to bargaining. However, in approving the Board's finding that the prices were within the category of "terms and conditions" and thus subject to bargaining, the Supreme Court upheld the NLRB's authority pursuant to *Borg-*

Warner to decide that a matter is a mandatory subject. (The question of whether an employer must bargain over the establishment of food services where none exist is unresolved.)

Mandatory subjects clearly include most aspects of the employer-employee relationship. However, mandatory subjects also include matters pertaining to the relationship of the union to the employer. Checkoff and union security clauses, the grievance procedure, and no-strike clauses are the most common and familiar of such subjects, and their impact on "conditions of employment" is obvious if not direct.

Subcontracting of Bargaining-Unit Work. An employer decision to contract out work previously performed by bargaining-unit employees has been an issue in many cases brought to the NLRB. The ability of an employer to take such action is a critical issue for unions. The decision may have an impact on the job security of the employees, and, more fundamentally, it may cause a narrowing of the bargaining unit and of the work over which the union can claim jurisdiction.

The Supreme Court held in *Fibreboard Paper Products Corp. v. NLRB* (1964) that a decision to subcontract is a mandatory subject and thus covered by the bargaining obligation. The case involved an employer announcement that at the expiration of the applicable contract, its maintenance work would be subcontracted due to cost factors and that maintenance employees in the unit would be terminated. The NLRB ruled that the employer was obligated to bargain not only about the effects of the subcontracting decision on the employees but about the decision itself. Bargaining was required even though the subcontracting did not have an anti-union motivation. The NLRB ordered the employer to terminate the subcontract, to reinstate its maintenance operation with the terminated employees, to pay them back pay, and to bargain with the union over any subsequent contracting decision.

The order was upheld by the Supreme Court, which said that the type of contracting out involved in this case—the replacement of employees in the existing bargaining unit with those of an independent contractor to do the same work under similar conditions of employment—is a mandatory subject of collective bargaining. The NLRB's remedial order was also approved. The *Fibreboard* decision imposed upon the employer only the obligation to bargain—to afford the union an opportunity to join with management in seeking less expensive and more efficient methods of accomplishing the maintenance work. The obligation to bargain does not prevent the employer from lawfully taking the very same action later if bargaining leads to an impasse.

Decisions subsequent to *Fibreboard* indicate that the NLRB and the courts interpret it narrowly and eliminate the requirement of bargaining on many subcontracting decisions. For instance, a subcontracting decision that is consistent with the employer's past practice does not require bargaining. Another criterion is whether the decision has any adverse impact on employees in the bargaining unit in terms of their job tenure, employment security, or reasonably anticipated work opportunities. This permits an employer to erode a union's control over work by subcontracting at a time when no employee is immediately adversely affected. In the long run, however, the union is weakened by having its jurisdiction narrowed. Once work is subcontracted out and later decisions are justified because it is consistent with past practice, the only method available to the union to reclaim the work is to seek to eliminate the practice in contract negotiations.

Other Organizational Changes. The NLRB and the courts have made distinctions between ordinary subcontracting decisions of the *Fibreboard* type and management decisions concerning the scope of an enterprise, business relocation, or subcontracting which contemplates an entirely different way of doing the work. For instance, a U.S. court of appeals found in *NLRB v. Adams Dairy* (1965) that a dairy had no duty to bargain over its decision to eliminate its own distribution system and to terminate its driver-salesmen and instead sell its product to independent distributors covering the same area.

An employer's decision to close its entire business is not subject to an employer duty to engage in collective bargaining prior to the decision to close. In *Textile Workers v. Darlington Co.* (1965), the Supreme Court held that "an employer has the absolute right to terminate his entire business for any reason he pleases." In the same case, the Court held that the union's legitimate interest in fair dealing prohibits partial closings motivated by anti-union animus. The principle the Court appeared to rely on is the broad purpose of the Act to secure industrial peace. Presumably, the Court saw no threat to industrial peace, and thus no duty to bargain, if all the workers of a company are thrown out of work on a companywide basis with a complete closure.

But what of the case of a partial closure unaccompanied by anti-union animus? In *First National Maintenance Corporation v. NLRB* (1981), the Supreme court concluded "(T)hat the harm likely to be done to an employer's need to operate freely in deciding whether to shut down part of its business purely for economic reasons outweighs the incremental benefit that might be gained through the union's participation in making the decision...." The facts before the Court were essentially that the employer, First National, held a maintenance contract with Greenpark Nursing Home and decided to terminate the contract by 30 days' written notice when, for financial reasons, the contract was thought by First National not to be advantageous. Distinguishing its decision from that in *Fibreboard*, the Court stated

> Petitioner's dispute with Greenpark was solely over the size of the management fee Greenpark was willing to pay. The union had no control or authority over that fee. The most that the union could have offered would have been advice and concessions that Greenpark, the third party upon whom rested the success or failure of the contract, had no duty even to consider.

The Court in a footnote in *First National* pointed out that it was not intimating a view as to the bargaining obligation regarding other management decisions necessitated by business considerations, such as relocations, sales, or automation. While an employer is free of the obligation to bargain with the union concerning decisions to close totally, merge, or sell an enterprise, or to partially close a business for economic reasons, there is an obligation to bargain concerning the impacts of such decisions on employees.

The bargaining obligation is independent of and in addition to any restrictions on operational changes that may be negotiated into a collective bargaining agreement, for example, relocation rights and severance pay. If an employer contractually limits its discretion in partial plant closures, relocations, and the like, the union can seek enforcement of its contract in the event of a breach. Unions are free to negotiate the strongest protections they can win against subcontracting, automation, relocation, or other management decisions.

Voluntary Subjects

Voluntary subjects may lawfully be included in contracts. Since mandatory subjects are those matters relating to "wages, hours, and other terms and conditions of employment," voluntary subjects include all legal issues not encompassed within that category. Voluntary subjects often involve the employer's and the union's relationship to third parties. For instance, a union demand that an employer participate in an industry promotion fund is a voluntary subject. The union's relationship to a third party, its members, was the context in which the *Borg-Warner* case arose. There the employer sought to condition agreement on a prestrike vote and a recognition clause with an entity of the union other than the certified bargaining agent. The NLRB found these issues to be matters of internal operation and hence not subject to bargaining, unless the union willingly consented to bargain on them.

The process of categorizing bargaining subjects as mandatory or voluntary is an ongoing one, achieved as the NLRB and the courts review specific issues brought before them in cases. A review of recent cases in which a subject has been ruled to be voluntary is helpful in understanding the limits of the "hours, wages, terms and conditions" standard.

A major case on the subject, *Chemical Workers v. Pittsburgh Plate Glass Co.* (1971), did not involve the nature of the demand (health insurance) but rather the status of the beneficiaries of the demand (retired workers). The Supreme Court rejected the NLRB's determination that the employer had unlawfully refused to bargain over a mandatory subject when it unilaterally changed the terms of an insurance program covering already retired workers. The Court held that retirees are not "employees" within the meaning of the LMRA. Since the law only requires bargaining concerning the interests of employees, there was no obligation on the employer to bargain concerning the benefits of already retired persons. A breach of contract action might have been appropriate here. Additionally, certain rights of retired employees may be vested under public law, thus limiting the employer's ability to make changes in such benefits. Under such circumstances, a unilateral change may be unlawful on other grounds but will not be the basis for a refusal-to-bargain charge. The Court further held that the interest of the employer's current employees were not so vitally affected by the change that it ought to be mandatory subject. This case underscores the distinction between industrial practice and legal interpretation. The fact that the company and the union had for many years bargained concerning the rights of already retired persons did not and cannot under the *Borg-Warner* case convert a voluntary subject into a mandatory one. (Bargaining over the rights of retired employees ought not to be confused with bargaining over the retirement rights of present employees. The retirement rights of present employees are most definitely a mandatory subject of bargaining.)

Although grievance arbitration clauses for resolving disputes on the interpretation and application of an existing agreement are a mandatory subject of bargaining, interest arbitration clauses establishing procedures for the negotiation of a future contract are voluntary. An interest arbitration clause requires disputes over the terms of a future contract to be submitted to an arbitrator for resolution, and the parties voluntarily sacrifice not only their opportunity for joint decisionmaking but the right to use economic leverage as well. Either party may willingly consent to such an arrangement. However, the Board found in *Columbus Printing Pressman* (1975) that the policy of the law would be undermined if one party was allowed to insist to the point of impasse on third-party determination for an agreement. The Board has noted in past decisions that the law favors collective bargaining free of outside interference. Basically, *Columbus Printing Pressman* was a finding that interest arbitration was not related to the so-called "rights" of employment—"wages, hours, and other terms and conditions"—but rather was related to the relative bargaining position of the parties.

Procedural rules pertaining to the conduct of negotiations, such as where to meet, had generally been held to be mandatory subjects of bargaining. For instance, a demand that a stenographer record negotiations would be examined by the NLRB to determine if the demand was made in bad faith to avoid or frustrate bargaining. Absent bad faith, the demand would be considered a mandatory bargaining subject. But in a reversal, the NLRB recently declared that procedural matters were preliminary and subordinate to substantive negotiations. The Board asserted in *Bartlett-Collins Co.* (1978) that if parties are permitted to stifle negotiations on such minor procedural issues as a request for a stenographer then the statutory policy of fostering meaningful collective bargaining cannot be achieved. The Board held the request for a stenographer to be a voluntary issue.

Another example of a voluntary subject is the requirement for one party to post a performance bond to secure the other party against a breach of contract. Security against a contract breach can legally be included in a contract, but the Board considers the issue to be too far removed from employees' interests to be a mandatory subject. Issues concerning the scope of the bargaining unit are also voluntary issues. The NLRB has the primary authority to define an appropriate bargaining unit. Beyond that, the parties are free to agree voluntarily to expand or restrict the unit, but neither can insist that it be changed.

Illegal Subjects

In the main, the law does not prescribe what terms can or cannot be included in a collective bargaining agreement. However, certain practices are considered to be so inimical to the public interest that the law forbids their inclusion in a contract even if both parties willingly consent to their inclusion. Most illegal subjects are those which violate the basic policy of the Labor Management Relations Act. Examples of this are closed-shop clauses, hot-cargo agreements, superseniority credit for certain workers, and provisions for disparate treatment of workers in violation of a union's duty of fair representation. Clauses violating other laws, such as the anti-trust laws, will also be considered illegal clauses.

Key Words and Phrases

Borg-Warner case
Fibreboard case
illegal subject
interest arbitration
management rights

mandatory subject
subcontracting
terms and conditions
voluntary subject
wages

Review and Discussion Questions

1. Is it appropriate for the law to require an employer to bargain on a union's demand that the employer establish a child care center for the children of its workers? Explain.

2. Defend the Supreme Court's decision in *Chemical Workers v. Pittsburgh Plate Glass Co.* that an employer has no obligation to bargain concerning the rights of already retired workers.

3. How does the right of an employer to negotiate a broad management rights clause promote or detract from the vitality of collective bargaining and bilateral decisionmaking?

4. Do you agree that an employer ought to be able to subcontract bargaining unit work if the subcontract does not deprive any of the employer's employees of work opportunities?

5. If someone described the concept of mandatory subjects as "floating" or "open-ended," what is meant?

6. Should an employer be required to bargain over its decision to go out of business?

7

Union Security

Although the law pertaining to collective bargaining primarily defines the procedures by which labor-management relations are to be carried out, it does contain some restrictions on the actual substance of bargaining. The law prohibits unions and employers from including certain provisions in a contract, regardless of their desires. These restrictions on the substantive content of collective bargaining agreements are supposed to achieve the greatest public good and therefore override the policies underlying free collective bargaining. The most significant of these restrictions are those on union security agreements.

Unions consider union security to be a fundamental aspect of any collective bargaining relationship, and its achievement is always a priority concern to a union which has not obtained it. A union security agreement is a negotiated contract provision requiring some form of union membership or payment to a union as a condition of employment. There are several arguments as to why such agreements are a necessary and even desirable component of stable collective bargaining relationships.

Probably most important from the union's standpoint is the fact that such an agreement permits it to consolidate its position as representative of a unit. The union is freed from continuous organizing activity directed at maintaining its majority status and its representation rights among the employees in a unit. New employees routinely become members, the employer is stripped of the ability to woo employees away from the union, other unions are discouraged from raiding the unit, and the union's bargaining position is strengthened because of its ability to discipline its members to obtain support of its positions.

In terms of the interest of the public and the employer, union security agreements tend to promote long-term stable relationships. Such agreements also minimize conflict, especially between workers where conflict often arises if some are members while others who work alongside them are not. Unions maintain that union security clauses prevent some workers from receiving the benefits of a union without bearing any of the costs of obtaining them.

The basic argument made against union security agreements is that they deprive individuals who do not want to join or support a union of the opportunity to obtain and keep a job in a workplace covered by such an agreement. A second argument against union security agreements is that compulsory union membership results in the entrenchment of unions and union leaders who are unresponsive to their membership. The elimination of union security arrangements is thus presented as a method for making unions more accountable to those whom they represent.

Union Security Clauses

The National Labor Relations Act, passed in 1935, was designed to protect and encourage strong unions. Consequently, it permitted the highest form of union security—the closed shop. An employer and a union could conclude an agreement under which the employer agreed to hire and retain only persons who were members of the union. This, in effect, permitted unions to participate in the hiring and retention process by their ability to confer or sever the membership of a person. However, in 1947, as part of the Taft-Hartley Act, Congress—believing that unions had come to exercise arbitrary control over the makeup of the work force—expressly prohibited the adoption of closed-shop agreements. This provision, Section 8(a)(3) of the LMRA, makes it an unfair labor practice for an employer

> . . . by discrimination in regard to hire or tenure of employment or any term or condition of employment to encourage or discourage membership in any labor organization: *Provided,* That nothing in this Act, or in any other statute of the United States, shall preclude an employer from making an agreement with a labor organization . . . to require as a condition of employment membership therein on or after the thirtieth day following the beginning of such employment or the effective date of such agreement, whichever is the later. . . .

Section 8(a)(3), while authorizing some forms of union security, completely removed hiring decisions from union influence. Thus, a union's members are chosen by the hiring decisions made by the employer. The strictest form of union security permitted by Section 8(a)(3) is the *union shop*. An employer must hire without regard to union membership. However, a union shop clause can require an employee to join the union after a grace period and to remain a union member during the agreement. The law prohibits a grace period from being shorter than 30 days *except* in the construction industry where, under Section 8(f), the period is shortened to seven days. Because the union security clause is negotiated, a grace period may be longer than 30 days.

An *agency shop* clause does not require a covered employee to become a union member but does require the employee to pay the union a fee for the services and benefits accruing to the employee because of the union. The law permits fees equivalent in amount to the initiation fees and dues paid by full union members.

A *maintenance of membership* clause does not require an employee to join a union or to pay a service fee. Rather, it requires an employee—once having voluntarily become a member of the union—to remain a member. It is not unusual to find a collective bargaining agreement containing two union security clauses, a union shop clause covering all new hires and a maintenance of membership clause for those employed prior to the signing of the contract establishing the union shop.

The statutory language of Section 8(a)(3) seems to approve a contract clause requiring an employee to become a member of the union. However, as interpreted by the Supreme Court, in *NLRB v. General Motors Corp.* (1963), a union security clause can require nothing more than the payment of dues and initiation fees. It cannot include an obligation to take an oath of membership. In the Court's words, "membership" as used in Section 8(a)(3) is "whittled down to its financial core." Thus, in practice, the highest form of union security permitted is an agency shop, even though it is usually called a union shop. Because a union can discipline only the persons who are members, an employee may shield him/herself from union discipline for violation of union rules by meeting the financial obligation but refusing to become a member. Employees who refuse to take the oath of membership are not subject to discharge as long as they are willing to meet all of the financial conditions for membership.

Employees who have religious objections to joining or financially supporting a union are covered by a special section of the law. Section 19 of the LMRA, which previously applied only to employees of private nonprofit hospitals, was amended in late 1980 to include all employees covered by the LMRA. Section 19 states:

> Any employee who is a member of and adheres to established and traditional tenets or teachings of a bona fide religion, body, or sect which has historically held conscientious objections to joining or financially supporting labor organizations shall not be required to join or financially support any labor organization as a condition of employment; except that such employee may be required in a contract between such employees' employer and a labor organization in lieu of periodic dues and initiation fees, to pay sums equal to such dues and initiation fees to a nonreligious, nonlabor organization charitable fund....

Section 19 does authorize a union to charge fees for grievance-arbitration services to persons who, for religious reasons, decline to support the union. This provision may be a crack in the structure of exclusive representation. If the aggrieved employee declines to "purchase" representation from the union, then might the employee be found to have a right to self-representation or to seek outside representation? Since Section 19 is new to the law, its meaning will develop in actual cases involving the extent of individual rights in the context of collective rights and union authority as guaranteed in other sections of the LMRA.

Deauthorization of Union Security. As originally enacted, Taft-Hartley required a union seeking to negotiate a union shop arrangement to first submit to an election to determine its right to enter into such an agreement. To secure such authorization, the union had to win a *majority* vote of the employees in a unit *eligible to vote.* This meant that any employee not voting was counted as voting against a union shop. These difficult election procedures were premised upon a congressional belief that employees would reject a union shop requirement if given an opportunity. Despite the unfavorable rule, the union shop was, in elections pursuant to this provision, authorized by an overwhelming vote in more than 97 percent of the elections conducted. This requirement was repealed in 1951, allegedly because the rule of a union shop authorization election was costly and burdensome. Some proponents of the union shop say it may have been repealed because it provided spectacular evidence of worker support for the principle of union security—a result in direct conflict to that which underlay the congressional purpose in imposing the requirement. Under the present law, a union shop clause negotiated by a union with majority status is presumed valid. However, upon petition of 30 percent of the employees in a unit, the NLRB will conduct a deauthorization election to determine whether a majority desire to rescind the union's authority to apply a union security agreement. In a deauthorization election, a majority of employees in a unit, as opposed to a majority of those voting, must vote to rescind the union's authority. The holding of a representation election within the previous year does not bar a deauthorization election, and the terms of a contract cannot bar such an election. If a deauthorization is successful, the NLRB will immediately declare the existing union security provision invalid.

Union Security in the Construction Industry. Due to conditions unique to the building and construction industry, the LMRA contains more lenient rules governing union security clauses in this industry. Section 8(f) authorizes collective bargaining between an employer and a union before any employees have been hired. Such a contract is called a prehire agreement. The justification for this special treatment is the transient nature of the industry in which an employer may operate in a variety of locations for varying periods of time.

The authorization of prehire agreements provides:

(1) A contract may be concluded before the majority status of the union has been established.
(2) The contract may require employees to join the union *seven* days after their employment or after the effective date of the contract, whichever is later.
(3) The contract may require the employer both to notify the union of opportunities for employment and to give the union an opportunity to refer qualified applicants (who need not be union members) for such employment.
(4) The contract may specify minimum training or experience qualifications or provide for priority in opportunities based upon *length of service with the employer, in the industry,* or *in the geographical area* (not on union membership).

Prehire contracts are subject to the following express limitations:

(1) The employer must be engaged primarily in the construction industry, and the employees covered must be engaged in the industry.

(2) The union must have construction employees as members.
(3) The union must not have been established or assisted by the employer.
(4) The employer may not discriminate against an employee for nonmembership in the union if it has reasonable grounds for believing that membership was not available to the employee on the same terms and conditions generally applicable to other members, or for believing that membership was denied or terminated for reasons other than the payment of required dues and fees (as provided in Section 8(a)(3)).
(5) The contract will not bar an election to determine representative status (the contract bar rule does not apply).
(6) The special status will not prevent an election to determine a union's authorization to maintain a union security clause.
(7) The execution and application of this type of union security agreement is, like all other forms of union security, not permitted in states which have forbidden such contract clauses.

The Supreme Court ruled in *NLRB v. Iron Workers* (1978) that a prehire agreement, although lawful, is voidable by either party until the union actually demonstrates its majority status. This decision increases the burden on construction trade unions in their efforts to negotiate and maintain collective bargaining agreements.

Section 14(b)

Section 14(b) of the Taft-Hartley Act permits a state to outlaw, through a statute or its constitution, the application of union security agreements, even those providing for agency shops, within its jurisdiction. It is the only statutory exception to an otherwise comprehensive federal scheme of labor-management regulation. These state laws are generally called "right-to-work" laws. This description obscures the nature of such laws, which have essentially no relationship to an actual right to work. Twenty states currently have right-to-work laws in effect. (States which outlaw union security agreements are: Alabama, Arizona, Arkansas, Florida, Georgia, Iowa, Kansas, Louisiana, Mississippi, Nebraska, Nevada, North Carolina, North Dakota, South Carolina, South Dakota, Tennessee, Texas, Utah, Virginia, and Wyoming.) These states are primarily in the South and Southwest, where unions historically have been weak and therefore less able to affect state legislation. A right-to-work law does not prevent unionization. Such a law does prevent a union from consolidating its position as representative of a bargaining unit, thus freeing its resources and energies for other activities, such as further organizing and legislative work. Consequently, there are fewer unions in right-to-work states. Standards laws in right-to-work states, such as workers' compensation and minimum wage laws, also generally afford less protection to workers than in states where union security clauses are permitted in labor agreements. The existence of these laws is proving to be a serious problem for organized labor, as employers increasingly move their facilities from unionized states to right-to-work states, seeking the supposed advantages of nonunion labor and of an overall less restrictive regulatory environment. Unions are continually seeking to protect union security both by fighting the adoption of right-to-work legislation in the states and by pushing for the congressional repeal of Section 14(b) to remove the power of the states to act on this issue.

Checkoff

A dues checkoff provision is a contract clause that is independent of any union security clause in a collective bargaining agreement. Checkoff is a negotiated provision which compels an employer to deduct union dues from an employee's earnings and to pay that amount directly to the union when authorized to do so by the individual employee. However, individual employees have the absolute right to decline to sign a checkoff authorization and instead may pay their dues directly to the union. Checkoff relieves the union of the burden of collecting dues from each employee.

Although the law permits the inclusion of checkoff clauses in contracts, Section 302(c) requires that a checkoff authorization be signed by the individual employee. Section 302(c) also provides that the authorization cannot be made irrevocable for more than one year or extend beyond the termination date of the applicable contract, whichever occurs sooner. This section is enforced by the U.S. Department of Justice rather than the NLRB, and willful violation is punishable by a fine of $10,000 and a year in jail.

A checkoff authorization is automatically renewed unless an employee revokes it during a specified annual escape period or during any period when no contract is in effect. The checkoff clause may apply to all lawfully imposed assessments as well as to dues.

Checked-off dues cannot be sidetracked to satisfy fines against a member and thereby cause that member to become delinquent in dues.

Hiring Halls

A hiring hall is an employment office conducted by a union to secure jobs for members and provide referrals to employers. Hiring halls are frequently confused with closed shops. Although the two are linked historically in that unions sought to control entry into their craft and to distribute work through both types of operation, they are not the same thing. The Supreme Court formalized the distinction in its *Teamsters, Local 357 v. NLRB* (1961) decision. A hiring-hall arrangement under which an employer agrees to hire through the union is not unlawful if it does not discriminate against applicants with regard to their membership or nonmembership in the union. However, a union may charge nonmembers a service fee to help pay the expenses of the hiring hall and the policing of the contract and may disqualify delinquent nonmembers from future referrals. The service fee cannot be equal to dues, for that would in effect create a union shop without the union having negotiated one. The hiring-hall provision may operate in conjunction with a union shop clause so that all workers, whether members or not, may be required to become members after the seventh day.

The hiring-hall provision as currently interpreted by the NLRB allows the negotiation of contracts which virtually assure that only union members will be hired. The Board determined in its *Interstate Electric Co.* (1977) decision that hiring halls could legally give priority in its referrals to those employees who have seniority either under an employer or under a particular contract. This decision bolsters a local union's ability to negotiate contracts and to keep its members at work in the local area.

The law governing the negotiation of union security arrangements is a clear example of the LMRA's regulation of the substance of bargaining. Although the law authorizes union security agreements, it places significant restrictions on their reach. Unions are by statute denied any form of security greater than a union shop irrespective of their ability to secure and enforce a greater form of security. Still further, the presence of Section 14(b) in the law, per-

mitting the individual states to abolish union security clauses altogether further weakens union efforts to build and maintain strong
unions. Case law has further narrowed the permissible scope of
union security so that in practice, the agency shop is the highest form
of security permitted to unions. In reducing the union-employee relationship to no more than a financial obligation, the law provides a
context in which union dues can be and often are perceived as little
more than the purchase price of the benefits and privileges of a union
contract. To the extent that this notion prevails and members fail to
recognize that the essence of the union is their collective strength,
unions are in an invisible yet powerful way weakened as the union
security principle is undermined.

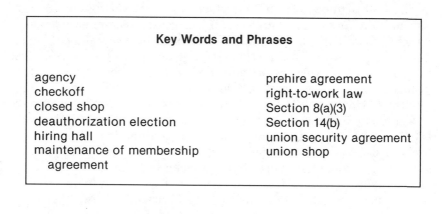

Key Words and Phrases

agency	prehire agreement
checkoff	right-to-work law
closed shop	Section 8(a)(3)
deauthorization election	Section 14(b)
hiring hall	union security agreement
maintenance of membership	union shop
agreement	

Review and Discussion Questions

1. Identify and discuss the *public*'s interest (not that of the union or
the workers) in authorizing the negotiation of union security clauses.

2. Counter the argument that the elimination of union security
clauses is necessary to make unions more responsive to their membership.

3. What are the practical differences to a union of the agency shop as
compared to the union shop, even though it collects the same amount of
money?

4. What are the advantages to a union of including a checkoff provision in a contract? Can you identify any negative impacts on a union that
result from the inclusion of a checkoff clause in a contract?

5. How does Section 14(b) of the Labor Management Relations Act
handicap union organizing efforts?

6. What is a prehire agreement? How does it work? What is its advantage to an employer? To a union?

8

Contract Enforcement

A collective bargaining agreement is a set of privately agreed-upon rules. The parties to the collective bargaining process have jointly determined the rules that will govern their relationship with each other for a prescribed period of time. As discussed in the chapter on the nature of collective bargaining, the public law, or the government, restricts the substantive terms of contracts in only limited ways. Otherwise, the parties are free to adopt those substantive rules upon which they agree are best protective of a stable and fair relationship. In this sense, collective bargaining is a private law-making process resulting in "laws" regulating the relationship of the parties. These privately made "laws" are embodied in the collective bargaining agreement.

Because collective bargaining free of governmental control is considered the cornerstone of U.S. labor relations policy, public authorities are cautious about disturbing this relationship or substituting their judgment for that of the parties. The result is that contract enforcement takes place primarily within a private arena, wherein privately made rules are privately interpreted and applied. Public law is, for the most part, no more than a backdrop against which such activity occurs. Nonetheless, questions concerning the law's impact on contract enforcement emerge in numerous contexts. These include the refusal of a party to submit to arbitration, the refusal to respect an arbitration award, and the role of the NLRB when a contract violation is also a violation of the law.

Enforcement of a Collective Bargaining Agreement

A collective bargaining agreement is made between an employer and a union and not between the employer and employees. It prescribes certain rights and responsibilities for each party. Though individual employee activities may be the substance of a breach of contract, officially the contract can be breached only by the employer or the union. A violation by one party of its contract obligation to the other party is typically called a grievance.

The contract procedure for resolving disputes about the interpretation and the application of the contract is called the grievance procedure. Many grievance procedures apply both to violations of contract language and to any other problems, such as a violation of an established practice, arising between management and the union during the term of the contract. The number of steps in a grievance procedure are defined in the contract. Because it is a negotiated item, both the range of problems covered and the procedure to be followed may vary somewhat from contract to contract but most are quite similar in their operation.

Observance of the grievance procedure is part of a party's legal obligation to bargain in good faith. Rejection of the contract altogether or a failure to observe procedural rules in the adjustment of grievances is a violation of the duty to bargain. But the violation of a contract is not in and of itself a violation of the duty to bargain in good faith. A violation of the contract may sometimes be a violation of public law or regulation but most are not. For instance, a complaint that the seniority system is not being observed or that a supervisor is doing bargaining-unit work is a contract violation if the contract provides for seniority or work classifications. However, neither of these complaints is a violation of any public law. These rights exist only because they are the "private law" achieved through collective bargaining. Therefore, the extent of such a right and its enforcement must be examined according to the procedure described in the contract.

Although a complaint concerning the meaning and extent of a contract right, such as seniority, is inappropriate for an unfair labor charge, the employer's unwillingness to respect the grievance procedure can be the basis for a refusal-to-bargain charge. For instance, if an employer refuses to accept a grievance on seniority, to meet and discuss its settlement, to meet the procedure's time limits, or to vest its representatives with authority to settle disputes, then there may be a basis for a refusal-to-bargain charge. The issue in the charge is whether the employer is respecting the grievance procedure's requirements. The merits of the grievance itself, such as whether the seniority provision has actually been violated, are not relevant to such a charge, and that issue will not be decided by the

NLRB. The Board's consideration is limited to the procedural issue of whether the employer met its obligation to bargain in the manner prescribed in the grievance procedure. If such a charge is successful, consideration of the merits of the grievance must then take place, as per the grievance procedure's requirements.

Arbitration

The grievance procedure affords an opportunity for an employer and a union to settle most breach-of-contract disputes by direct negotiations. However, when negotiations fail, most collective bargaining agreements provide for arbitration. This type of dispute settlement involves the submission of the dispute to a neutral third party, with an agreement that the decision of the arbitrator will be binding on both parties.

Arbitration is a form of private decisionmaking. Formal arbitration is a well-established process, with definite rules and patterns, and is applied to disputes in other arenas besides labor relations. In private-sector labor relations, it is an entirely voluntary method of settling disputes. For instance, a dispute concerning the interpretation of language in a collective bargaining agreement is subject to arbitration only if a contract so provides or if parties on a case-by-case basis decide to use it to settle their differences. Since arbitration is a negotiated item in a collective bargaining agreement, the details concerning its operation may be specified in the agreement. For example, the method of selecting an arbitrator and the manner of paying for the arbitrator's services will vary from contract to contract. When arbitration is included in a contract, it is usually described as final and binding. This means that both parties agree to live by that decision, whatever it is, and that they will not seek an alternative solution.

Voluntary arbitration that is final and binding should not be confused with "compulsory" arbitration. Compulsory arbitration refers to a method of dispute settlement that is imposed from outside the collective bargaining process. For instance, the laws in some of the states establishing collective bargaining rights for public employees require the submission of both unsettled contract terms and grievances to an officially designated decisionmaker, or arbitrator, as a substitute for the use of economic weapons. This arbitration is "compulsory" because the parties are not free to choose or reject its use.

Within voluntary arbitration, there is also a distinction between grievance or rights arbitration and interest arbitration. Grievance arbitration is concerned with the enforcement of contract terms and interest arbitration is concerned with the determination of future contract terms. The most dramatic example of interest arbitration is the Experimental Negotiating Agreement adopted by the United Steel Workers union and 10 companies in the basic steel industry in 1974. The Experimental Negotiating Agreement provided that at the end of the 1974 agreement, the companies and the union would submit all unresolved points of bargaining on national issues to arbitration and would forego the use of economic weapons to obtain new contract terms. However, in the private sector, interest arbitration, like grievance arbitration, is strictly voluntary, and the parties may in any future contract choose to discontinue its use for settling contract issues.

Arbitration is widely accepted in labor relations as an alternative to civil court suits over breaches of a collective bargaining agreement and to the industrial strife that potentially could result if disputes were not settled. Arbitration is attractive because it is considered to be quicker, cheaper, and less complicated than formal legal proceedings. To those who have experienced arbitration, it may not seem to fit this description. But compared to court actions, it does meet these criteria, although increasingly less so. Furthermore, unions and employers generally believe that arbitrators are more familiar with labor-management relations and that this expert knowledge assures the dispensing of a better brand of justice than that obtainable in a court action. This argument is especially made in connection with the use of a permanent arbitrator, umpire, or panel selected by the parties to settle all disputes under a particular agreement. The art of contract interpretation as developed and practiced by arbitrators in the labor-management field is frequently referred to as "industrial jurisprudence."

Legal Framework of Contract Enforcement

The Wagner Act did not make any provision for the enforcement of collective bargaining agreements, leaving this aspect of labor relations to state jurisdiction. However, in many states the common law of contracts did not recognize unions as having the capacity to sue or to be sued and did not consider collective bargaining agreements true contracts. Consequently, court enforcement of obligations contained in collective bargaining agreements was spotty and lacked uniformity. The Taft-Hartley Act, in Section 301, empowered the federal courts to hear disputes concerning alleged violations of collective bargaining agreements. This section was deemed necessary to make unions more cognizant of their responsibilities under a labor agreement. If a union could be sued for damages resulting from its breach of an agreement, then Congress believed it would be less likely to engage in conduct violative of the agreement.

Section 301 of the Labor Management Relations Act provides as follows:

> Suits for violation of contracts between an employer and a labor organization representing employees in an industry affecting commerce as defined in this Act, or between any such labor organizations, may be brought in any district court of the United States having jurisdiction of the parties, without respect to the amount in controversy or without regard to the citizenship of the parties.

Initially, the meaning of Section 301 and the nature of the powers which it bestowed on the federal courts were the subject of considerable controversy. Section 301 clearly empowered federal courts to hear suits involving breaches of a collective bargaining agreement. However, the actual substantive law such courts were to apply was not at all clear. Some labor law commentators believed that Section 301 was merely a grant of jurisdiction to federal courts and that conventional contract law as developed in state courts ought to govern such disputes. The Supreme Court, however, adopted a differing view in a landmark decision in Section 301 interpretation.

Textile Workers v. Lincoln Mills (1957) involved an employer that had refused to submit to arbitration certain disputes admittedly subject to the grievance-arbitration procedure. In ordering specific performance of the employer's promise to arbitrate, the Court explained:

> The legislation does more than confer jurisdiction in federal courts over labor organizations. It expresses a federal policy that federal courts should enforce these agreements. . . . We conclude that the substantive law to apply in suits under 301(a) is federal law, which the courts must fashion from the policy of our national labor laws. . . . Federal interpretation of the federal law will govern, not state law.

The Court viewed the employer's promise to arbitrate as the *quid pro quo*, or the trade-off, for the union's promise not to strike over grievances. Therefore, it upheld the authority of the courts to order the employer to submit the dispute to arbitration. This remedy would not have been available to the union under ordinary principles of contract law. But in the Court's view, the industrial peace which the labor law was designed to achieve could only be accomplished by compelling the parties to abide by the procedures in the agreement.

Pursuant to this decision, the law governing contract actions under Section 301 has been judge-made federal law. This means that the courts view collective bargaining agreements as a special type of contract outside of the principles of ordinary contract interpretation. Collective bargaining agreements operate within a framework reflecting a governmental view of a desirable labor-management relationship and the uses of the law in achieving that relationship.

The Supreme Court later ruled in *Charles Dowd Box Co. v. Courtney* (1962) that Section 301 had not divested state courts of the power to hear breach-of-contract disputes. State courts have concurrent jurisdiction, *i.e.,* the power to hear, Section 301 actions. However, the rights at issue are federal rights, and state courts are therefore required to apply federally established principles of labor contract interpretation instead of their own traditional principles of contract law.

Judicial Deference to Contract Procedures. One of the central features of U.S. labor relations policy is a preference for arbitration as a means of settling disputes. The exalted position that arbitration enjoys in U.S. labor relations policy was first enunciated by the Supreme Court in a group of cases known as the *Steel Workers Trilogy.* In these cases, the Court developed a policy favoring limited judicial intervention into, and oversight of, decisions resulting from a grievance procedure, particularly those made in an arbitration proceeding. The Supreme Court expressed its belief that full freedom for the operation of privately agreed-upon methods for dispute resolution would best foster labor stability.

In *Steelworkers v. American Mfg. Co.* (1960), the contract contained a standard arbitration clause providing for the arbitration of all disputes "as to the meaning, interpretation, and application of the provisions of this agreement." The employer had refused to submit to arbitration the union's claim that an employee was improperly denied reinstatement to his job. The employer's decision to refuse reinstatement was based on the fact that the employee had been found permanently partially disabled in a compensation proceeding. In an action to compel arbitration, both the federal district court and the U.S. court of appeals ruled that the union was not entitled to arbitration, since its grievance was without merit. The Supreme Court reversed, declaring that courts ought not to substitute their judgment on the merits of a grievance for that of an arbitrator, whose determination was the one which the union and the employer had mutually agreed to accept. The Supreme Court stated that judicial review of contract issues should normally be limited to a procedural review—to ensure that the parties abided by the agreed-upon process. Judges were directed to refrain from deciding whether a substantive provision of a contract had or had not been violated. In the Court's words:

> The function of the court is very limited when the parties have agreed to submit all questions of contract interpretation to the arbitrator. It is confined to ascertaining whether the party seeking arbitration is making a claim which on its face is governed by the contract. Whether the moving party is right or wrong is a question of contract interpretation for the arbitrator.
>
> The Courts, therefore, have no business weighing the merits of a grievance, considering whether there is equity in a particular claim, or determining whether there is particular language in the written instrument which will support the claim. The agreement is to submit all grievances to arbitration, not merely those which the court will deem meritorious.

In deciding whether to order arbitration, the role of the court, then, is to determine whether the dispute is one which the parties have agreed to submit to arbitration in their bargaining agreement.

Presumption of Arbitrability. Another *Trilogy* case involved the range of disputes covered by the arbitration clause. In *Steelworkers v. Warrior and Gulf Navigation Co.* (1960), the union had sought arbitration of a dispute over the employer's contracting out of work. The company refused to submit to arbitration, maintaining that the decision to subcontract was strictly a function of management, and as such, the decision was exempt from arbitration under the terms of the bargaining agreement. The Supreme Court declared that on a question of whether an issue is arbitrable, there exists a presumption of arbitrability. This means that all disputes arising under a collective bargaining agreement are presumed to be covered by the grievance procedure and are subject to resolution under that procedure unless excluded by specific contract language. The Court declared:

> An order to arbitrate the particular grievance should not be denied unless it may be said with positive assurance that the arbitration clause is not susceptible of an interpretation that covers the asserted dispute. Doubts should be resolved in favor of coverage.

Thus, the Court concluded that the decision involving the contracting out of work was arbitrable. In the Court's view, the arbitrator must decide whether subcontracting was a decision exclusively reserved to management under the management rights clause of the contract.

Subsequent cases have bolstered the strength of this presumption of arbitrability concept. Generally, as far as the unions are concerned, only those matters specifically exempted from the grievance procedure escape the presumption. In *Gateway Coal v. Mine Workers* (1974), the Supreme Court rejected the argument that Section 502 of the LMRA embodies a general policy of exempting safety issues from arbitration. Section 502 states:

> Nor shall the quitting of labor by an employee or employees in good faith because of abnormally dangerous conditions for work at the place of employment of such employee or employees be deemed a strike under this Act.

Nonetheless, the Court extended the presumption of arbitrability to safety issues.

In *Nolde Brothers v. Bakery Workers* (1977), the Supreme Court ruled that a party's obligation to arbitrate may survive the termination of a collective bargaining agreement. If the dispute is over an obligation arguably created by the expired contract, then the obligation assumed under the contract continues. The case involved the claim of workers to severance pay from an employer that had permanently closed its operation after a contract had expired. The employer contended that the obligation to arbitrate had ended when the contract expired. But the Court found that the substantive disagreement on the right of the workers to severance pay involved an interpretation of the contract, a decision reserved to an arbitrator. Therefore, the Court ruled, the presumption of arbitrability continues beyond the expiration of a contract, unless clear contract language terminates the obligation.

Judicial Enforcement of an Arbitration Award. The final case of the *Trilogy* raised the issue of the judicial role when an arbitration award has already been obtained. In *Steelworkers v. Enterprise Wheel & Car Corp.* (1960), an arbitrator had reduced a discharge to a suspension and had ordered reinstatement and back pay to the affected workers. The employer refused to comply with the award. The union sought a court order to compel the employer to abide by the arbitrator's decision. A lower court denied enforcement of that portion of the award covering the period after the contract under which the employees worked had expired. It also refused to enforce the order of reinstatement. The Supreme Court overturned this decision, finding that the court had substituted its own view of the meaning of the contract for that of the arbitrator. The Supreme Court was concerned that a judicial judgment on the merits of a dispute would undermine the federal policy favoring the settlement of disputes by privately agreed-upon methods. The Court believed:

> The question of interpretation of the collective bargaining agreement is a question for the arbitrator. It is the arbitrator's construction which was bargained for; and so far as the arbitrator's decision concerns construction of the contract, the courts have no business overruling him because their interpretation of the contract is different from his.

Thus, the Supreme Court directed courts to respect arbitration awards and to defer to them as well as to routinely order compliance with arbitration awards, since they result from a process to which the parties have voluntarily consented. As long as an arbitrator's decision is justified by the wording in the contract—or can be justified on other grounds, such as bargaining history or industry practice—courts cannot alter an arbitrator's findings or decision.

Although voluntary compliance with an arbitrator's award is the norm, the losing party sometimes refuses to comply with the arbitrator's directive. Since an arbitrator does not have the power to compel compliance with his/her decision, the prevailing party must initiate a Section 301 court action seeking a court order requiring compliance.

Despite judicial deference to arbitrators' awards, courts are not entirely excluded from reviewing the merits of an arbitrator's decision. A court may decline to enforce an award if it is plainly unsupportable by the contract or if the arbitrator has exceeded the authority granted by the contract. An award may also be challenged on the basis that the arbitrator has been bribed or was biased by some personal interest in a case. Furthermore, lower courts, asked to review arbitrators' awards, may not understand the limited role which the Supreme Court has delineated for them. Occasionally, a judge may disagree with the federal policy favoring arbitration or may strongly believe that a particular decision is grossly wrong. The judge might, therefore, refuse to enforce an award. Even though a court's decision may be inconsistent with the law, it stands unless successfully challenged in an appeal. Such instances, however, represent a very small fraction of court decisions in arbitration enforcement cases. As a rule, the parties abide by the results of arbitration, and relatively few arbitration awards are subject to a court enforcement or review proceeding. The primary means of changing an arbitration decision can be, and is often, through future contract negotiations, when the parties' entire relationship is subject to reassessment. Through contract negotiations, the parties have an opportunity to establish a different policy to cover an issue ruled on by an arbitrator.

Arbitration of Legal Rights. Although contract proceedings, particularly arbitration, are generally accorded a high degree of respect by both courts and public agencies, arbitration awards on certain issues are not absolutely "final and binding." Certain matters that are covered by a collective bargaining agreement and its procedures may at the same time be the subject of public law. Unlike awards on other issues, arbitration decisions on such matters are not accorded persuasive significance.

In *Alexander v. Gardner–Denver Co.* (1974), the Supreme Court held that an employee who obtains an adverse ruling is an arbitration proceeding can nevertheless institute a claim raising the same issue under Title VII of the Civil Rights Act of 1964. The Court noted that the rights under a contract and the statute have distinctly separate sources. In the Court's view, the right to be free of unfair discrimination is absolutely guaranteed by Congress and cannot be waived in the collective bargaining process. Therefore, in the Supreme Court's opinion, use of contract processes ought not to deprive an employee of the right to pursue a public remedy via an action under Title VII. (The employee might, however, voluntarily waive the right to legal action in settlement of a contract claim.) Thus, an employee does not have to choose between contract and legal procedures and may pursue a remedy via two independent routes. Employers view the *Gardner–Denver* decision with some hostility, arguing that while arbitration binds the employer, it affords the employee a "second bite at the apple."

The Supreme Court did qualify its decision somewhat by directing courts to consider an arbitration award as evidence, particularly if:

(1) the contract rights parallel the Title VII right;

    (2) the Title VII issue is considered in the arbitration proceeding;

    (3) the arbitrator has some special competence to consider the issue; and

    (4) the arbitration was procedurally sound.

A further distinction between "the law of the shop ... and ... the law of the land" is contained in the Supreme Court's decision in *Barrentine v. Arkansas–Best Freight System* (1981). The case involved the application of the Federal Labor Standards Act (FLSA), a federal wage-hour law. Employees sought a remedy under the FLSA following an adverse arbitration decision on a grievance arising out of the same set of facts. The Court ruled that a statutory guarantee of substantive rights to individual employees includes a right to a public forum in disputes concerning those rights. This right to a forum cannot be compromised by the existence or use of a procedure or forum designed to achieve collective interests.

    Since *Gardner–Denver*, there has been extensive controversy over its application. Most particularly, discussion has focused on a long-standing debate—whether arbitrators ought to consider only the issue raised under the applicable contract or whether the relevance of public laws ought to be considered in an arbitral decision. The primary argument against arbitrators considering issues raised under public laws is that they are not public officials, are in no way publicly accountable, and therefore ought not to have the power to decide legal rights. The opposing argument maintains that as more laws are passed with an impact on substantive job rights, it becomes difficult to consider issues strictly under contract language and interpretation. This view asserts that failure to consider the legal as well as the contractual issues increasingly erodes the finality and the legitimacy of arbitral awards, thereby diminishing the importance of arbitration—and derivatively collective bargaining—as a dispute settlement method.

Violations of the LMRA That Are Also Grievances

    Section 301 of the Labor Management Relations Act (the "Act") gives the courts the power to adjudicate claims that a collective bargaining agreement has been breached. The NLRB's authority to adjudicate claims of unfair labor practices is independent from the powers given to the courts in Section 301. Occasionally, a breach-of-contract action may also be an unfair labor practice. For instance, the discharge of an employee may violate the contract's "just cause" provision and at the same time may violate the Act's ban on discrimination because of union activity. Disputes involving representation questions may also raise issues that are covered by contract language as well as by the Act.

A run-of-the-mill contract violation—although arguably a refusal to bargain—has never been considered an unfair labor practice. Contract violations, as such, are not adjudicated by the NLRB. Section 10(a) of the Act emphasizes that the NLRB's authority over unfair labor practice cases "shall not be affected by any other means of adjustment or prevention that has been or may be established by agreement, law, or otherwise." This unrestricted authority means that an NLRB decision made pursuant to the public law supersedes any conflicting decision reached through privately established dispute settlement channels. Although it enjoys unrestricted authority to act on certain statutorily defined issues, the NLRB, like the courts, has carefully used its authority so as not to undermine the federal policy favoring private settlement of disputes.

The statutory language of the Act does not specify the extent to which privately agreed-upon methods of dispute settlement ought to or can substitute for public processes. The legislative history of the Act does lend significant support to a policy favoring private resolution of disputes subject to a contract. This policy has been applied both to disputes involving alleged unfair labor practices and to disputes raising a question of representation rights. This permits the parties to seek a settlement under a grievance procedure without regard to whether the dispute involves a violation of the Act.

However, the assertion of NLRB jurisdiction does sometimes foreclose or limit the opportunity for decisionmaking by an arbitrator. For instance, the Supreme Court upheld the finding of an unfair labor practice against an employer who refused to release requested information pertaining to a grievance. In *NLRB v. Acme Industrial Co.* (1967), the employer had argued that the union had by contract waived its right to the information and that the extent of the waiver was subject to arbitration. The Court permitted the NLRB to engage in limited interpretation of the substance of the contract for the purpose of determining whether the union had waived its statutory right to information. The Court ruled that limited contract interpretation by the NLRB was in this instance not an improper intrusion into the workings of a grievance-arbitration procedure. Because a statutory right was involved, the Court viewed the possible existence of an alternative method of settlement as irrelevant.

NLRB v. C & C Plywood Corp. (1967) involved the Board even more directly in the business of contract interpretation. The agreement authorized the employer to pay "a premium rate over and above the contractual classified wage rate to reward any particular employee for some special fitness, skill, aptitude, or the like." In reliance on this provision, the employer unilaterally established an incentive pay scale. The NLRB interpreted the contract provision and found the the contract did not authorize the employer's action. Therefore, the Board ruled that the employer's change of conditions without bargaining was an unfair labor practice. The court of appeals refused to enforce the bargaining order, since the existence of the unfair labor practice could not be determined strictly by reference to the Act but also required an interpretation of contract language, a role foreclosed to the NLRB. The Supreme Court reversed, finding that the NLRB had gone no further than necessary to enforce the statutory right to bargain, one of the very rights which it was created to safeguard. This decision affirmed the power of the Board to construe a contract where necessary to decide a pending unfair labor practice charge. It does not mean that the NLRB has any authority to enforce contracts or to act on their alleged violation independent of its authority to act on unfair labor practice charges and on representation issues.

Even though the NLRB clearly has broad authority to act when an unfair labor practice is involved, it has sought to accommodate the operation of contractual grievance procedures by curtailing the use of this authority. The Board has shown an unwillingness to disturb arbitration awards once made. The policy of respecting arbitration awards *already rendered* and the criteria for refusing to act despite its legal authority to do so were set forth in a 1955 decision. In *Spielberg Mfg. Co.* an arbitrator had upheld an employer's refusal to reinstate four strikers accused of misconduct. When unfair labor practice charges were then filed against the employer, the NLRB deferred to the arbitrator's decision that the discharges were legitimate. The Board has announced four standards necessary for Board deferral to an arbitrator's decision. They are:

(1) The proceedings appear to have been fair and regular;
(2) All parties had agreed to be bound;
(3) The decision of the arbitration panel is not clearly repugnant to the purposes and policies of the Act; and

(4) The issue must have been presented to and considered by an arbitrator.

The Board's attitude toward complaints where arbitration is *pending* or has not been invoked has been a changing one. In 1963, the Board extended its deferral policy to disputes that were the subject of pending contract proceedings. However, if no proceeding had been instituted under the contract, the Board's inclination prior to 1971 was to proceed with charges. In 1971, it reversed its position in *Collyer Insulated Wire* (1971) and announced a policy of not acting on unfair labor practices subject to contract resolution, even when no proceeding under the contract was pending. This policy of pre-arbitral deferral did not mean that the NLRB totally relinquished its authority. It meant that the Board "put off" exercising its authority until the contract machinery had an opportunity to work. However, it retained jurisdiction in case the matter was not settled, or was not submitted to arbitration, or the result obtained did not meet the *Spielberg* requirements for deferral to an arbitration award. In requiring the exhaustion of grievance remedies, the effect was to substitute private decisionmaking for legal enforcement of publicly guaranteed rights.

The *Collyer* doctrine was announced in a case involving an employer's unilateral changes in working conditions. The employer maintained that bargaining was not required, since the changes were authorized by the contract and consistent with the parties' practices under it. The Board explained its reasons for deferring action until arbitration was attempted. These were:

(1) The parties had a long and productive collective bargaining relationship and had for 35 years mutually and voluntarily resolved the conflicts which inhere in collective bargaining.
(2) There was no claim of enmity by the company to the employees' protected rights, no unlawful conduct or aggravated circumstances of any kind, and no employer design to undermine the union.
(3) The employer was willing to submit the matter to arbitration and had urged the union to do so.
(4) The contract obligated parties to submit contract disputes to binding arbitration, and the matter in dispute was unquestionably subject to that contract obligation.
(5) The contract and its meaning lay at the center of the dispute.
(6) The arbitrator can construe the agreement so as to resolve

both the contract dispute and the unfair labor practice charge.

The *Collyer* decision was a split one and was roundly criticized by the dissenting Board members as well as by outside forces. The AFL-CIO accused the NLRB of abdicating its responsibility to enforce the law. This criticism was especially prevalent after the deferral policy was extended to Section 8(a)(3) cases charging employer discrimination on account of union activity. Unlike *Collyer*, which involved an employer's claim of privilege under contract language, such cases did not in any way depend upon interpretation of a contract.

Although the Board consistently engaged in pre-arbitral deferral for several years, it did refuse to defer in a significant number of cases. For instance, complaints of outright and total repudiation of a contract or a grievance procedure were not considered appropriate cases for deferral. The Board also refused to defer if arbitration was not actually available, if arbitration was not binding, and if the parties were unwilling to honor an award. Nor did it defer when the charging party stood in an adversarial relationship to both the employer and the union or when it could be shown that the union could not adequately represent the charging party's interest. The Board also would not defer if the legality of a contract provision was the basis for a complaint proceeding—even if arbitration was available to the parties.

Finally, a change in the NLRB makeup resulted in a narrowing of the *Collyer* doctrine. In 1977, the NLRB held in *General American Transportation Corp.* that deferral is proper only in cases alleging a refusal to bargain on issues that are also covered by contract language. Complaints of discrimination on account of union activity or complaints of interference with Section 7 rights are considered without regard to the availability of contract procedures. In its last consideration of the deferral policy, two members believed that the NLRB has no power to "Collyerize" at all, while two others believed that it has unlimited power to engage in pre-arbitral deferral. Thus future changes in NLRB makeup may lead to other changes in the application of the deferral doctrine.

Since the application of the *Collyer* doctrine has been restricted, some types of disputes may actually be submitted simultaneously to two independent channels for settlement. If an NLRB proceeding is initiated first, the aggrieved may still compel the employer to abide by the grievance procedure, including submission of the dispute to arbitration. The parties are considered to have bargained for the right to have issues settled through the grievance procedure and, therefore, are entitled to their full bargain—a decision through those channels. However, as mentioned earlier, if a decision is obtained under the public law, it takes precedence over any obtained pursuant to private proceedings.

Liability for Breach of a Contract

Although a union is clearly liable for the actions it authorizes, encourages, or ratifies, many activities taken in the name of the union do not have any official status or support. These unauthorized or wildcat actions may nevertheless subject the union to liability. When all or most employees of an employer strike in violation of a contract, generally a union will be found liable, on the theory that a functioning union must be held responsible for the mass actions of its members. A union can shield itself from liability for the actions of its members only if it takes affirmative steps to secure compliance with the contract. The mere declarations by the union that a strike is illegal, that the issue is subject to a grievance procedure, or that workers ought to return to work are generally an insufficient defense if an employer pursues a suit over an illegal work stoppage.

However, a recent Supreme Court decision relieves a parent organization of liability for strikes conducted by its constituent locals unless it has accepted specific responsibilities for contract enforcement. Employers wanted to attach such liability to the unions, because it would have created a "pocketbook" incentive for unions at the national level to become actively involved in achieving labor stability. *Carbon Fuel Company v. United Mine Workers* (1979) involved a suit against three locals, a district subdivision of the international union, and the international union of the United Mine Workers of America. The three locals had over a five-year period engaged in numerous unauthorized strikes over grievable issues. The Court read Section 301(b), which makes a union liable for the actions of its "agents," as a limitation on union liability. Because the international and the district had not in any manner supported or condoned the strikes, the Court ruled that the locals could not have been acting as agents of the parent bodies. An additional employer argument for finding liability was based on a contract promise that required the international and the district to "maintain the integrity" of the contract. The Court examined the bargaining history behind this provision and concluded that the international had specifically achieved deletion of language that directed certain action in response to unauthorized strikes. Consequently, the Court ruled that neither the law nor the applicable contract established a basis for international or district liability in this case. Without a specific contract obligation, the current law thus relieves parent unions of responsibility for unauthorized activities by their locals.

A local union, however, remains liable for the unauthorized activities of its membership unless it uses available measures to compel compliance with the contract. Included in these measures are the discipline and removal of union officials, the imposition of fines, and the suspension of members who organize and participate in unauthorized strikes. Such activities obviously put a union in an ambiguous role both in terms of how it views itself and of how it is viewed by its members. Even though employers have a wide range of available measures to punish illegal strikers, the threat of a suit against a union may force union participation in the discipline of striking workers. Union efforts toward maintaining stability can blunt worker hostility toward an employer and can obscure the actual balance of power that the employer has in the employment relationship.

Responsibility of Union Officers. The responsibilities of union officers during an unauthorized work stoppage have been the issue in several recent cases. The cases involved the more severe disciplinary action taken against union officers for participation in illegal strikes than that taken against ordinary union members for participating in the same strike. Arbitrators often recognize that such a distinction exists as a basis for the selective discipline of officers.

Even though an employer may discipline any or all workers who engage in an illegal strike, the NLRB does not approve of selective disciplinary action of employees based solely on their union status or activities. This reasoning has also applied to selective discipline of officers for the mere participation in an illegal work stoppage. The selective discipline of officers is generally found to be a violation of the right of employees to be free of discrimination on account of union activity. However, when an officer leads a strike or encourages others to participate, the NLRB generally agrees that greater punishment for the officer than for other participants is appropriate. However, the NLRB's distinction between participation and leadership has recently been rejected by several courts of appeals. For example, in *Gould, Inc. v. NLRB* (1979) a court reversed the NLRB and upheld the discharge of a steward singled out from a group of about 50 illegal strikers. The employer justified its discipline of the steward on the ground that he failed to carry out his contractual duty as a union official to attempt to restore order and to terminate the strike.

Individual Liability. Individuals are not liable for a breach of a labor agreement by their union or for their own breach by participation in an unauthorized work stoppage. This notion is consistent with a basic principle of labor relations under the Labor Management Relations Act—that a collective bargaining relationship is between a union and an employer. Any resulting contract is between those parties, and its breach is enforceable only against those parties.

The issue of individual liability for a union's breach of a contract was resolved in a 1962 Supreme Court decision. *Atkinson v. Sinclair Refining Co.* involved a suit against a union and 24 individual members—all of whom had an official role in the union—for a strike in breach of a contract. The individuals were sued for wrongful interference with contractual relations, a claim ordinarily recognizable under state law applying to contracts other than labor agreements. Because the individuals were being sued as agents of the union, to find the individuals liable would have meant, in effect, that under state law the union could be found to be liable as well. The Supreme Court rejected this possibility. The Court noted that Section 301 had displaced other avenues for suit against a union for breach of a labor agreement, whether attributed to the union as an entity or to actions of particular officers or agents.

A persuasive consideration in the Court's decision is Section 301(b), providing that:

> Any money judgment against a labor organization in a district court of the United States shall be enforceable only against the organization as an entity and against its assets, and shall not be enforceable against any individual member or his assets.

The Court found the legislative history of Section 301 to embody a deeply felt congressional reaction against the 1908 *Danbury Hatters* case, in which many union members, held liable for their union's action, lost their homes. The Court reiterated its congressional mandate to formulate the law to govern Section 301 suits. Quoting an earlier decision, it declared that Section 301 evidenced "a congressional intention that the union as an entity like a corporation, should . . . be the sole source of recovery for injury inflicted by it." In the Court's words, "This policy cannot be evaded or truncated by the simple device of suing union agents or members . . . in a separate action for damages for violation of a collective bargaining contract for which damages the union itself is liable."

The issue of attaching liability to individual officers and members for their own breach was addressed, or readdressed, in a more recent case. Union members, concerned that their union was not adequately handling negotiations for amendments to their contract, engaged in a wildcat strike in breach of a no-strike promise. The three struck employers each sued the employees as individuals for losses resulting from the strike. The suits alleged that the strike was not authorized or approved by the union, and the union was not named in the action. The Supreme Court, in *Complete Auto Transit v. Reis* (1981), found no basis for a suit and again emphasized that Section 301 shielded employees from suit for breach of a contract, whether or not their union authorized or approved their breach. This case appears to establish firmly the rule that contracts are agreements between unions and employers and that only those parties are liable for their breach, regardless of the specific individual responsibility for a breach.

Some lawsuits will purport to sue individuals both in their representative capacity and as individuals. Naming individuals as individuals in a suit is often an employer tactic designed to intimidate and to provide an incentive for persons so-named to apply themselves to the prevention of any future breaches of the contract. Individuals may be named as union representatives or as individuals in injunction proceedings—often initiated at the same time as a 301 damage suit—and may be enjoined as named individuals from certain activities. Therefore, failure to comply may result in penalties for which the individual is personally liable.

Contract Enforcement by Injunction

The primary means of enforcing a labor contract is the private dispute settlement method created by the contract itself. Since the 1970s, however, the courts have assumed an increasingly dominant role in contract enforcement through the use of injunctions. Because this is a trend that will likely intensify in coming years and will have an enormous impact on labor relations, the use of injunctions is discussed in detail.

Historically, injunctions have been the favored legal means to cripple workers' efforts to further their collective interests. An injunction is simply an "order" which mandates that the enjoined party either perform a certain act or refrain from engaging in certain activity. An injunction is known in the law as an "equitable remedy." It is based on a concept in early English law in which the Chancellor of Equity was empowered to make orders to achieve fairness regardless of the legalities of a situation. The purpose of an injunction is to *maintain the status quo, i.e.,* to keep things the way they are, *until legal issues can be decided* so as to prevent irreparable harm to one party's rights. Injunctions are applied to all types of disputes—not simply to labor disputes—and are in most cases a reasonable exercise of a court's authority.

A simple example illustrates the basic idea behind an injunction. Suppose that *A* and *B* own adjoining properties. *A* has on his property a large, rare, and unusually beautiful tree near the dividing line. Suddenly *B* announces that investigation has revealed that the supposed property line is wrong and that his property actually extends onto that which *A* believes to belong to him and on which the tree is situated. *B*, who has never liked the tree, announces that he is planning on removing it now that he has determined that it is on his property. At this point, *A* might seek an order from a court enjoining *B* to refrain from cutting the tree until the true owner of the disputed tract can legally be determined. *A* argues that he is entitled to the injunction because if *B* is permitted to cut the tree, it is irrelevant that *B* is later found to be wrong, because the tree will already be gone. *A* further argues that *B* will suffer less harm from having to wait (since he can cut down the tree later if it is determined that he owns it) than *A* will suffer if *B* is permitted to cut it now, but it is later determined that the tree in fact belonged to *A*. *A* also maintains that the tree is invaluable in the sense that its worth cannot be measured in dollars, meaning that money damages from *B*, if *B* is wrong, cannot adequately compensate *A* for the loss of the tree. This is the notion of *irreparable* harm, *viz.,* it cannot be repaired.

Every petition for an injunction, including one relating to a labor dispute, is based on an argument similar to that in the above example. An injunction is based not on the merits of a party's position, or on legal rights, but on the need to preserve the existing relationship until the point when the merits or legalities can be determined. An injunction must be obeyed as long as it is in effect regardless of the circumstances under which it was granted and is enforced through a court's power of contempt. Violation of an injunction is punishable not only because the enjoined party continues to violate the rights of the party which obtained the injunction but also because the enjoined party has challenged the authority of the court. Therefore, a contempt fine or sentence for the purpose of securing compliance with the court's order is proper, even if an appeals court later decides that the injunction was not appropriately granted.

In the latter part of the nineteenth century, injunctions became the preferred method of combating unions because of the speed with which they could be obtained and the flexibility they offered. The reach of the injunction was virtually unlimited in terms of the conduct that could be enjoined, and it was less cumbersome than criminal prosecution. Because only a judge is involved in issuing an order, the injunction procedure also avoided a hearing before a potentially hostile jury, one sympathetic to workers and their organizations. Similarly, on the issue of a contempt citation for the violation of an injunction, usually only a judge is involved in deciding whether to impose a citation. The use by the federal courts of the injunction in labor disputes was held constitutional by the Supreme Court in 1895. The case (*In re Debs, Petitioner*) involved the imprisonment of Eugene V. Debs for violating an injunction against the American Railway Union's strike against the Pullman Company.

The use of injunctions by federal courts in labor disputes was severely restricted by Congress when it passed the Norris-LaGuardia Act in 1932. Although the Norris-LaGuardia Act remains on the statute books, its meaning has been seriously eroded by later developments in labor management relations law. Both the Wagner Act and the Taft-Hartley Act made some express exceptions to the Norris-LaGuardia Act in the areas of unfair labor practices and national emergency situations. However, Section 301 of the LMRA authorizes parties to file suits over labor contract violations in federal courts, and it has provided federal courts with the primary route by which they have assumed authority to routinely issue injunctions in labor disputes.

Section 301 was initially believed to be no more than a grant of jurisdiction, that is, the vesting of power in the federal courts to hear a type of case traditionally reserved to the state courts. This concurrent jurisdiction interpretation meant that the federal courts could hear an action but would be required to apply the law of the state governing the contract. This interpretation prevented the formulation of a uniform federal labor policy.

Ten years after Taft-Hartley was passed, the Supreme Court, forced to resolve the varying interpretations, decided that Section 301 was more than a simple grant of jurisdiction to hear a case. *Textile Workers v. Lincoln Mills* (1957) involved a union seeking a

federal court injunction to compel an employer to arbitrate a grievance in accordance with the procedure established in a contract. A
literal reading of Norris-LaGuardia's ban on federal court injunctions in labor disputes would have precluded the granting of the injunction. However, the union argued that Section 301 amended
Norris-LaGuardia insofar as the enforcement of contracts was concerned. The union viewed Section 301 as empowering the federal
courts to develop a federal labor policy—a federal common law to
govern collective bargaining agreements. Only this argument could
overcome the obvious restriction of the Norris-LaGuardia Act.

In the case under review, the collective bargaining agreement
contained a no-strike promise by the union and a mandatory final-
and-binding arbitration provision applying to all disputes between
the employer and the union on the meaning and application of the
agreement. It was in this context that the Supreme Court first articulated a principle that is the foundation for present-day contract interpretation and application. "Plainly, the agreement to arbitrate
grievance disputes is the *quid pro quo* [trade-off] for an agreement
not to strike," the Court observed. Surely, it reasoned, Section 301
must mean that the federal courts have the power to enforce such
agreements—to compel the parties to abide by their obligations.
How otherwise could the national policy favoring industrial stability
be achieved if the federal courts were powerless to secure actual performance of contract promises that parties made to each other? The
ability of a court to award damages after the breach of contract
would not achieve the stability which the law was supposed to foster.

The Court noted that the failure to arbitrate was not the kind of
abuse at which Norris-LaGuardia had been aimed and that its limitation on injunctions by federal courts therefore ought not to apply.
Thus, in spite of the unequivocal language of Norris-LaGuardia, the
Supreme Court approved the use of injunctions in this type of contract enforcement proceeding.

In 1962, the Supreme Court was forced to answer a question it
had avoided in *Lincoln Mills*. Did Section 301 of the LMRA repeal
Norris-LaGuardia so as to permit federal courts to issue injunctions
against a union striking in violation of the collective bargaining
agreement? *Sinclair Refining Company v. Atkinson* involved a
union-authorized strike over a grievable issue in violation of an express no-strike promise accompanied by a mandatory final-and-
binding arbitration provision. In a split decision, the Court found
that the injunction sought was squarely within the prohibition of the
Norris-LaGuardia Act. After considering the legislative history of

Section 301, the Court declared that although the law as applied to the case seemed unfair, the judiciary could not do what Congress had declined to do—that is, empower federal courts to issue injunctions against a striking union. The decision was an invitation to Congress to act if it disagreed with the Court's holding that Norris-LaGuardia prevented the issuance of an injunction in such circumstances.

Another Supreme Court decision that same year has also had important consequences for unions. In *Teamsters v. Lucas Flour Co.* (1962), the Court ruled that a final-and-binding arbitration clause *implies* a no-strike clause, the breach of which entitles an employer to sue the union for money damages under Section 301. With this decision, the Court wrote a no-strike clause into virtually every collective bargaining agreement in the country. This means that a strike over any matter covered by a grievance procedure subjects the union to a damage suit for breach of contract—unless the contract expressly provides for the right to strike. This concept is referred to as an implied no-strike promise.

Norris-LaGuardia, by its own terms, is inapplicable to state courts, which have concurrent jurisdiction with the federal court over Section 301 suits. Even after *Sinclair*, employers could, if state law permitted, seek injunctions from state courts against unions striking in breach of a contract. However, a procedural right of defendants in any action arising under a federal statute, such as Section 301, permits the removal of the action to a federal court. In *Avco Corp. v. Areo Lodge 735* (1968), the Supreme Court upheld a union's right to remove an action against it from state court to federal court. Because the federal courts had no power to grant the requested relief, the practical effect of this independent procedural right was to eliminate the availability of injunctive relief to an employer seeking to enjoin a union striking in breach of a contract.

Congressional inaction after a controversial Supreme Court holding such as *Sinclair* is typically taken to mean that Congress agrees with the decision that the Court reached. If Congress disagrees with the Supreme Court on the interpretation of a congressional statute, it may exercise its legislative power to clarify the law. Congress, in spite of urgings to do so, did *not* act to legislatively overrule the *Sinclair* decision.

Congressional inaction meant that the law governing injunctions would change only if the Supreme Court decided that it had erred in its previous decision. That is exactly what the Court eventually did. The facts of *Boys Markets, Inc. v. Retail Clerks* (1970) were identical to those in *Sinclair*—a strike by a union over a grievable issue in the face of an express no-strike promise accompanied by a final-and-binding arbitration procedure. The Court used as its starting point the fact that the right of removal stripped state courts of their power to grant injunctive relief in Section 301 suits. Even if injunctive relief were available in state courts, the Court observed, the differing degrees of availability from state to state would encourage "forum shopping" by employers seeking the state most willing to permit injunctions in labor disputes. This reasoning led to the inescapable conclusion that the only way to ensure uniformity in the standards under which injunctive relief might be granted would be for the federal courts to have the authority to issue injunctions.

But what of the Norris-LaGuardia Act's limitations on federal court injunctions? Pointing back to *Lincoln Mills* and *Lucas Flour*, the Court reiterated its conclusion that a no-strike agreement, express or implied, was the *quid pro quo* of a mandatory grievance-arbitration procedure. The Court reasoned that the incentive for employers to enter into an agreement providing for arbitration is diminished if the most expeditious way of securing compliance with the promise to arbitrate—the injunction—is unavailable to them. Furthermore, the Court said, even if employers are not discouraged from entering into such agreements, the unavailability of injunctions to enforce them undermines the national labor policy favoring arbitration and the peaceful resolution of labor disputes. With this reasoning, the Court maneuvered itself into a position that logically found Norris-LaGuardia inapplicable when injunctions are sought against strikes in violation of a contract's no-strike promise or a promise to submit disputes to final-and-binding arbitration.

The Court justified its decision by pointing to social conditions radically different in 1970 from those existing when Norris-LaGuardia was passed in 1932. At that time, employers—aided by courts using their injunctive powers—could effectively thwart unions. By 1970, however, unions were mature, strong organizations with an institutionalized role in labor relations and society. Unions no longer required protection against abuses of the type which Norris-LaGuardia was designed to correct. Public policy favoring the protection of an infant labor movement had now shifted to an emphasis on collective bargaining between relatively equal parties. Therefore, the Court reasoned, the public's interest in the peaceful resolution of disputes required that the principles of Norris-LaGuardia be accommodated to the interests of contract enforcement embodied in Section 301.

The Court emphasized that its holding in *Boys Markets* was a narrow one, not meant to undermine the overall vitality of Norris-LaGuardia. An injunction was to be available only when a contract contained a mandatory grievance adjustment procedure, and the Court stated, "It does not follow . . . that injunctive relief is appropriate as a matter of course in every case of a strike over an arbitrable grievance."

In practice, however, courts have, since *Boys Markets*, routinely granted injunctions against any strike during the term of a contract. The immediate, serious consequences of violating injunctions have meant that unions seldom—if ever—authorize strikes over grievances (unless they have a contract right to use that method). Prior to 1970, a union would occasionally strike in breach of a contract, because its risk was limited to a damage action that might eventually be dropped by the employer in exchange for some other concession. Since *Boys Markets*, the reluctance of unions to use the strike to defend contract rights gave rise to a greater number of unauthorized, or wildcat, strikes in the 1970s.

In *Gateway Coal Co. v. Mine Workers* (1974) the Supreme Court further delineated the extent of federal court authority to grant injunctions in labor disputes. The Court examined the applicability of the *Boys Markets* rule to a work stoppage under a contract which provided for arbitration but which did not include an outright no-strike promise. The case involved a work stoppage by a United Mine Workers local over an alleged safety hazard. The union relied not on its contractual safety provision but on Section 502 of the LMRA which states that "the quitting of labor . . . in good faith because of abnormally dangerous conditions" shall not be considered a strike. The company sought an injunction against the work stoppage, claiming that the broad grievance arbitration clause of the applicable contract governed the dispute. In upholding an injunction against the strike, the Supreme Court rejected the argument that Section 502 embodied a public policy disfavoring arbitration. The Court, pursuing the reasoning developed in *Lucas Flour*, found that arbitration *implies* a no-strike promise *sufficient to justify* an injunction as well as damages.

The Court further announced that the presumption favoring arbitration applies to safety disputes in the same way as it does to any other dispute unless the parties by specific language in the contract indicate otherwise. By placing safety disputes into the same category as any other grievance, this decision places the burden on a union to negotiate into the contract any particular protections or procedures it desires on safety issues. Essentially, the Court gutted Section 502 by holding that it protects a refusal to work only when "ascertainable objective evidence" of an abnormally dangerous working condition exists. This test of objective evidence is far more stringent than the "good faith" requirement specified in the statutory language.

Both *Boys Markets* and *Gateway Coal* involved disputes over matters subject to collective bargaining—the employer's relations to a group of workers and their union concerning their wages, hours, and terms and conditions of employment. Typically, it is disputes on these matters covered by a contract that are subject to a grievance-arbitration procedure. It is these matters to which a no-strike clause ordinarily applies, and it is in regard to these matters that a no-strike promise is implied when they are subject to a mandatory grievance procedure.

A 1976 Supreme Court decision clarified the reach of *Boys Markets* in disputes over *nonarbitrable* issues. *Buffalo Forge Co. v. Steelworkers* involved a sympathy strike by a union operating under a contract which contained both a no-strike clause and a mandatory grievance-arbitration procedure. The strike was not addressed to any dispute that the union or its members had with the employer. Rather, the strike sympathized with the legal strike of a sister local representing other employees of the same employer at the same facility.

The employer argued that the strike violated the no-strike promise and that the interpretation and application of the no-strike clause were themselves subject to the broad arbitration provision in the contract. Thus, the employer maintained that *Boys Markets* entitled it to an order enjoining the strike and compelling the union to submit the issue of the breadth of the no-strike clause to arbitration. The Supreme Court disagreed, noting that the basis of *Boys Markets* had been the implementation of a strong congressional preference for the operation of private dispute mechanisms agreed upon by the parties. Since this dispute was not over any issue between the union and the employer remotely subject to the grievance procedure, the strike had neither the purpose nor the effect of evading the contract obligation to arbitrate and therefore could not be enjoined.

With respect to the employer's argument that the strike breached the no-strike promise, the Court emphasized that *Boys Markets does not authorize* courts to enjoin contract violations. *Boys Markets* is aimed at securing compliance with the agreed-upon method of settling disputes and does not allow courts to decide the merits of a dispute or to interpret and apply agreements. It is confined to forcing the parties to use contract processes to whatever extent they have agreed to use them.

Thus, the Court found that Norris-LaGuardia has continuing vitality in that it prevents federal court injunctions against strikes involving matters other than those upon which the parties have agreed to use a specified dispute settlement method. Since the courts will enforce whatever the parties agree to, it is obvious that a union can by contract waive the right to engage in sympathy strikes and thereby make them enjoinable. Since *Buffalo Forge*, many employers have sought and obtained no-strike clauses broad enough to cover any type of work stoppage.

At this time, there are unanswered questions as to the availability of damages to employers when a strike is over nonarbitrable issues, such as that in the *Buffalo Forge* case. The Supreme Court has not addressed this issue. However, courts of appeals decisions indicate that if the no-strike obligation is one *implied* from the existence of a mandatory grievance procedure, then the union will not be liable for damages resulting from strikes over nongrievable issues. However, when a union has *expressly* promised not to strike, it may be liable for damages when it engages in a strike over a nonarbitrable issue.

The Substantive/Procedural Dichotomy

As first developed in the *Steel Workers Trilogy* in 1960 and regularly re-emphasized in later cases, particularly *Buffalo Forge*, the Supreme Court views the judicial role in contract enforcement as limited to securing compliance by the parties with the method they have agreed upon for settling disputes. This reasoning has a deceptive plausibility to it. Why should the parties to a collective bargaining agreement not be compelled to live up to their promise to settle differences by a certain method? In practice, however, its reasonableness is less apparent.

For the most part, only an employer can breach the substantive provisions of a contract. The union does not possess any independent authority with respect to any of the substantive issues covered by a contract. The only power it possesses is that derived through collective bargaining. Via bargaining, a union can impose limits on an employer's otherwise unrestricted ability to make decisions on the substantive aspects of work—hours, wages, and conditions.

Through a union and a contract, workers can enjoy some control over their work lives. But despite these limits, it is nevertheless the employer who makes the decisions. For example, a union cannot violate the job-bidding procedures of a contract, since it does not do the hiring and promoting. The union cannot breach the overtime and classified-work rules, since it does not direct workers as to what work they are to perform and at what time they are to perform it. The same is true of all the substantive matters covered by a contract.

A contract also typically contains a procedure which the parties agree to use to settle any disputes which may arise concerning the application of the substantive rules on which they have mutually agreed. The failure to observe the proper procedure is the basis of virtually every breach of contract by a union. Employers, on the other hand, seldom breach the procedural requirements of a contract. Consequently, injunctions in practice affect unions more harshly, because, as a rule, only procedural breaches of a collective bargaining agreement are enjoinable. As the Court emphasized in *Buffalo Forge*, injunctions are not available against violations of a contract but are available to secure compliance with the agreed-upon method of settling disputes.

It is this distinction between a substantive breach (typically by an employer) and a procedural breach (typically by a union) that makes the use of injunctions such a travesty of fairness as perceived by unions and their members. Consider an oversimplified example. An employer permits a supervisor to perform bargaining-unit work in violation of the contract. The union's remedy is to grieve the violation, pursuing the remedy all the way to arbitration if necessary. Suppose the union wins. Thereafter, the employer permits the supervisor again to perform bargaining-unit work. Again, the union's remedy is to pursue the matter through the grievance procedure, the entire route if necessary. Each violation is an independent grievance, and its correction must be sought independently. If a grievance on an issue is won, the victory may become "precedent" for future, similar cases. But "precedent" is like the contract itself. If an employer chooses to violate it, its correction must be pursued through the grievance procedure.

Regardless of the merits of a dispute—regardless of how wrong the employer may be and how right the union may be—the courts consider only the procedural issue. That issue is whether the parties are observing the procedure they agreed upon for settling disputes. An employer will be ordered to submit to arbitration or to respect an arbitration award. A union will be ordered to refrain from using any method, such as striking, other than the one specified in the contract and to respect any decision obtained through the contract process. An employer will not be ordered to refrain from engaging in the activity which the union maintains is a violation of a substantive provision of the contract, since that involves the merits or the substance of the dispute—a matter of contract interpretation. Because the parties agreed upon a method to settle their disputes, courts refuse to consider the merits of claims, since that would usurp the agreed-upon method. The substantive right or wrong is irrelevant to injunction proceedings in labor disputes. In other words, to go back to the earlier example of the nature of an injunction, it does not matter who really owns the tree. From a union's point of view, a promising departure from this concept of the government's enforcement role in collective bargaining agreements is contained in a recent court of appeals decision. In *OCAW v. Ethyl Corp.* (1981), the court approved the granting of an injunction against the substantive conduct of an employer that has been the subject of an arbitration award expressly forbidding future "like" conduct.

Obviously, in contract enforcement, a union is always on the defensive. Its sole goal is to preserve, protect, and clarify the rights won at the bargaining table. It generally does not win new rights in this process. The failure to diligently protect the contract means that the employer is able to erode the rights of the employees as well as union strength and to take back through contract violations that which it had to concede to the union when the contract was negotiated.

The relative powerlessness of the union and workers to defend their rights via contract methods against an employer who deliberately and routinely violates the contract often causes them to attempt redress by other methods. And invariably employers obtain injunctions against them. The one protection for unions who want to use other methods is to negotiate the right to use such methods, since courts only compel adherence to a particular method if a union has agreed to use that method.

The difference between procedural and substantive rights harshly affects unions. Yet, it is based on a policy which most unions support. If courts decided the merits of disputes, privately established methods for settling disputes—a notion central to the concept of "free" collective bargaining—would certainly be undermined.

Arguably, an employer's substantive breach could be temporarily enjoined until an arbitrator decided whether the employer had the right to take the action in question. This may work when major problems, such as the elimination of jobs, are concerned. But the concept is difficult to apply to the somewhat piddling yet crucial matters, such as following the overtime schedule, that are the heart of day-to-day contract enforcement. In fact, unions have on occasion successfully enjoined some employers' actions, arguing that the employer will be less harmed by the delay until an arbitrator can decide the merits than the union and its members will be if the employer is permitted to take the action immediately. However, such cases are definitely a rarity, but they do offer opportunities for future reform.

In terms of union interests, grievance-arbitration procedures can be amended to work more efficiently. "Expedited" procedures work more quickly and more cheaply, and they are usually designed so as not to result in "precedent." However, as mentioned earlier, when an employer chooses to deliberately violate an agreement, establishing precedent has doubtful value anyway. Procedures for consolidating cases can be designed. Penalties for repeated violations can be authorized. But efficient procedures do not guarantee effective contract enforcement. Improvement could be made by convincing courts that once a union has established the terms and the application of an issue under a contract, the employer ought to be enjoined from future violations on that issue. However, no amount of reworking can exempt a procedure from the context of Section 301 and its distinction between substantive and procedural rights.

However, any attempt to tamper either with the injunction power of the courts or with the workings of arbitration must ultimately confront a basic fact. Although unions and government do exercise some control—via collective bargaining agreements and standards legislation—on an employer's discretion, it is ultimately employers and not government, unions, or workers who have the power to make most decisions about work: An employer may choose to manufacture jewelry for pets rather than a needed drug because the profit margin is higher; an employer may choose to manufacture in Singapore instead of Connecticut for the same reason; and an employer may in a contract agree to post and fill vacancies in a certain manner. But the employer retains the authority to make the actual decision. Even though it fails to act as promised, the employer's decision stands until successfully challenged.

Thus, while some commentators tout unions as co-partners, or at least junior partners, in the decisionmaking of the workplace, their status is really more that of the aspiring office boy—sometimes favored, sometimes abused, and never certain enough of his position to take anything for granted. The use of injunctions during the latter half of the 1970s has increasingly reminded unions of this fact.

Key Words and Phrases

arbitration	irreparable harm
Boys Market case	*Lincoln Mills* case
Buffalo Forge case	*Lucas Flour* case
collective bargaining agreement	*NLRB v. C&C Plywood Corp.*
Collyer doctrine	Norris-LaGuardia
compulsory arbitration	presumption of arbitrability
deferral	*quid pro quo*
Gateway Coal case	rights arbitration
grievance	Section 301 of the Labor Manage-
grievance procedure	ment Relations Act
implied no-strike clause	*Spielberg* doctrine
industrial jurisprudence	status quo
injunction	*Steel Workers Trilogy*
interest arbitration	voluntary arbitration

Review and Discussion Questions

1. Explain how a collective bargaining agreement may be referred to as private law.

2. How did the Taft-Hartley Act change the law concerning the enforcement of collective bargaining agreements?

3. What impact did the Supreme Court's decision in *Textile Workers v. Lincoln Mills* have on the law concerning the enforcement of collective bargaining agreements?

4. Do state courts have authority to hear cases alleging a breach of a collective bargaining agreement? Explain.

5. Who may be sued for the breach of a collective bargaining agreement?

6. Does a breach of a collective bargaining agreement also breach the public law on labor-management relations? Explain.

7. Describe the manner in which a contractual grievance procedure operates. Compare this method of conflict resolution to that used by the National Labor Relations Board in an unfair labor practice proceeding and that used by courts in civil suits. What are its advantages to a union? Disadvantages to a union?

8. What is the relationship of the Labor Management Relations Act and the judicial system to the enforcement of contractual rights under a grievance procedure, including one which has arbitration as a final step?

9. Who determines the rules governing an arbitration proceeding?

10. What action may a party which has won an arbitration award take if the losing party fails to comply with the arbitrator's award?

11. May a court overturn an arbitrator's award? If so, under what circumstances?

12. What is the Board's authority over unfair labor practices which are also matters subject to a contract procedure?

13. Explain the Board's policy of deferral. Defend this policy. Does this policy differ depending on whether an award or a final decision has been obtained via a contract proceeding or on whether the matter is pending under the contract procedure?

14. Under what circumstances may the Board engage in contract interpretation?

15. Should arbitrators be permitted to interpret and apply the public law to an issue raised in the context of a contract proceeding, such as discrimination on account of sex? If so, should the authority exist even if such consideration forecloses the right to seek redress of an alleged wrong through the appropriate public agency or court? Explain.

16. Trace the history of the application of injunctions to breach-of-contract disputes under the Labor Management Relations Act.

17. Why can't an employer be adequately compensated by money damages if a union strikes in breach of its contract? Stated otherwise, how does an employer demonstrate the "irreparable harm" that is supposedly a condition for an injunction?

18. What impact did the Supreme Court's *Boys Markets* decision have on the Norris-LaGuardia Act's prohibition of injunctions by federal courts in labor disputes?

19. What is the only issue a judge considers when an employer requests an injunction against a union striking in breach of the applicable collective bargaining agreement?

20. Explain how contract enforcement as practiced presumes an employer to be innocent until proven guilty. Does this same presumption apply to unions and their members? Explain. Is there any relatively easy way that the imbalance can be at least partially corrected?

21. How does the mere availability of injunctions in labor disputes significantly expand the ability of judges to apply discretion or personal standards—irrespective of the legal standards—to a dispute?

22. What does the Supreme Court's decision in *Boys Markets* reveal about the role of the law in labor relations? Do you think that the U.S. Congress disagrees with the Court's interpretation of Section 301 on the issue of injunctions? Explain.

23. Describe the difference in judicial treatment of procedural breaches of a contract as compared to that accorded to substantive breaches.

9

Collective Action

Historically, the right to engage in collective action has been at the heart of the right of workers to organize and to bargain in furtherance of their goals. The use of economic weapons particularly has enabled organized labor to gain its immediate goals vis à vis employers. Collective economic action has also had a significant impact on the achievement of political goals as well, as public officials have reacted to the demonstrated economic strength of workers. Today, labor increasingly relies on direct legislative activity to further its goals. This reflects both a change in the philosophy of the appropriate role of government in labor relations and the emergence of problems, such as runaway shops, that are not easily solved by the collective bargaining process. For the most part, however, collective economic action remains a viable and necessary weapon for labor.

The right to engage in collective action is guaranteed in Section 7 of the Labor Management Relations Act. Although collective action is generally synonymous with a strike or picketing, the term encompasses a broader range of activity. An organized effort to discourage the purchase of a particular product or bargaining for a contract that limits an employer's dealings with third parties are forms of collective action. A concerted effort of workers to control the pace of production or to regulate the amount of overtime is likewise collective activity.

Despite Section 7's guarantee of the right to engage in concerted activity, not all collective action by employees is legal. Nor does the law leave an employer powerless when employees engage in collective activities that are legally protected.

Under the LMRA, an employer is prohibited from restraining or interfering with employees when they are exercising rights guaranteed under that law and is prohibited from discriminating against employees because of union activity. However, an employer has the right to take certain countermeasures in response to employees who exercise their legal right to engage in concerted activities. The most significant responses that an employer may make to employees engaged in *legal* concerted activity are the hiring of permanent replacement workers for economic strikers, the use of a lockout that denies employees the opportunity to work, and the right to go out of business altogether to avoid a union. Apart from the countermeasures that an employer may take against legal concerted employee activity, the distinction between "protected" and "unprotected" concerted activity is of critical importance. Employees who engage in unprotected activity do not enjoy any of the protections of the LMRA and are subject to discharge by their employer.

The Section 7 right to engage in concerted activity is modified by the secondary boycott prohibitions of the LMRA that expressly limit the right of employees to engage in virtually every form of collective action against any but their own immediate employer. The NLRB and the courts have also placed restrictions on the right of collective action against the direct, or primary, employer. Most collective bargaining agreements include limitations on the right to use collective action. In addition, concerted activity that is accomplished through certain methods, directed at certain goals, accompanied by violence, or that constitutes insubordination or disloyalty to the employer is also considered unprotected.

Like so many other rules in labor law, the line between protected and unprotected activity is ambiguous. The determination of illegality is made in the context of particular situations, each with its own set of facts. The decision on the legality of a concerted activity is made by an enormous number of individuals at various levels of the administrative and judicial structure. These decision-makers may, in some instances, apply differing rules of law from jurisdiction to jurisdiction. Furthermore, judges may have differing legal interpretations of what the applicable rule of law requires as well as differing subjective views of what the appropriate impacts of law on particular situations ought to be. Thus, because the eventual legal status of particular concerted activity is frequently uncertain, workers and unions must gamble to some extent when pursuing a course of collective action.

Constitutional Protection of Collective Action

The extent of a constitutional right of private employees to strike has never been determined. The Supreme Court held in *Dorchy v. Kansas* (1926) that the U.S. Constitution does not confer an absolute right to strike. Since the right of private-sector employees to strike is protected by statutory law, the constitutional question is seldom raised. Absolute governmental bans on strikes by public employees have been sustained against constitutional challenge.

Constitutional interpretation has had significant impact in the past 40 years on the right of employees to picket to secure organizational and bargaining demands. Picketing can be defined as the physical presence of persons gathered to advertise particular facts. Prior to the Norris-LaGuardia Act of 1932, courts routinely enjoined picketing associated with labor disputes on the theory that picketing was either an unlawful method or that it sought to achieve an unlawful end. However, after the adoption of the Norris-LaGuardia and the Wagner Acts, the Supreme Court held in *Thornhill v. Alabama* (1940) that peaceful picketing was a legitimate exercise of the right to speech and therefore insulated from governmental restriction. However, the Supreme Court has continued to uphold restrictions on the manner and the time of picketing and to approve absolute prohibitions on picketing for certain purposes, *e.g.,* in support of a secondary boycott, on the grounds that the public interest outweighs the right to picket.

Apart from the unprotected nature of picketing, the location of picketing is important. Since the Constitution limits governmental regulation, picketing on public premises enjoys a degree of protection not available to picketing conducted on privately owned premises. Private landowners historically have enjoyed the right to prohibit the presence of other parties on their premises. When the property of a private employer adjoins a public roadway, picketers can remain on publicly owned property (the road right-of-way) and yet effectively communicate their message. However, the advent of the shopping center as the hub of much of the commercial life of communities has created a problem. Shopping center access roads and parking lots are usually private property but yet are freely open to the public, thereby assuming a quasi-public nature. This public-like quality led the Supreme Court to overturn an injunction in *Food Employees v. Logan Valley Plaza* (1968) against the picketing of a supermarket located in a shopping center. The Court ruled that the injunction violated the

First Amendment rights because the supermarket had become the "functional equivalent" of a municipal business district. Therefore, the shopping center could not be closed to persons who wished to picket the supermarket and to communicate to its patrons information concerning its employment practices.

This rule was narrowed in 1972, when the Supreme Court—with new members—reviewed an NLRB decision raising a similar issue. An employer had been found guilty of an unfair labor practice for expelling union organizers from its parking lot, open to both employees and customers. In *Central Hardware Co. v. NLRB*, the Supreme Court reversed this decision, finding that private property rights give way to the First Amendment speech right only when the private property has assumed a quasi-governmental nature (such as a company town), a condition not satisfied when an employer merely invites the public onto its premises. A subsequent case gave the Court's new majority an opportunity to clarify the status of *Logan Valley* in light of *Central Hardware*. In *Hudgens v. NLRB* (1976) the facts were as follows: Striking warehouse employees picketed a shoe company's retail store, located in a shopping mall; pickets, threatened with arrest by the mall owner, filed an unfair labor practice charge against the owner; the NLRB distinguished the picketing to communicate in *Logan Valley* from the solicitation of membership in *Central Hardware* and found the owner guilty of interfering with a constitutionally protected right. The Supreme Court, however, declared that *Central Hardware* had implicitly overruled *Logan Valley* and that the right of a landowner does not give way to the right to speech unless the private land assumes substantially all of the functions of a governmental entity. (Remember: the First Amendment protects speech only against governmental intrusion; the question here was whether the employer's private actions could assume the role of the government and thereby subject its intrusive behavior to the constitutional restrictions applied to governmental conduct.)

The Supreme Court did, however, remand the *Hudgens* case to the NLRB for consideration of the issue arising under the LMRA: is there a statutory Section 7 right of employees to picket on private property? In this supplemental proceeding, *Scott Hudgens* (1977), the NLRB found that the pickets had engaged in the type of lawful, economic picketing different from the organizational activity associated with a solicitation for membership. The Board's distinction exempted economic picketing from the Court's rule in *NRLB v. Babcock & Wilcox* (1956) that employees' organizational rights cannot impinge on private property rights *except* when the union has no other reasonable access to the employer's employees. Thus, the NLRB appears willing to extend Section 7 protection to some speech activity lacking constitutional protection.

The Right To Strike

Section 501 of the LMRA defines a "strike" as "any ... concerted stoppage of work by employees and any concerted slowdown or other concerted interruption of operations by employees." Although Section 13 of the LMRA specifically guarantees the right to strike, the most relevant provisions concerning the right to strike are Section 7 and Section 8(a)(1). Section 7 guarantees the right to engage in concerted activities. Section 8(a)(1) prohibits employer interference, restraint, or coercion in the exercise of Section 7 rights. As interpreted by the NLRB and the courts, a strike must entail a complete cessation of work to be legal. A less drastic interruption of an employer's production is generally considered unlawful on the theory that employees should not be able to engage in economic warfare and still be able to compel their employer to pay for their labor.

Legal strikes are categorized as either unfair labor practice strikes or economic strikes. Simply defined, an unfair labor practice strike is one *caused or prolonged by an employer's unfair labor practices*, while an economic strike is one *in support of collective bargaining demands*, including any negotiated right to strike over issues covered by a contract. The difference is important in that unfair labor practice strikers have greater job security than do economic strikers.

Strikes in Support of Economic Demands. Employees have a broad right to strike in support of collective bargaining demands when there is no contract in effect. The major limitation on this right is the notice requirement contained in Section 8(d) of the LMRA. Though a procedural formality, the notice requirements hold severe consequences for employees who strike without proper notice in that the strikers lose their employee status and thus all protection under the LMRA. The notice requirement does not apply to strikes over unfair labor practices or to strikes based on a negotiated right.

Although the LMRA guarantees the right to strike in support of contract demands, employees may give up that right through collective bargaining. One example is the agreement between the

United Steelworkers of America and the basic steel industry, in which workers agreed to forego the use of the strike to support demands on economic issues in return for certain benefits. Failure to settle on issues results in their submission to a third-party neutral, who must resolve the differences and, in effect, write the contract.

Although contract enforcement is legally an extension of collective bargaining, the right to strike over disputes on contract interpretation and application does not parallel the right to strike over contract terms. One of the fundamental purposes of the LMRA was to achieve orderly methods of resolving conflicts between employers and employees in order to minimize disruptions to the economy. A grievance procedure, by which parties agree to settle disputes over the interpretation and application of a collective bargaining agreement, is considered to be a substitute for economic warfare. In the event of impasse, the procedure usually provides for the submission of the dispute to a neutral third party whose decision is binding on both parties. The inclusion of such a procedure in a contract is considered by law to constitute a waiver of the right to strike over issues covered by the procedure. In addition, many contracts contain an explicit no-strike clause. Such a clause may obligate the union not to strike over matters subject to the grievance procedure or may by broad language give up the right to strike on other issues as well. However, a union may specifically reserve the right to strike over grievances.

Strikes Against an Employer's Unfair Labor Practices. Employees have a legal right to strike in response to unfair labor practices committed by an employer. An unfair labor practice strike can be conducted only as a reaction to an employer's violation of the LMRA. A strike in protest of an employer's violation of other laws or an employer action that is unfair in a moral rather than a legal sense is not protected concerted activity under the LMRA.

The right to engage in an unfair labor practice strike is limited but not totally barred by a contractual no-strike promise. The Supreme Court held in *Mastro Plastics v. NLRB* (1956) that a no-strike promise in a contract does not, without clear language to the contrary, bar a strike over serious unfair labor practices by an employer. However, the Board reads this rule narrowly to cover only those strikes caused by flagrant violations of the LMRA, such as the total repudiation of contract procedures, as in *Arlans Dept. Store* (1961). The Board will usually find that a strike conducted over unfair labor practices is unjustified when there are contract provisions which provide for other forms of resolution. A serious limitation in striking over unfair labor practices is the union's uncertainty as to whether the employer's conduct will eventually be adjudged to be illegal conduct under the LMRA. Even if the conduct is a violation, predicting whether the NLRB will classify it as serious enough to justify a strike is a risky proposition for employees subject to a no-strike obligation.

An economic strike may turn into an unfair labor practice strike because an employer's unlawful conduct prolongs the strike beyond the point where it otherwise would have ended. At that point, an economic strike assumes the status of an unfair labor practice strike. For example, an employer's demand for bargaining on a nonmandatory subject will likely convert an economic strike into an unfair labor practice strike, whereas a discharge for union-related activity likely will not. The Board's decision about the nature of a strike is made within the context of each case. Therefore, a strike does not automatically fall into the category of an unfair labor practice strike simply because employees call it one.

Replacement of Strikers. A primary weapon available to an employer whose employees are engaged in a legal strike is to hire replacements for strikers. The distinction between economic strikes and unfair labor practice strikes becomes critical in terms of the protections afforded to employees. The Supreme Court decided in *Mastro Plastics v. NLRB* (1956) that at the end of a strike, unfair labor practice strikers have an absolute right to reclaim their jobs if their jobs still exist—even though it requires the dismissal of the employees hired as their replacements. An early Supreme Court decision, *NLRB v. Mackay Radio and Telegraph Co.* (1938), determined that an economic striker retains the status of "employee" and is consequently protected against employer discrimination based on participation in a strike. The Court later decided in *NLRB v. International Van Lines* (1972) that an employer may hire *permanent* replacements for economic strikers. Generally, economic strikers who are replaced have a right to reclaim their jobs only if they win a strike settlement that includes such a right. If strike replacements are hired on a temporary basis, economic strikers are entitled to reinstatement upon request.

In *NLRB v. Fleetwood Trailer Co.* (1967), the Court found that the law does afford some protection to permanently replaced economic strikers by entitling them to preference over new hires when the employer fills future openings. The Supreme Court based this decision on the LMRA's definition of "employee" which includes strikers who have not obtained regular and equivalent employment elsewhere. This right to reinstatement exists only so long as a striker has not secured regular and substantially equivalent employment elsewhere and indicates a desire to return to employment with the employer. A replaced economic striker must apply for re-employment when the strike ends. The duration of this right to reinstatement must be "reasonable"; the NLRB has found that the right exists for periods of only a few months to more than a year.

Employer responses to a strike that cannot be justified by legitimate business concerns are not lawful. For instance, in *NLRB v. Erie Resistor Corp.* (1963) a grant of 20 years of seniority credit to persons who worked during a strike was found to be unlawful. Because this action allowed nonstrikers to improve their job security substantially, it was found to be inherently destructive of employee rights and thus could not be justified by the employer as a business necessity. The NLRB believed that such a system of superseniority—to a much greater degree than outright replacement—would induce employees to abandon a strike and would create continuing hostilities among workers. In other words, an employer can hire new employees but can't "sweeten the pie" to lure current employees away from a strike.

The ability of an employer to replace economic strikers also has implications for the union as to its status as bargaining representative. An economic striker is entitled to vote in any representation election conducted during the 12-month period after a strike begins. Permanent replacements for economic strikers are permitted to vote in any representation proceedings conducted after their hire. In the NLRB's view, therefore, an employer who hires permanent replacements may justifiably doubt the union's majority status at some point and, as a result, refuse to bargain. This can bring about an election to determine the union's status as bargaining representative. An employer, through a skillful response to an economic strike, may use the election as an opportunity to oust the union altogether. Consequently, a union which undertakes an economic strike risks not only the jobs of the strikers but its own status as well. There is, therefore, a strong incentive for strikers to maintain a successful strike and particularly to prevent the hiring of permanent replacements into their positions. (Unfair labor practice strikers have an unrestricted right to vote in representation elections whenever they are conducted. Replacements of unfair labor practice strikers may not vote in any representation election.)

Refusing to Cross a Picket Line. The effectiveness of a strike often depends on the degree of respect that employees have for the picket line that advertises the strike. Generally, employees have a right to respect *lawful* picketing of their own immediate employer regardless of whether or not the picketing is being conducted by their own union and of whether or not they are union members. For example, unorganized clerical workers have a legal right to refuse to cross a lawful picket line conducted by unionized employees of their employer. This is consistent with the idea that the person who refuses to cross a picket line makes common cause with the picketers. But the same logic denies protection to employees who refuse to cross an unlawful picket line, such as one in violation of a contract. An employee cannot lawfully make common cause with other employees who are themselves engaged in unlawful activity. This rule obviously puts a heavy burden on the employee to determine whether the picket line is a legal one.

Similarly, employees have a legal right to respect a lawful picket line against an employer other than their own. However, just as a struck employer may maintain operations by using replacements for striking workers, so may an employer respond to the gap created when its employees observe picket lines against other employers. In *Redwing Carriers, Inc.* (1962), the NLRB upheld the discharge of employees who honored a picket line located at the premises of another employer because the discharges were necessary to maintain the efficient operation of the employer's business. In later cases, a number of factors have been considered in deciding what a legitimate business purpose is. One of these factors is the ability of the employer to switch work around to accommodate the right of employees who choose not to cross a picket line. Another factor is the proportion of work lost by an employee's refusal to cross a picket line against another employer. Thus, while an employee may not be fired for "exercising the right to respect a lawful picket line," an employer may fire employees to maintain operations. The situation is one in which the legality of an employer's action may depend on how the employer characterizes the discharge of the employee. (A collective bargaining agreement may afford greater protection in this area, but it cannot protect an employee who refuses to cross a picket line that is illegal.) In *Newberry Energy Corp.* (1976), the Board determined that employees who respect a legal picket line against their own employer have a status like that of economic strikers: They may be replaced but not discharged. In this situation, the employer was not thought to have a business necessity as great as that created by a relationship to another employer, as was present in the *Redwing* case. In *C. K. Smith & Co., Inc.* (1977), the Board found that employees who respect a picket line protesting unfair labor practices acquire the status of unfair labor practice strikers and cannot be replaced.

Although observance of a picket line may be protected under

the law, the Court stated in *NLRB v. Rockaway News Supply Co.* (1953) that it can lose such protection if it breaches a collective bargaining agreement. However, a waiver of the right to honor a picket line will not be inferred in the absence of clear and unmistakable contract language supporting the waiver. A broad nostrike clause does not ordinarily constitute a waiver of the right of covered employees to refuse to cross a lawful picket line of another union. The NLRB recently interpreted a clause stating that "no employee . . . shall be required to cross a picket line . . . of any other subordinate union of the International Typographical Union" as not implying a waiver of the right of employees to honor a picket line of other unions. In *Keller Crescent Co., Div. of Mosler* (1976), the appeals court refused to enforce the Board's decision, finding that the question of whether employees could honor an unaffiliated union's picket line was arbitrable and in the absence of an arbitration award establishing the right, that employees were properly disciplined.

An interesting case is the Fourth Circuit's decision that the refusal to cross a picket line at one's own place of employment because of fear for one's physical safety is not protected activity. The court's logic in *NLRB v. Union Carbide* (1971) was that an employee who acts from fear is not acting on principle, does not make common cause with other employees, and therefore does not contribute to the mutual aid and protection of employees. (Fear for one's safety may justify refusal to cross a picket line if a collective bargaining agreement so provides.) Refusing to cross a picket line is a Section 7 right belonging to *individual* employees. It is somewhat different from the right of unions to engage in sympathy actions that also may involve the job status of employees whose union is conducting a sympathy action, particularly if it is illegal.

Lockouts

A lockout is a purposeful withholding of jobs by an employer. The legality of a lockout depends primarily on its purpose. The NLRB considers a lockout to be illegal if it seeks to prevent union organization or to interfere with rights of employees under the LMRA. However, a lockout in response to a union's strike or threatened strike or a lockout to improve the employer's bargaining position is considered by the Board to be comparable to the use of economic weapons by a union. Within certain limits, a lockout can be a legitimate self-help measure.

For many years, the NLRB distinguished between offensive and defensive bargaining lockouts, finding only the latter lawful. An offensive lockout is an affirmative economic attack by an employer in support of its bargaining position. A defensive lockout is one necessitated by unusual economic hardship on the employer that would occur if the union were to strike, such as the potential spoilage of materials or the interruption of a continuous process operation.

NLRB v. Truck Drivers Local 449 (1957) was the first lockout case to reach the Supreme Court. The case involved the lockout by all members of an employer association in response to a union strike against one member of the association. A union sometimes prefers a selective strike because it minimizes the financial hardship on its members while putting pressure on the struck employer by undermining its competitive position in the industry. This whipsaw strike threatened disintegration of the multi-employer unit, which the employers wanted to preserve as a means of bargaining on an equal basis with the union. The Supreme Court approved the Board's finding that the lockout was a permissible defense tactic for the employers in the association.

In another case, *NLRB v. Brown* (1965), a union struck one of six retail stores in a multi-employer bargaining group. The struck store continued to operate, using management personnel and temporary replacements. The other stores in the association, considering a strike against one of the association members to be a strike against them all, then locked out their permanent employees and continued to operate on the same basis as the struck employer. The NLRB, believing that the employers acted not merely to protect the integrity of the multi-employer unit but rather to inhibit a lawful strike, found a violation of the law. The Supreme Court disagreed, holding that without an anti-union motive, the lockout was a permissible exercise of the employers' economic power. The Court reasoned that to allow the struck employer to lock out and to operate but to deny that right to the other members of the association would likely destroy the association, which the employers had a legitimate reason to preserve.

The Supreme Court in *American Shipbuilding Co. v. NLRB* (1965) also approved the use of the offensive lockout by an employer to support its bargaining position. After an impasse in bargaining and in anticipation of a strike, the employer laid off most of its employees. The Court differentiated between actions in support of a bargaining position and actions based on hostility toward collective bargaining, finding only the latter unlawful. The NLRB subsequently applied this interpretation in *Darling & Co.* (1968) and found that a pre-impasse lockout was lawful where there was no evidence of anti-union purpose and where the lockout was undertaken for legitimate business reasons.

During any lockout an employer may continue to operate with management personnel or other of its employees, and during a defensive lockout, it may continue to operate also with temporary replacements hired from outside the company. However, an issue that has not been resolved is whether an employer may hire temporary replacements during an offensive lockout. In *Johns-Manville Product Corp. v. NLRB* (1977), the NLRB held that hiring permanent replacements during an offensive lockout is inherently destructive of employees' rights and therefore a violation of the law. On review of this case, the Fifth Circuit failed to reach a decision on the issue, finding instead that the employees in question had foregone protection of the law by engaging in sabotage and other unlawful activity, and were on these grounds subject to replacement.

The law pertaining to lockouts balances employer economic interests against employee rights. Even though a lockout or a threat of lockout may discourage employees in the exercise of Section 7 rights and may even directly have an adverse effect on employees, it is a legally acceptable form of employer self-help.

Strikes Creating a National Emergency

Even when a strike is legal under all the laws usually applied to strikes, the government may seek to prevent or end a strike because of its adverse impact on the nation. Widespread interruptions of work in critical industries following World War II served as the backdrop for the inclusion in the LMRA of Sections 206–210, which apply to actual or threatened strikes that endanger the national health or safety. These provisions permit the President, under prescribed conditions and procedures, to seek and obtain an injunction ordering an end to an otherwise entirely lawful strike.

These provisions—called the national emergency provisions—apply to strikes which affect an entire industry or a substantial part of it and which "imperil the national health or safety." No greater guidance is given in the statute as to which strikes are covered, *i.e.,* under what conditions the public health and safety are imperiled. Are they imperiled by mere inconvenience or by human suffering, or by an interruption affecting the national security, or by a strike which has a deleterious effect on the nation's economy?

In practice, the "national health or safety" is quite broadly construed. The economic well-being of the nation, or even portions of it, falls apparently under the category of "national health or safety." In his abortive effort to end the national coal strike in 1978, President Jimmy Carter relied in large part on the unemployment caused for workers other than coal miners to secure an injunction under the national emergency provisions. Presidential intervention in strikes may be prompted more by a perception of political expediency, particularly as promoted by the media, than by the actual impact of the strike on the public.

The most that the President can delay a strike is 80 days. If a settlement is not achieved during that time, the parties are free to resume or institute economic actions in support of their respective bargaining positions. However, the entire mechanism operates in a manner that may blunt or undercut the effectiveness of a party's bargaining position. Both the participation of the Federal Mediation and Conciliation Service in negotiations and the formation of public opinion by the publication of the reports of the President's board of inquiry can create pressures for settlement.

The constitutionality of the national emergency provisions was challenged in *United Steelworkers v. U.S.* in 1959. The union argued that the provisions permitted courts to exercise powers that are legislative or executive in nature because in each case a court is permitted to decide what is a threat to the "national health or safety." The union asserted that the vesting of such power in a court violated the constitutional division of power among the three branches of government. The Supreme Court disagreed, finding instead that a district court exercises authority permissibly delegated to it by Congress. This decision implicitly approved a broad construction of "national health or safety." The union had maintained that since only one percent of steel production was for defense purposes, only that portion of the industry ought to be covered by a national emergency injunction. The Supreme Court rejected this narrow view and the partial application of a national emergency injunction (or of any of the national emergency provisions).

Seizure. The seizure of an enterprise describes an act by which the government completely takes over a business operation to end or prevent strikes. In effect, seizure means that the government becomes management. This method of ending strikes was not uncommon during World War II. Like strikes against the government by its employees, strikes against a seized operation are unlawful.

The last instance of government seizure was during the Korean War, when President Truman seized the steel industry to avert a threatened strike. The steel companies brought suit against the President, charging that he lacked the authority to seize since neither the Constitution nor Congress had so empowered him. In *Youngstown Sheet and Tube Co. v. Sawyer* (1952), the Supreme Court agreed with the companies, finding that the President may seize an enterprise only at the direction of Congress.

Compulsory Arbitration. Another proposed method of dealing with labor-management disputes affecting the national welfare is to adopt compulsory arbitration legislation—either in general or to apply to specific disputes. Such legislation could require the submission of unsettled contract issues to a third party for binding resolution. This method, it is argued, would create an incentive for parties to resolve their problems through negotiation, since the failure to do so would mean that they lose control over the outcome. Unlike seizure and the national emergency provisions of the LMRA, which are only temporary in nature, compulsory arbitration would explicitly introduce a third party (the public) into labor-management relations. Conceptually, this would be a radical departure from long-standing notions about the appropriate parties to collective bargaining. Compulsory arbitration would make the public more than a mediator, which is its present, occasional role.

Illegal Methods of Collective Action

Even though a strike or picketing may be for a lawful purpose, it may be unprotected because of the methods used. Unions may resort to a wide range of methods that will render collective action unprotected and that will make employees subject to discharge for their participation. Collective action characterized by violence, sabotage, or trespass is considered unprotected activity. Generally, any attempt of employees to work on their own terms will be considered unprotected activity. Some of these illegal methods of activity are slowdowns, partial strikes, quickie strikes, and sitdowns.

Slowdowns. The NLRB holds that workers participating in a slowdown are engaging in unprotected activity, because the employees are attempting to obtain the benefits of a strike without giving up their wages. The Board has held that an employer has no duty to bargain while a slowdown is in progress. Even the threat of a slowdown is sufficient grounds for an employer to refuse to bargain until the threat is withdrawn. An employer has wide latitude in disciplining employees who engage in slowdowns. It is not illegal for an employer to make an example of a few employees while permitting others equally guilty to continue in their jobs as long as the employer does not discipline or discharge for other unlawful, discriminatory reasons.

Partial Strikes. While the NLRB believes that workers have a right to strike, it does not believe that workers have a right to select what parts of the assigned work they will do. For example, employees who refuse to handle "struck" goods are not protected, unless their contract gives them this right.

Quickie Strikes. These are short, intermittent strikes conducted at irregular intervals for the purpose of imposing maximum inconvenience and confusion on the employer while minimizing the burden on the employees.

Sitdown Strikes. In *NLRB v. Fansteel Metallurgical Corp.* (1939), the Supreme Court determined that employees who remain on the employer's premises but who refuse to do their assigned work are not protected by the LMRA. The degree of interference with the employer's legal right to the possession and the control of the premises is the key to the determination of whether such activity is protected. Unless a "takeover" element is present, a sitdown may be protected activity. For example, the Court found in *United Merchants & Manufacturers v. NLRB* (1977) that a 15-minute work stoppage by a group of *unorganized* employees to protest the discharge of two fellow workers was protected activity.

Strikes in Violation of a Contract

Strikes that are in direct violation of a contract obligation not to strike are unprotected activity—whether authorized by the union or not. If a contract contains a no-strike promise, most strikes during its term will be in violation of that promise and therefore unprotected. If a contract contains a final and binding arbitration clause, the courts will rule that a strike over a matter covered by the clause violates the contract, unless the contract specifically reserves the right to strike over the issue.

Wildcat strikes are strikes that are initiated by union members who have not secured approval of the action through official union procedures. These protests are unprotected because they conflict with a basic tenet of the LMRA—the notion of exclusive representation by the union. While earlier decisions have sometimes found such activity protected if it complemented and furthered the union's position, a recent Supreme Court decision, *Emporium Capwell v. WACO* (1975), reaffirms that activity conducted by individual union members which detracts from the union's status as representative is unprotected. (This case did not involve strike activity but rather picketing conducted by employees on their own time.)

Secondary Boycotts. Striking and picketing may be considered unprotected because of the union's objective. The LMRA specifically prohibits some of these objectives, *e.g.,* the prohibition of secondary boycotts. The NLRB has developed other restrictions. Any strike which itself is an unfair labor practice on the part of the union or which seeks to force the employer to commit an unfair labor practice is unprotected because of its purpose. A secondary boycott is an example of the former. An action to force an employer to discriminate against a worker because of his/her failure to support the union is an example of the latter.

Historically, much of labor law litigation has focused on activity that could broadly be described as secondary activity—attempts to influence *one* party by exerting pressure on *others* who deal with that party. For instance, the famous *Danbury Hatters* case involved a union that organized a boycott of stores selling the company's hats. (A boycott is concerted economic or social pressure to express disapproval or force a change in behavior. The term comes from Captain Boycott, an English land agent, whose ruthless eviction of tenants led them to refuse all cooperation with him and his family.) The courts, in applying the principles of common law and later of the anti-trust statutes, were quite hostile to such activity. However, the Norris-LaGuardia Act of 1932 exempted unions from the anti-trust laws. The act introduced a period which could allow the Supreme Court to find in *U.S. v. Hutcheson* (1941) that unions could use secondary pressure "so long as the union acts in its self-interest and does not combine with non-labor groups." This rule, combined with Norris-LaGuardia's substantial ban on injunctions in labor disputes, meant that unions enjoyed wide freedom to use secondary boycotts to further their goals. However, one of the fundamental changes made by the Taft-Hartley Act of 1947 was the prohibition of most forms of "secondary" economic pressures by unions. Section 8(b)(4) provides that it is an unfair labor practice for a labor organization or its agents

> ... to engage in, or to induce or encourage any individual employed by any person engaged in commerce to engage in a strike or a refusal in the course of his employment to use, manufacture, process, transport, or otherwise handle or work on any goods, articles, materials, or commodities or to perform any services; or ... to threaten, coerce, or restrain any person engaged in commerce or in an industry affecting commerce, where in either case an object thereof is: ... forcing or requiring any person to cease using, selling, handling, transporting, or otherwise dealing in the products of any other producer, processor, or manufacturer, or to cease doing business with any other person, or forcing or requiring any other employer to recognize or bargain with a labor organization as the representative of his employees unless such labor organization has been certified as the representative of such employees under the provisions of Section 9: ....

A *primary* employer is one with which a union deals concerning the rights of its employees. A *secondary* employer is any other employer that a union involves in a labor dispute where there is no question or dispute concerning that employer's treatment of its own employees. Frequently, secondary employers are implicated in a dispute between a union and a primary employer because the secondary employer is associated with the primary employer. In the construction industry, the relationship is most commonly that of a general contractor and a subcontractor. In a manufacturing context, the secondary employer may be a supplier or a distributor of the primary employer.

A union may pressure the secondary employer to cause it to exert pressure on the primary employer. For example, a union on strike against a manufacturer of furniture might pressure a sawmill operator to stop delivery of wood to the furniture maker. If no wood is available, then the furniture maker cannot produce furniture. However, the law attempts to shield the secondary, or neutral, sawmill operator from such pressure on the basis that it does not possess any power to resolve the dispute between the union and the primary employer, the furniture maker. This is a legal fiction, because the secondary employer in fact possesses very real power against the primary employer and may *voluntarily* decide to use it. The law protects the secondary employer from pressures that would *compel* it to use its power against the primary employer. Simply stated, the law asserts that an employer ought to be insulated from the labor problems of other employers.

The NLRB's authority over secondary boycotts is substantially different from that over other unfair labor practices. Section 10(1) of the LMRA requires the NLRB to immediately investigate a charge that a union is committing a secondary boycott. Such a complaint takes priority over any other current business of the regional NLRB office that receives the charge, except for other charges of a similar nature. If after a surface investigation, the facts alleged in the charge appear to be true, the regional director is required to issue a complaint and to seek immediately an injunction against the accused union. The judge's role in reviewing the petition for an injunction is limited to a determination of whether the Board has reasonable cause to believe that an unlawful secondary boycott is occurring. The judge cannot consider the basic issue of whether a statutory violation has in fact occurred.

This procedure is radically different from the normal procedure applying to charges of unfair labor practices. Normally, an injunction is obtained only after a finding of actual wrongdoing in violation of the LMRA. Until that process is completed, the accused is presumed innocent and is permitted to continue the same conduct, regardless of how outrageously violative of the law it may be. It is notable that Congress does not consider any alleged employer violation of the LMRA to be serious enough to warrant the drastic measures imposed on unions accused of secondary boycott activity.

Section 303 of the LMRA provides that a private party can sue a union in federal court for damages resulting from an unlawful secondary boycott. In interpreting the statutory language "whosoever shall be injured," the courts have read it as conferring a right of action on neutral employers and on primary employers where their business is injured by the unlawful activity. However, absent physical damage, damages are not available to anyone other than employers. Only damages to compensate for actual loss and not punitive damages can be awarded under Section 303. In addition, only those losses resulting from the illegal activity can be counted, and a union is not ordinarily liable for the individual acts of its members. The right to sue under Section 303 is entirely independent of any unfair labor practice proceedings related to the same conduct.

Only activity with a specified objective is prohibited by Section 8(b)(4). Other activity, though secondary in its effect, is not in violation of *this* provision. The Supreme Court specifically considered this issue in a case involving drivers, employed by a neutral employer, who were physically prevented from entering a rice mill by pickets seeking union recognition. The Court found this picket activity aimed at individual drivers to be different from activity aimed at securing concerted activity by the employees of a neutral employer. Although secondary in its impact because it affected the operations of an employer other than the struck employer, the Court ruled in *NLRB v. International Rice Milling Co.* (1951) that Congress had not intended to prohibit this incidental secondary effect of an ordinary strike. (Note that the physical prevention used in the case, although not an unlawful secondary boycott, might be the basis for other charges of unlawful activity.)

Common Situs Questions. Although the nature of the activity determines whether it is unlawful secondary activity, its situs, or location, is sometimes a factor in that determination. Picketing the premises of the employer with whom a dispute exists is usually primary, and picketing at the premises of a neutral employer is usually secondary. In some cases, however, the location of the primary employer and the neutral employer is the same—a common situs. Section 8(b)(4)(B) specifically states that it is not to be construed as making unlawful any primary picketing, and the *International Rice Milling* decision recognized that some effect of primary picketing on secondary employers is probably inevitable. However, the NLRB has engaged in extensive review of primary picketing in order to shield secondary employers from its effects.

The restrictions on picketing a common site have their greatest impact in the construction industry—characterized by the participation of several different employers on a job site. Since industrial sites can be picketed without regard to the incidental effects on neutral employers, construction unions argue that the imposition of a different rule on construction sites denies the unions and workers in that industry equal rights—relegating them to second-class status. Nonetheless, early on the Supreme Court approved the application of secondary boycott rules to construction sites.

NLRB v. Denver Building and Construction Trades Council (1951) involved a strike against a general contractor with the purpose of forcing the contractor to terminate a subcontract with a nonunion electrical subcontractor operating on the job. After unsuccessful discussions, the Denver Building Trades Council placed a picket at the site, with a sign stating that the job was unfair. Each affiliated union was notified of this decision, in effect ordering members of those unions to refuse to work as long as the nonunion subcontractor operated at the site. When the subcontractor was removed from the job, even though the electrical work had not been completed, it complained to the NLRB that the Building Trades

Council had engaged in strike action to force the general contractor to cease doing business with it—activity prohibited by Section 8(b)(4). The union argued that its picketing was simply to force the general contractor to make the job an all-union one and that the picketing was therefore primary. However, the Supreme Court agreed with the NLRB that the strike had the proscribed object of forcing an employer to cease doing business with another employer—squarely an unfair labor practice, as defined in Section 8(b)(4). The fact that the general contractor and the subcontractor worked on the same site and the fact that the general contractor had some supervision over the subcontractor's work did not change their status as independent employers. The Court emphasized:

> In the views of the Board as applied to this case we find conformity with the dual Congressional objectives of preserving the right of labor organizations to bring pressure to bear on offending employers in primary labor disputes and of shielding unoffending employers and others from pressure in controversies not their own.

To date, this decision stands as the clearest statement of the limitations imposed on any economic actions construction trades unions may take to maintain a fully unionized operation.

The Moore Dry Dock *Standards.* In implementing the decision in *Denver Building and Trades Council,* the NLRB developed rules that seek to protect the right of employees to boycott a primary employer and that try to insulate other employers on the same location from the effects of the picketing. The rules emerged from the NLRB's decision in *Sailor's Union of the Pacific and Moore Dry Dock Co.* (1950) and have become known as the *Moore Dry Dock* standards. The standards provide that picketing may be conducted at a common situs if:

(1) It is limited to times when the primary company's employees are actually present at the site;
(2) It is limited to places reasonably close to the operations of the primary employer's workers;
(3) The pickets show clearly that their dispute is with the primary employer alone; and
(4) The primary employer's employees are engaged in the employer's normal business.

Compliance with these rules does not protect a union from secondary boycott charges if the union—by other actions or the totality of its conduct—indicates that its dispute is not confined to the primary employer. For example, in *Garst Receveur Construction Co.* (1977), the union business agent's remark, "If the primary is off the job, then everything can be cleared up" was found to demonstrate that picketing had an unlawful purpose. The Board's finding was that the purpose of the picketing, despite the union's compliance with the standards, was to cause a general contractor to cease doing business with a subcontractor with whom the union had a dispute.

The nature of some employers' operations, *e.g.*, trucking, is such that there is no single indentifiable site of operations. The law permits picketing at any place where the primary employer's employees work as long as the *Moore Dry Dock* standards are met. For example, trucks may be followed to pick-up and delivery points and picketing may be conducted at the site of a neutral employer so long as the primary employees are present and the other standards are observed.

Reserved Gates. Another aspect of a shared situs is the use of separate entrances on both industrial and commercial sites to shield the different employers working on a site from each other's labor problems. The secondary boycott rules may be applied to a union that pickets a gate established for use by employees of a neutral employer.

In a case involving a large manufacturing facility of General Electric, independent contractors were used for a variety of tasks, including general maintenance, retooling of machines, and construction of new buildings. To insulate its own employees from the labor disputes of these outside contractors, GE posted a gate for use by employees of contractors and directed GE employees to use other gates. When GE's own employees went on strike, they picketed all entrances, including the separate gate, causing most employees of the contractors to refuse to enter the premises. In reviewing this case, the Supreme Court focused on "the type of work that is being performed by those who use the separate gate." The Court's standard, expressed in *Electrical Workers, Local 761 v. NLRB (General Electric)* (1961), provides:

> There must be a separate gate, marked and set apart from other gates: the work done by the men who use the gate must be unrelated to the normal operations of the employer, and the work must be of a kind that would not, if done when the plant were engaged in its regular operations, necessitate curtailing those operations.

In the GE example, retooling and general maintenance were both part of normal operations. Even though performed by employees of independent employers, any gate used by these employees was subject to picketing because their work was a part of the routine operation of the primary employer. A reserved gate may be established to protect employers doing work unconnected to the normal operations of the struck employer, such as new construction. It is immaterial that a reserved gate is not established until after a strike begins.

In *United Steelworkers v. NLRB (Carrier Corp.)* (1964), a union picketed on property owned by a railroad company at a gate on a spur line running into the struck employer's premises. The gate was accessible only to railroad employees involved in deliveries to the struck plant. The Court upheld the NLRB's finding that the work of railroad employees was connected with the normal operations of the struck employer and that the picketing was therefore primary and lawful. The Court commented, "We think Congress intended to preserve the right to picket during a strike a gate reserved for employees of neutral deliverymen furnishing day-to-day service essential to the plant's regular operations." However, the Board found in *Markwell v. Hartz, Inc.* (1965) that in the construction industry, the rationale did not permit picketing which was aimed at all employees of employers involved in a joint undertaking.

The Allied Employer Doctrine. Some independent and apparently secondary employers may have a relationship with a primary employer that creates for them an interest in a dispute between a primary employer and its employees. The law holds that such an employer foregoes its neutral status and in essence stands in the shoes of the primary employer. This permits the union and the employees of the primary employer to use economic weapons against the allied employer to the same degree they lawfully can use them against the primary employer.

The allied employer may be one with whom the primary employer has a continuing relationship and who receives more work because of a strike or it may be one with whom the primary employer has had no prior dealings. The most common example is an arrangement by which a secondary employer takes on the struck work which the employees of a primary employer would be doing but for a strike against the primary employer. For example, in *NLRB v. Business Machine and Office Appliance Mechanics, Local 459 (Royal Typewriters)* (1955), an employer, faced with a strike by its servicemen, advised customers with whom it held service contracts to select another repair company if service was needed and to send a receipt for any services rendered to the primary employer for reimbursement. The court of appeals held that these independent repair shops were allied employers and subject to picketing despite the lack of a subcontract or any direct arrangement between them and the primary employer. In *Kable Printing Co. v. NLRB* (1976), an employer orchestrated a system for its customers to contract directly with other companies for services during a strike. The primary employer retained no role and was not financially liable. However, an appeals court found that the employers who assumed the primary employer's business were allied employers and therefore subject to economic pressure by the primary employer's employees.

A normal subcontracting relationship may be maintained during a strike and is shielded by the secondary boycott rules. Employees can follow only that work which they normally perform *and would be performing* but for a strike. An employer's decision to subcontract work previously done in the bargaining unit does not make a subcontractor an allied employer—that is, one subject to economic pressure for performing the subcontracted work. If a subcontract causes a strike instead of results from a strike, the allied employer rule does not apply.

Unions and the NLRB have sought, without much favor from reviewing courts, to extend the ally doctrine to other operations owned and controlled by the same persons who own and control a primary employer. The NLRB's current policy reflects that judicial caution. In *Los Angeles Newspaper Guild, Local 69 (Hearst Corp.)* (1970), the Board decided that separate corporate subsidiaries—having no continuing influence over the operations of each other and not subject to such control by the parent corporation—are separate and distinct employers. Therefore, subsidiaries of a single company are usually protected against economic pressure caused by the labor relations problems of a sister company. However, the primary employer is vulnerable to economic pressure at all of its operations wherever located. The fact that facilities may be geographically separated, involved in different kinds of industry, or represented by different unions, does not negate the fact that the primary employer has the ability to resolve the matter in dispute. Consequently, the secondary boycott rules do not apply.

Consumer Picketing. A union may follow the product of an employer with whom a dispute exists and advise potential consumers of the product that the dispute exists. *NLRB v. Fruit and*

Vegetable Packers, Local 760 (Tree Fruits Labor Relations Committee) (1964) was a major case involving a union that had picketed stores selling apples supplied by packers with whom the union had a dispute. The stores were advised that the sole purpose of the picketing was to induce customers not to purchase the apples: picketing was confined to customer entrances; picket signs urged customers not to buy Washington State apples. The NLRB found the union guilty of a secondary boycott. The Supreme Court reversed, distinguishing between consumer picketing to shut off all trade with the secondary employer and picketing merely to persuade customers not to purchase a particular struck product. The Court found the latter type to be a permissible extension of a primary boycott, since it did not involve the "threatening, coercing, or restraining" conduct that is requisite to a secondary boycott violation. This decision firmly established the right of a union to engage in picketing aimed at consumers of a particular product. Such picketing must clearly identify the unfair product and must avoid any implication of a dispute with the secondary employer which is handling or selling the product.

A *merged* product, *i.e.*, one which is integrated with a product of the secondary employer such that it loses its independent identity, may make consumer picketing unlawful. In *American Bread Company v. NLRB and Teamsters, Local 327* (1969), a Court of Appeals found that the picketing of a restaurant using struck bread was a secondary boycott, since its effect was to urge a boycott of the entire secondary operation, which utilized the bread in every sandwich made.

Furthermore, the economic impact on a secondary employer also appears to be a proper consideration in determining the legality of picketing aimed at consumers. The Supreme Court found union picketing of five land title companies that derived more than 90 percent of their income from the sale of insurance underwritten by the primary employer to be unlawful in *NLRB v. Retail Clerks, Local 1001 (Safeco Title Insurance Co.)* (1980). Because it left consumers no alternative but to boycott the neutral employers altogether, the picketing was considered to create a separate dispute with the secondary employers.

Political Boycotts

Refusing to distinguish between labor and political goals, the Supreme Court upheld in *ILA v. Allied International, Inc.* (1982) the application of secondary boycott rules to a refusal by the Longshoremen's Union to handle Soviet cargo. In protest of the Russian invasion of Afghanistan, union employees of a stevedoring company refused to unload shipments belonging to an importer of Russian wood products. Upholding the importer's right to sue the union for damages, the Court declared that when an action can reasonably be expected to impact heavily on neutral parties, the pressure on secondary parties must be seen as one of the boycott's objectives. Noteworthy here is the fact that the secondary party's relationship to its employees—its labor relations policies—had no bearing on the case.

Hot Cargo Agreements

A clause in a collective bargaining agreement providing that the covered employees cannot be required to handle nonunion or struck goods of other employers is commonly known as a *hot cargo* agreement. Such clauses were the basis of secondary boycott cases after 1947, the issue being whether such a clause was a legitimate defense against a secondary boycott charge. The Supreme Court eliminated most of the effectiveness of such contract clauses in *Local 1976, Carpenters v. NLRB* (1958) when it held that a secondary boycott is a secondary boycott regardless of what a contract provides.

The question of whether a contract clause could legalize otherwise prohibited secondary activity and, furthermore, whether such clauses were themselves legal was legislatively answered by Congress in 1959. The answer to both questions was "No." Section 8(e), commonly known as the hot cargo provision, makes clauses which seek to limit subcontracting to unionized operations unlawful. It is presumed that the purpose of such clauses is to affect the labor relations policies of the subcontractor and that its purpose is, therefore, secondary. The NLRB has interpreted Section 8(e) broadly to make the mere "entering into" of a hot cargo agreement illegal, regardless of whether either party actually implements the clause. Picketing or other boycott pressure to force an employer to enter into such an agreement is also an unfair labor practice. In the construction industry, a contract clause that restricts subcontracting out of site work except to employers signatory to an agreement with the union is lawful and may be included in collective bargaining agreements. A union can strike to obtain such a clause and may sue or arbitrate to enforce such a clause. However a strike to enforce such a clause is considered unlawful. The NLRB narrowly interprets the construction industry exception to apply only to work actually done at a construction site. It does not apply to work which could conceivably be done at the site but in fact is done elsewhere. For instance, in applying the exception standard in *Teamsters, Local 294 (Island Dock Lumber)* (1963), the NLRB decided that the mixing, delivery, and pouring of ready-mixed concrete at a construction site is not on-site work.

Work Preservation Clauses. Contract clauses that prohibit the subcontracting of bargaining unit work and clauses that restrict the kinds of work that can be subcor.'racted are lawful. Clauses which seek the preservation of bargaining unit work and the maintenance of union standards are also lawful. The reasoning behind this policy is that such clauses are primary in nature because they are directed at the protection of the jobs and the conditions of employment of an employer's own employees. Where the object of a contract clause is the preservation of work customarily performed by unit employees, the clause is primary in nature and lawful despite its being a literal violation of the hot cargo ban. The Supreme Court approved this formulation in *National Woodwork Mfgrs. Assoc. v. NLRB* (1967) which involved a provision negotiated by the carpenters' union that permitted members to refuse to handle prefabricated doors. The provision was found lawful since it sought to preserve work customarily performed by carpenters at a job site, and it did not have a motive of affecting the labor relations of any secondary employer.

A union may also bargain for recapture of work that its members previously performed but which has since been subcontracted out. Work that is different in nature but a direct substitute for the work previously done in the unit is subject to the work preservation doctrine. A union may not strike to acquire additional work even though it may be the type its members are capable of performing. In *NLRB v. Plumbers, Local 638* (1977), the Supreme Court determined that a union cannot strike to enforce a work perservation clause if the primary employer does not have the right to control how particular work is to be done. The situation arose when a union whose collective bargaining contract with a subcontractor provided that pipe threading and cutting was to be performed at the jobsite violated the LMRA when it sought to enforce the contract by refusing to install pipe which had been cut and threaded at the manufacturer's factory according to the job specifications prescribed by the general contractor. The Court upheld the NLRB's finding that the union's refusal to install the pipe was based on a valid work-preservation clause in the agreement with the subcontractor and was for the purpose of preserving work that the union had traditionally performed. Applying its "right to control" test, however, the Board concluded that the union was exerting prohibited pressure on the subcontractor with an object of either forcing a change in the general contractor's way of doing business or forcing the subcontractor to terminate its contract with the general contractor. The situation where an owner/builder or a general contractor may specify to its subcontractors that only certain materials produced off-site are to be used is a frequent one in the construction industry. An employer can thereby avoid its contract obligations to the union by accepting work that must be performed in a manner inconsistent with the agreement that it has made with the union representing its employees. Although the union cannot seek direct enforcement of its contract in such cases, it may seek redress of the contract violation through other means, such as arbitration.

There is also a developing ambiguity over the meaning of the concept of *work traditionally done.* One court decision, *Carrier Air Conditioning Co. v. NLRB* (1976), involved a contract clause which prohibited members of an employer association in the New York area from subcontracting work relating to plenums, a part attached to air conditioning units. One employer developed a new air conditioner that used prefabricated plenums that could be produced only at its Texas plant. The union objected to the installation of the units unless the plenums were fabricated by its members in the New York area. The court found that the object of the union's protest was to acquire the work performed in Texas rather than to preserve work opportunities and was therefore unlawful. The court emphasized that the product was new and different and that production of the plenums was not of the sort traditionally performed by the union's members on conventional air conditioners. This decision, if generally adopted, might seriously impair the ability of unions to negotiate the preservation of work opportunities for their members in the face of technological changes.

Struck-Work Clause. A union may negotiate a contract clause that permits its members to refuse work acquired by their employer from another employer whose employees would be performing the work if they were not on strike. Such a contract clause allows employees to refuse to do work which is itself struck work. A contract can also protect employees in a refusal to do struck work from another of the primary employer's own operations. For example, employees covered by a struck-work clause can refuse to assemble television sets that would be assembled by other workers were they not on strike. Struck-work clauses are different from clauses that attempt to protect employees who refuse to handle or work on struck goods or goods made by nonunion employees. The latter type of clause is the type prohibited by Section 8(e). Employees cannot pick and choose the parts of their work they will perform with the object of forcing their employer to put pressure on a secondary employer. For example, employees who normally assemble television sets cannot refuse to do so because the components have been made by nonunion workers. In contrast, a refusal to perform struck work itself is considered to be a protest over the relationship to the immediate employer. However, a refusal to do struck work is similar to a refusal to cross a picket line in that an employer has reason to take measures to maintain efficient business operations, such as the hiring of temporary replacements.

Picket Line Clauses. Contract clauses that immunize employees against discipline for refusing to cross a picket line at their own or another employer's site of operations are also the subject of Section 8(e) proceedings. Such clauses are lawful if they apply to primary picket lines which support strikes by unions which the picketed employers are required to recognize. But these clauses are in violation of Section 8(e) if they seek to protect employees who observe unlawful secondary picket lines. For instance, in *Bricklayers, Local 2 v. NLRB* (1977), the following contract clause was found unlawful:

> *Pickets, Banners and Strikes.* The employer may not request or instruct any Employee except Watchmen or Supervisory personnel to go through a picket line except to protect life or property. The Unions agree that there shall be no cessation of work or any recognition of picket lines of any union without first giving prior notice to the Employer or his Association.

The conclusion was that the language of the clause was broad enough to protect observance of unlawful secondary picketing. The court also affirmed the NLRB's holding that an arbitrator's favorable ruling on the clause did not make it legal.

Recognitional/Organizational Picketing. Sometimes a union which has not organized a majority of an employer's employees will picket the employer to further its organizing effort or will picket to induce the employer to recognize the union despite its lack of majority status. Because picketing may interrupt deliveries or pickups and disrupt operations, it may encourage employees to join the union or persuade the employer to recognize the union.

Although condemned by the common law, such picketing gained legal recognition in the 1930s as long as the union involved had a legitimate economic interest, such as the elimination of competition from nonunion employers with lower standards. However, both the Taft-Hartley Act and the 1959 amendments to the LMRA restrict such picketing. Section 8(b)(4)(C) made it an unfair labor practice for a union to engage in—or induce employees to engage in—a work stoppage with the object of forcing or requiring any employer to recognize or bargain with a particular union if another union has been certified to represent the employees involved. Section 8(b)(7), added in 1959, further limited the right of a union to picket for recognitional or organizational purposes unless it is certified as the representative of the affected *employees* as follows:

(1) Where the employer has lawfully recognized in accordance with this Act any other labor organization and a question concerning representation may not appropriately be raised under Section 9(c) of this Act;

(2) Where within the preceding twelve months a valid election under Section 9(c) of this Act has been conducted; or

(3) Where such picketing has been conducted without a petition under Section 9(c) being filed within a reasonable period of time not to exceed thirty days from the commencement of such picketing.

Theoretically, recognitional picketing is aimed at an employer, urging recognition of the union as the bargaining agent for its employees without regard to their desire to be represented. Organizational picketing is, on the other hand, directed at employees and seeks to convince them to support the union. In practice, the distinction is virtually meaningless. Section 8(b)(7) does not distinguish between the two purposes.

The term *picketing* is not defined in the law, and in several cases, the question has been whether certain conduct constitutes picketing. The key to whether picketing exists is the potential for confrontation between persons who post themselves near a premise and others who typically would be entering the premises and whom the picketers desire to discourage from entering. Handbilling for the simple purpose of advising the public is not regarded as picketing. However, handbilling, which signals a dispute and has the same effect as picketing will constitute a violation of Section 8(b)(7).

Area Standards Picketing. The NLRB determined in *Houston Building and Construction Trades Council (Claude Everett Con-*

struction Co.) (1962) that picketing with the purpose of encouraging an employer to observe area standards in the industry is not a violation of the Section 8(b)(7) ban on recognition and organizational picketing. This kind of picketing—mostly utilized by unions in the construction industry—is permitted because a union is considered to have a justifiable interest in protecting standards in its contracts from being undermined by competing substandard operations. It is lawful even though it may result in disruptions to the employer's business, such as interrupting deliveries. The wording of picket signs must carefully delineate the nature of the picketing.

If picketing has the dual purpose of preserving area standards and striving for employer recognition, the picketing will usually be a violation of Section 8(b)(7). Other union activities during the time of picketing will determine the nature of the union's purpose. For instance, the gathering of authorization cards or a demand for recognition is considered evidence that simultaneous picketing has as its objective union recognition rather than the preservation of union standards. Picketing will more likely be considered legitimate standards picketing if it is limited to demands that total wages and fringe benefits be equal to, or at least comparable to, those achieved by the union elsewhere. If a union engages in standards picketing, it must be able to show the disparity between the standards maintained by the picketed employer and those prevailing under union contracts. If demands relate to other than money items, such as seniority or grievance procedures, then the NLRB will likely find that the union is seeking recognition through the back door—that is, cloaking a forbidden activity and purpose behind the appearance of lawful demands.

Featherbedding

Featherbedding describes a requirement that an employer pay for services not performed. It is made an unfair labor practice in Section 8(b)(6) for a union "to cause or attempt to cause an employer to pay or deliver or agree to pay or deliver any money or other thing of value, in the nature of an exaction, for services which are not performed or not to be performed." This section has been narrowly interpreted to apply only to services not performed or not to be performed. It does not prevent a union from bargaining for actual employment of its members or the hiring of more employees even if the employer does not want or need the extra services. As long as some work is performed for the compensation paid, there is no violation of Section 8(b)(6).

Payments sought by a union for time not worked but which are incidental to employment are lawful. These include payments for lunch periods, vacation, and call-in, as well as payments to workers who continue to be employed despite the elimination of their jobs by labor-saving equipment.

In *American Newspaper Publishers Assn. v. NLRB* (1953), for example, the Supreme Court found that the typesetting of copy that the employer did not need and in fact never used was not unlawful featherbedding. The Court ruled that the employees were paid for a service actually performed although the employer would not have provided the work opportunity had the contract not obligated it to do so.

Jurisdictional Disputes

Disputes over the assignment of work are a source of tension both between employers and unions and between unions, each of which claims the right for its members to do particular work. Such disputes are especially prevalent in the construction industry. When two unions, or two groups of workers, are the contenders, the employer is caught between their conflicting demands with little ability to satisfy both. Because of the seriousness and frequency of work stoppages resulting from such disputes, the Taft-Hartley Act included Section 8(b)(4)(D) dealing specifically with this type of economic disruption.

When a violation of Section 8(b)(4)(D) is alleged, Section 10(k) of the LMRA provides for a special hearing. The NLRB decides whether the dispute is a jurisdictional one and, if so, which group of workers is entitled to the work. If the losing union, or group of workers, refuses to abide by the NLRB's Section 10(k) determination, then the matter is treated like a secondary boycott violation. The effect of the Section 10(k) award is to permit the prevailing union to strike or picket to obtain the work while the losing union is prohibited from such activity. However, an award pursuant to Section 10(k) does not impose any obligation on the employer to assign the work to one or the other of the competing unions. Employers have substantial flexibility to assign work as they wish unless clear contract language restricts their ability to do so.

While the LMRA theoretically protects the rights of employees to engage in concerted activities, in practice there are innumerable restrictions. These restrictions are generally greater for workers covered by contract procedures than for unorganized workers. However, at the same time, the legal right is less important to workers covered by a contract than to unorganized workers. Through the collective bargaining process, workers may gain protection which the law does not provide. For instance, the settlement of a legal strike, such as one in support of contract demands, is frequently accompanied by an agreement that the employer will not take any action against employees based on their participation in the strike. This kind of agreement protects employees who may otherwise be subject to discharge because of violence or other unprotected activity during the strike. Strikes in violation of a contract are usually also settled with an agreement that the employer will not retaliate. Thus, workers acquire protection through bargaining—based on their collective strength—that they do not enjoy under the law. Although there is a firm right to strike in support of contract demands, the most certain protection for strikers at any other time and over any other issue is one negotiated into a contract.

The law on secondary boycotts has a significant impact on labor solidarity. By channeling collective action by workers into narrow and legalistic categories, the law successfully obscures the common interests that workers of different employers, or even different subsidiaries of the same employer, may have with each other. Probably more than any other, this provision has shaped modern-day industrial relations, because it discourages collective action by workers as a social group in taking action in behalf of group interests or in behalf of particular workers who alone are unable to win their demands. By shielding third parties, the secondary boycott rules require workers to focus on their own immediate concerns vis-à-vis their own employer. In essence, the law has made the concept of "one for all, all for one" illegal and has in the long run helped to change the very way workers view the role of unions vis-à-vis employers.

Key Terms and Phrases

allied employer
area standards picketing
boycott
common situs
compulsory arbitration
consumer activity
defensive lockout
Denver Building Trades Council case
economic strike
featherbedding
hot cargo agreement
jurisdictional dispute
merged product rule
national emergency provisions
national health or safety
offensive lockout
organizational picketing
partial strike
picketing

primary employer
protected concerted activity
recognitional picketing
reserved gate
right to control
secondary boycott
secondary employer
seizure
sitdown
slowdown
strike
struck work
struck work clause
Tree Fruits decision
unfair labor practice strike
unprotected concerted activity
wildcat strike
work preservation
    doctrine

Review and Discussion Questions

1. How does invoking the national emergency procedures usually adversely affect the union?

2. Is the poll of the membership on an employer's final offer required by the national emergency provisions consistent with the notion of exclusive representation? Does this procedure promote democracy?

3. How would compulsory arbitration of contract issues differ from the use of the national emergency provisions as a public response to strikes having a substantial impact on the society?

4. What does the Supreme Court's reversal of its *Logan Valley Plaza* decision in the *Hudgens* case reveal about the social context in which the Supreme Court acts?

5. What is the current status of constitutional protection for picketing relating to a labor-management dispute?

6. What are some methods of collective action which will render an action "unprotected" or unlawful?

7. What are some purposes which will render collective action unlawful?

8. Why should slowdowns be considered "unprotected" concerted activity?

9. What is the difference in the law's view of slowdowns as compared to sitdowns?

10. Workers who are not unionized can legally strike over any unfair labor practice, whereas workers covered by a contract can only legally strike over an unfair labor practice that is "flagrant." Is there a justification for this distinction? Explain.

11. Explain how the rule that wildcat or unauthorized strikes are unprotected is consistent with the basic principles of the Labor Management Relations Act (particularly as developed in the materials on collective bargaining).

12. Why may the term "minority" be appropriately used to describe an unauthorized strike even though it may in fact be supported by an actual majority of the affected workers?

13. Justify the greater level of protection the law affords to workers engaged in an unfair labor practice strike as compared to that afforded to economic strikers.

14. Explain and defend the rule denying permanently replaced economic strikers the right to vote in representation elections conducted more than 12 months after the economic strike began.

15. What is the principle behind the rule that an employee may refuse to cross a lawful picket line even if the demands of the picketers are not specifically relevant to that employee?

16. How is the employer's right to lockout similar to a union's right to strike? How are the two actions fundamentally different?

17. Can workers legally refuse to work overtime as a method of protest against an employer?

18. Are there any conditions that would justify a strike by workers to protest a change in supervisors? Identify the considerations that impact on the answer to this question.

19. Should a union have a legal right to picket an entire construction site when its dispute is with only one of several independent employers operating on the site? Explain.

20. When the United Farm Workers conducted a boycott of Safeway Food Stores instead of limiting their boycott to specific products, how did the union escape secondary boycott charges?

21. Do work preservation clauses in construction agreements add to inflation? Explain.

22. How do the secondary boycott rules cripple worker solidarity among all of the workers in a community?

23. Do secondary boycott rules prevent any union activity which may have an impact on a secondary employer?

24. For what purposes may a reserved gate be used by an employer? Does the same rule apply to both construction employers and employers in general industry? Explain.

25. Does the allied employer doctrine provide a union with a workable means of economic action against a struck employer? Explain.

26. Logically, why is an allied employer different from a secondary employer? Based on that reasoning, why is a sister subsidiary of a struck employer considered a secondary rather than an allied employer? Do you agree with this reasoning? Explain.

27. Legally, how is a subcontracting clause that prohibits the contracting out of bargaining unit work different from a clause that restricts contracting out to unionized subcontractors?

28. How does the right to control test allow an employer to circumvent or avoid a lawful work preservation agreement?

10

The Individual and the Union

The preceding material has focused on the collective rights of workers and the rights of unions. For example, the principle of exclusive representation gives *exclusive* authority to a union to act on behalf of a bargaining unit with regard to wages, hours, and terms and conditions of employment. This strips the individual of any authority to act on his/her own behalf. The right of a union to negotiate a contract clause requiring that an employee join a union as a condition of retaining a job also subordinates individual rights to collective interests. Even though collective bargaining makes the employee subject to power shared by the employer and a union, the law does not ignore the use of this power as it affects individuals, particularly as exercised by the union.

This concern is manifested in numerous ways. These include rules developed by the NLRB on the operation of union security clauses, the imposition of discipline by a union against a member, and the union's duty of fair representation. The conduct of union affairs is also the focus of another federal law, the Labor Management Reporting and Disclosure Act (LMRDA), popularly known as the Landrum-Griffin Act. In addition, the common law is occasionally applied to the relationship between a union and its members.

The Duty of Fair Representation

A judicially developed corollary of a union's exclusive right to represent a bargaining unit is its obligation to represent the unit's members fairly. A union acts on behalf of a bargaining unit regardless of whether individual workers support the union. Because the law denies individuals the right to act on their own behalf, the Supreme Court has imposed a duty on a union to represent fairly and fully the interests of all members of a unit for which it holds representation rights. This duty of fair representation applies to all functions that a union performs on behalf of a bargaining unit, including the negotiation of contracts, the processing of grievances, and the intra-union activities that affect an employee's job rights. Because the duty of fair representation arises out of union's right to represent a unit, it applies to *members of the bargaining unit*, irrespective of whether they are union members.

The duty of fair representation was first developed in *Steele v. Louisville & Nashville Railroad* (1944), a case arising under the Railway Labor Act (RLA). The union had won contract provisions limiting the access of black workers to jobs in the unit. Black workers ousted from their jobs by this contract sued to recover their jobs. The Supreme Court held that it would be an anomaly for Congress to strip workers entirely of the right to bargain for themselves and to bestow that right on a union which refused to accept that responsibility. Therefore, the Court grafted the duty of fair representation onto the RLA. Later, in *Syres v. Oil Workers, Local 23* (1955), the Court applied the principle of fair representation to the Labor Management Relations Act, and has continued to do so.

In 1962, the NLRB determined in its *Miranda Fuel Co.* decision that the breach of the duty of fair representation constituted an unfair labor practice by a union. The Board held that the right to be fairly represented was implied in Section 9 and was to be read into Section 7 of the LMRA, thereby making violation of the right an unfair labor practice. The Supreme Court has implied, but never expressly held, that the NLRB has jurisdiction over such cases. However, courts, both state and federal, retain authority to act on cases involving the duty of fair representation. This is a rare type of unfair labor practice which does not come under the exclusive jurisdiction of the NLRB. When a union is charged with failing to adequately handle a grievance, it is generally through a lawsuit because that is the only way to get a remedy from the employer.

The Supreme Court in *Vaca v. Sipes* (1967) declared that in order to meet its duty of fair representation, a union must "serve the interests of all members without hostility or discrimination toward any, to exercise its discretion with complete good faith and honesty, and to avoid arbitrary conduct." To prove a breach of this duty, an employee must show that the union engaged in conduct more serious than simple mistakes, errors in judgment, or even negligence. The duty of fair representation does not prevent a union from taking actions that may have a differential, or even an un-favorable, impact on some members. A union can exercise discretion in the furtherance of its goals even when its activities draw distinctions among groups of employees. The very nature of collective bargaining requires the compromise of specific individual and subgroup interests for the overall well-being of the group. For example, pension rights may be of greater concern to senior workers than to younger employees, particularly those who do not expect to work long enough to collect a pension. Yet the union, in protecting long-term interests, may compromise the short-term interests of some by bargaining for pensions rather than for, say, greater wage increases. The Supreme Court in *Ford Motor Co. v. Huffman* (1953) described it in this way:

> Inevitably differences arise in the manner and degree to which the terms of any negotiated agreement affect individual employees and classes of employees. The mere existence of such differences does not make them invalid. The complete satisfaction of all who are represented is hardly to be expected. A wide range of reasonableness must be allowed a statutory bargaining representative in serving the unit it represents, subject always to complete good faith and honesty of purpose in the exercise of its discretion.

It is in the area of grievance handling that the fair representation principle is currently having its greatest impact. Some unions have mistakenly assumed that the obligation is fulfilled if they carry *all* grievances through *all* channels of the grievance resolution procedure. However, the key is not how far a union pursues a grievance. Nor is the issue one of whether the union wins or loses a grievance. Rather, the issue is the manner in which the union carries out its grievance representation function: It is the quality of representation and not the quantity that determines whether a union has met its obligation.

There is also a misconception that employees have an absolute right to have a grievance arbitrated. Such a right would directly conflict with the union's right to act as exclusive representative of collective interests. A union may determine that one grievance is meritorious and pursue it. It may drop another grievance despite the objections of the employee concerned. The duty of fair representation requires the union to fully investigate and consider a matter before making a decision. The union must be able to articulate sound reasons for making a particular decision. An individual dissatisfied with either a decision or the underlying investigation may file an action against the union and seek to prove that it ought to have acted otherwise.

Because most case development of fair representation is fairly recent and the law is still in flux, it is difficult to authoritatively state any rules. It is clear that a union breaches the duty if it discriminates on the basis of race, sex, union membership status, intraunion activities, or personal hostility. Less obvious discrimination involves the *swapping of grievances, i.e.,* dropping one grievance as a trade for winning another without regard to the merits of the dropped grievance. Discrimination charges can also arise when a union's activities, intended to protect the interests of one group in a bargaining unit, adversely affect the interests of other groups, *e.g.,* employees who have been merged into the existing unit.

Arbitrary union action can also be a breach of the duty of fair representation. Instead of simply prohibiting intentional wrong doing, the prohibition of arbitrary action positively requires the union to provide an acceptable level of representation to its members. Most court decisions have said that simple negligence or poor judgment are not a breach of the duty of fair representation. However, a court can still find that a violation exists if a union's conduct is negligent rather than intentional. For instance, the failure to raise a particular argument or issue in an arbitration may be a good-faith oversight but has nevertheless been found to be sufficient basis for maintaining a suit. In discharge cases where the impact is immediate and dramatic and where the individual may be left in desperate circumstances, unions need to be most cautious to assure that representation is of the highest quality.

Arbitration decisions are ordinarily final and binding and cannot be reviewed or reconsidered in any public forum. Suits involving the duty of fair representation, however, are exceptions to that rule. In *Hines v. Anchor Motor Freight, Inc.* (1976), the Supreme Court recognized a suit against an employer despite the fact that the plaintiffs had lost on the same issues in arbitration. The case involved truck drivers who were discharged for seeking reimbursement for expenses greater than those they had actually sustained. In arbitration, the employer showed that the grievants' receipts claimed an amount greater than that noted on their motel registration cards. The union presented no evidence to contradict these documents and the discharges were upheld. Subsequently, the grievants, alleging that they had been terminated on false charges of dishonesty, instituted a suit against the employer and the union. The grievants claimed that the falsity of the charges could have been discovered with a minimum of investigation, but that the union had made no effort to determine the truth of the matter. The grievants' own investigation had revealed that the motel clerk was the culprit—they had in fact paid the amount on the receipts, but the clerk had entered a lesser amount in the motel records. In accepting the suit, the Supreme Court said that an employer cannot hide behind final and binding arbitration if the proceeding was a sham and failed to protect the rights of the grievant.

The remedies available in a fair representation suit are varied. They include injunctions, orders to arbitrate, and reinstatement. Money damages can be assessed against both the employer and the union depending on their relative responsibility for the harm caused. Only compensatory damages for back wages and other losses caused by the breach are available. The Court in *IBEW v. Foust* (1979) has determined that punitive damages, intended to punish a union for its breach, are not available in a fair representation suit.

The principle of fair representation can also be applied to the internal operations of a union. A democratically adopted directive which authorizes a particular action does not relieve a union of its responsibility to each employee, or to the employees as a group. For example, some unions have established a policy whereby the membership votes on which grievances to send to arbitration. This practice would generally not protect a union against a charge that it has breached the duty of fair representation. Fair representation is a legal obligation of the union as an institution, and it cannot escape or avoid the responsibility.

The length of time in which a person may file suit varies from state to state. The reasons for this variation are rooted in differing theories of law on which such claims are based. Breaches pursued as unfair labor practices must be filed within six months of the alleged violation. If an employee seeks to sue an employer in court based on a union's breach of its duty of fair representation, the Supreme Court has ruled in *UPS v. Mitchell* (1981) that the filing period is that prescribed by a state's arbitration statute for vacating, or dismissing, an arbitration award, usually 30 to 90 days.

Union Discipline of Members

The ability of a union to maintain a united front is central to its ability to further the collective interests of the employees it represents. Likewise, the observance by its members of mutually agreed-upon rules is important if a union is to operate effectively, efficiently, and democratically. A union's ability to compel individuals to act in a collectively prescribed manner is affected by the requirements of the LMRA, the LMRDA, and the union's own rules of internal governance.

Discipline Under the LMRA. The Labor Management Relations Act affects a union's relationship to its members primarily through Section 8(b)(1)(A), which makes it an unfair labor practice for a union:

> (1) to restrain or coerce (A) employees in the exercise of the rights guaranteed in section 7: Provided, That this paragraph shall not impair the right of a labor organization to prescribe its own rules with respect to the acquisition or retention of membership therein.

The role of the NLRB in interpreting and applying this provision is one of finding an appropriate balance between, first, the conflicting claims of employees and their unions and, second, the extent of the power this provision gives unions over their members.

NLRB v Allis Chalmers Mfg. Co. (1967) was a major case on this issue. The case involved the ability of a union to impose sanctions against members found guilty of breaching the union's constitution. Workers, in violation of the union's constitution, crossed the union's picket line to work during a strike. The workers refused to pay the fines levied by the union for this infraction of rules. When the union secured court enforcement, the members filed an unfair labor practice charge against the union, alleging "restraint and coercion" of their rights. In upholding the NLRB's dismissal of the complaint, the Supreme Court approved a union's right to secure a court judgment against a member. In interpreting Section 8(b)(1)(A), the Court found no distinction between the right of a union to impose fines and the right to expel a member, which the proviso to Section 8(b)(1)(A) clearly would have permitted. The ability of the union to maintain a united front in performing its collective bargaining function was central to this decision.

When union discipline arises out of a matter involving only a member's relationship to the union and raises no question about the union's relationship to the employer, a union's disciplinary actions are more closely scrutinized. For example, in *NLRB v. Marine & Shipbuilding Workers* (1968), a member had been expelled by the union because the member had filed an unfair labor practice charge against the union without first exhausting internal union remedies in an effort to resolve the complaint. The union was found to have violated Section 8(b)(1)(A). In its decision, the Supreme Court held that the ability of a union to establish rules of membership is protected activity only when those rules protect the "legitimate" union interests. What is "legitimate" is decided on a case-by-case basis by the NLRB and by the courts rather than by the union.

In *Scofield v. NLRB* (1969), the Supreme Court listed four requirements that a union must meet when disciplining its members in order to protect itself against a charge of restraint and coercion of the member's Section 7 rights. The Court requires that a union disciplinary rule:

(1) be a properly adopted one,
(2) reflect a legitimate union interest,
(3) impair no congressional policy established in the LMRA, and
(4) be reasonably enforced against members who are free to leave the union and to escape the rule.

The case involved suspension from membership and the imposition of a fine on members who, while working on a piecework basis, violated a union rule that total daily earnings could not exceed a certain level. The discipline was found lawful in that the union's ruling was found to be consistent with the listed requirements and therefore was not a violation of Section 8(b)(1)(A).

Applying these rules in *NLRB v. Textile Workers, Local 1029* (1972), The Supreme Court upheld a finding of a violation against a union that fined employees who engaged in strikebreaking *after* resigning from the union. In *Sheet Metal Workers, Local 29* (1976), the union had fined workers, both union members who had resigned and nonmembers, for crossing a picket line because both groups of employees had by written agreement promised to honor any picket line established by the union. The NLRB based its finding that a violation existed on the fact that the agreement provided no escape for employees which would allow them to exercise their Section 7 right to refrain from engaging in strike activity. According to the NLRB, the publicly established right to refrain from engaging in strike activity cannot be waived by a private agreement without a very clear intent on the part of the employee to do so. In *Carpenters Local 1233* (1977), the NLRB also unanimously held that a union violated Section 8(b)(1)(A) when it imposed fines in accordance with the terms of a restriction that prohibited members from resigning at any time so as to be able to perform nonunion work. The NLRB believed that the result of such a restriction would be to impede forever the exercise of the Section 7 right to refrain from union activity. However, in *NLRB v. Machinists, Local 1327* (1979), a court overturned an NLRB finding of a violation against a union which fined members who had resigned and then continued to work even though their union constitution expressly forbade resignation during a strike or during the 14 day period prior to a strike. The Court distinguished between restrictions on resignation and restrictions on post-resignation conduct and found only the latter to be unlawful.

Union discipline of members for refusal to engage in unlawful or unprotected activity is generally a violation of Section 8(b)(1)(A). Examples of such violations are fining members for crossing a picket line that is part of an unlawful secondary boycott and penalizing members who fail to support a strike that breaches an applicable no-strike clause. In most cases, discipline of members because they exercise a legal right, such as filing a charge with the NLRB or another public agency, is a violation of the law. However, the policy that forbids union discipline of members for taking claims to the NLRB does not apply when the member is involved in the filing of a decertification petition. Decertification threatens the union's very existence, and the union does not have to extend the privilege of membership to those who seek to destroy it. However, a fine, unlike expulsion, is considered to have a punitive rather than a defensive purpose and is therefore unlawful. Consequently, in *NLRB v. Molders, Local 125* (1971), the court confirmed the Board's finding that a union was in violation of the law when it fined a member for filing a decertification petition. Similarly, in *Independent Shoe Workers* (1974), the Board found that fining members who signed authorization cards for a rival union was unlawful.

The Board determined in *Plasterers Local 521* (1971) that a union may lawfully maintain a constitutional provision requiring members to exhaust the internal remedies available to them within the union structure before taking a matter to court or to a public enforcement agency. However, attempts to enforce such a provision are often found to be illegal, since such attempts deny members the exercise of their right to public processes. This would appear to make exhaustion voluntary insofar as the member is concerned.

A second provision in the LMRA affecting a union's relationship to its members is Section 8(b)(1)(B), which makes it an unfair labor practice for a union to restrain or coerce "an employer in the selection of his representatives for the purposes of collective bargaining or the adjustment of grievances." This provision has been held to outlaw union efforts to force an employer to dismiss an industrial relations consultant, to force an employer either to join or to resign from a multi-employer association, and to force an employer to hire or fire certain supervisory personnel. Additionally, numerous cases involving this provision have arisen when a union has disciplined members employed as supervisors who work during a strike. The Supreme Court held in *Florida Power & Light Co. v. IBEW, Local 641* (1974) that a union did not violate Section 8(b)(1)(B) when it disciplined its supervisor-members for performing "rank-and-file bargaining unit work" during a strike. However, in *ABC v. Writers Guild* (1978) the Supreme Court did uphold an NLRB finding against a union that fined and disciplined supervisor-members who crossed a picket line and "performed only managerial work" during a strike.

Union-imposed discipline for intraunion activities, such as op-position to incumbent officers, is sometimes the basis for a Section 8(b)(1)(A) charge. However, the removal of the appointed chairman of the union safety committee for supporting an unsuccessful candidate for international president was found not to be a violation of the LMRA in *Shenango, Inc.* (1978). The Board declared that a union may demonstrate hostility to dissident members who hold positions where "teamwork, loyalty and cooperation" are necessary to enable the union to administer its collective bargaining contract with an employer.

Discipline of Members Under the LMRDA. The LMRDA, in Section 101(a)(5), contains safeguards against improper disciplinary action by unions against members. These safeguards are in addition to and sometimes overlap those contained in Section 8(b)(1)(A) of the LMRA. A union can, of course, discipline its members only to the degree that its own internal governing rules permit. Beyond that, the LMRDA creates "due process" rights. These require that a member not be fined, suspended, expelled, or otherwise disciplined unless served with written specific charges, given a reasonable time to prepare a defense, and afforded a full and fair hearing. Any provision of a union's constitution and by-laws that is inconsistent with the requirements of the LMRDA is not valid. The LMRDA rights relating to discipline are strictly procedural rights. Unlike the LMRA, Section 101(a)(5) does not apply to the scope of offenses for which the union may impose discipline. Nor does it apply to the appropriateness of penalties imposed.

The requirements of the LMRDA do not apply to actions taken against members due to their failure to pay dues required by a union security clause. Members may be summarily expelled for failure to pay required dues as long as the policy is uniformly applied. No form of discipline, other than termination for failure to pay dues as required by a union security clause, may affect a member's job rights.

The Supreme Court has ruled in *Finnegan v. Leu* (1982) that the LMRDA's protection against discipline for exercising rights under that law does not extend to the termination of a member's status as an appointed union employee. The case arose when a newly elected president of a local union, under authority granted him by the local's by-laws, discharged union business agents who had supported the defeated incumbent. The Court reasoned that discharge from union employment does not impinge on union members as members, the core of rights which the LMRDA seeks to protect.

State Regulation of Internal Union Affairs

Although state regulation of conduct subject to the NLRB's exclusive jurisdiction is generally prohibited, there is an exception for cases where conduct is only of peripheral concern to the LMRA, such as certain disputes arising out of the internal operations of the union. In some states union constitutions are treated as a contract between the institution and its members. The extent of a union's obligation to its members is, therefore, sometimes at issue in state civil proceedings.

States may also permit suits by members against their union for a variety of actions that are outside the range of conduct in which a union might reasonably be expected to engage. For example, *Farmer v. Carpenters, Local 25* (1977) involved a state court action by a union officer who alleged that, as a result of political disagreements with other union officers, he was denied referrals to jobs by the union's hiring hall. After complaining to other union officers of discrimination in job referrals, he claimed also to have been further subjected to a campaign of personal abuse and harassment by union officers. One of the central questions addressed in the case was whether the union member had the right to sue the union for these wrongs in a state court. The Supreme Court noted that the union member's allegations of discriminatory conduct could arguably form the basis for an unfair labor practice charge before the NLRB. The Court noted that the LMRA ordinarily preempts the application of state law in order to protect federal labor policy from potential conflicts with state laws. But, in this case, the Court ruled the state court should not be preempted when the union's intentionally "outrageous" conduct resulted in the infliction of emotional distress. It viewed this rule as prevailing although the LMRA could be applied to other aspects of the union's conduct.

Direct Regulation of Internal Union Affairs

Because the LMRA is violated only when a union restrains or coerces its members in the exercise of Section 7 rights as employees, it does not cover many internal activities of a union. In 1959, after extensive hearings on the alleged abuse and misuse of power by unions, Congress enacted the Labor Management Reporting and Disclosure Act (LMRDA). This law created a mechanism for the federal government to police the internal affairs of unions. It created a "bill of rights" for union members, established rules regarding the conduct of elections and the imposition of trusteeship on local unions, and prescribed the responsibilities of union officers. It also requires reports by employers on payments to unions and to employees and on other expenses related to labor relations. Labor consultants must also file reports. (The Landrum-Griffin Act also contained some amendments to the LMRA particularly on secondary boycotts and on recognitional and organizational picketing.)

The Union Member's Bill of Rights

Title I of the LMRDA is designed to guarantee democratic procedures in the operation of a union's internal affairs. Because it partially parallels the rights that citizens enjoy under the Bill of Rights of the U.S. Constitution, Title I is generally referred to as the union member's "bill of rights." It mandates that union constitutions and bylaws give members an equal right to nominate candidates for union office, to vote in union elections, to attend membership meetings, to discuss the issues raised in union meetings, and to express views concerning the union outside of meetings. It also establishes standards to govern the adoption of any increase in dues and fees, protects the right of members to sue the union, establishes procedural standards for the imposition of discipline on members by the union, and guarantees access of members to certain information.

Title I rights are enforceable only in a private action filed by an aggrieved union member. The costs and difficulty of maintaining a private action are supposed to discourage frivolous and harassing claims against a union. However, the Supreme Court in *Hall v. Cole* (1972) found that a successful claim may entitle the member to attorney's fees because upholding individual rights renders a substantial service to the union as an institution for which it ought to pay.

Equal Rights. The equal rights section of Title I does not entitle a person to become a union member. It simply requires that members be afforded equal rights on prescribed matters: nominating officers, voting, attending meetings, and participating fully in them. Each of these rights is subject to "reasonable" rules necessary for the orderly conduct of union business. Unions are free under the LMRDA, as they are under the LMRA, to establish admission standards. For instance, a union may deny membership rights to a strikebreaker. Other public laws, such as Title VII of the Civil Rights Act of 1964, do in limited ways restrict a union's ability to decide membership qualifications.

Member's Right to Information. Section 105 of the LMRDA requires every union to inform its members of the provisions of the law. It does not specify the manner in which this is to be done. Distribution of the text of the law is clearly the surest means of satisfying this obligation.

Section 104 requires the secretary or equivalent officer of a union to "forward" a copy of each collective bargaining agreement made by a local union to any employee who requests a copy and to any whose rights as an employee are directly affected by the agreement. A union, other than a local (such as an international or a joint council), is required to forward a copy of any agreement which it makes to each constituent unit having members directly affected by such agreement. The secretary, or equivalent officer, must also maintain copies of any agreement made or received for inspection by affected members. This requirement also applies to welfare/pension agreements and to apprenticeship training agreements. Section 104, unlike other Title I provisions, is enforceable by filing a complaint with the Secretary of Labor, as well as by a private action by the member.

Section 201(a) requires every union to adopt a constitution and bylaws, a copy of which must be filed with the Secretary of Labor. This copy is available for inspection by union members. However, the law does not require a union to furnish its members with a copy of its constitution and bylaws.

Dues, Fees, and Assessments. The LMRDA specifies procedures which must be followed when a union seeks to increase its dues, fees, or assessments. Federations of unions, such as the AFL-CIO, are not bound by these procedures.

Local unions may execute increases in either of two ways: (1) by a majority vote in a secret ballot of members in good standing at a general or a special membership meeting after reasonable notice of the intent to vote on the issue, or (2) by a majority vote in a secret ballot membership referendum. National unions, international unions, and intermediate bodies may approve increases in any of three ways. First, an increase may be approved by a majority vote of the delegates voting at a regular convention or at a special convention of which constitutent bodies have received at least 30 days written notice. A second acceptable method is a majority vote in a secret ballot membership referendum. Finally, an increase may be effected by a majority vote of the governing body of the union if such authority has been vested in that body by the union's constitution and bylaws. However, an increase adopted by this method can be effective only until the next regular convention of the union.

The amount of initiation fees is addressed by the LMRA. Section 8(b)(5) makes it an unfair labor practice for a union to charge excessive or discriminatory initiation fees.

Protection of the Right To Sue. A union may not limit the right of its members to institute an action in any court or before a public administrative agency regardless of whether the union or its officers are named in the action. (For instance, an action might be solely against an employer.) Nor may a union limit the right of members to appear as witnesses in any judicial, administrative, or legislative proceeding. A union member also has the right to petition a legislative body and to communicate with legislators.

Members may be required, for a period not to exceed four months, to seek redress of problems with the union via internal union means before taking legal or administrative action against the union or its officers. This exhaustion requirement is not an absolute prerequisite to the beginning of an action. Because the statute uses the words "may be required," the public tribunal has the discretion of proceeding without requiring exhaustion of internal remedies. Because enforcement of an exhaustion requirement by the union may constitute unlawful coercion under the LMRA, internal remedies are effective to the degree that members voluntarily utilize them or to the degree that public officials, rather than unions, require union members to use internal procedures before providing them with a public forum.

Reports Required by the LMRDA

Title II of the LMRDA pertains to reports that must be filed with the Secretary of Labor by unions, their officers, employers, and labor relations consultants.

Every union must annually file with the Secretary of Labor a financial report with information on the union's assets, liabilities, receipts, and disbursements. Every union must adopt a constitution and bylaws and file a copy with the Secretary of Labor accompanied by a report containing detailed information about the union, its internal structure and rules, and its activities. This information must be supplemented by an annual report. A union must make the information required in these reports available to its members. With just cause a member may maintain a suit to compel the union to permit the member to examine any books, records, and accounts necessary to verify the report. The reports filed with the Secretary of Labor are available to the public also.

Employers are required to file annual reports detailing:

(1) any payments or loans to union representatives;
(2) any payment to employees (other than their ordinary compensation) for the purpose of causing the employees to lobby against the union;
(3) any expenditures with the object of interfering with employees' rights to organize and collectively bargain or of obtaining information regarding employees or the union in connection with a labor dispute; and
(4) any arrangement or payment to a labor relations consultant whose responsibility is to interfere with employees' right to organize and bargain or to supply information in connection with a labor dispute.

Labor relations consultants are required to report within 30 days of entering into an agreement for the purpose of interfering with organizational and bargaining rights of employees or for the purpose of obtaining information on labor disputes. Labor relations consultants must also file an annual financial report.

The willful violation of the reporting requirements is a criminal violation punishable by a $10,000 fine, or one year of imprisonment, or both. Knowingly making false statements, misrepresentation, or omission of material facts in a report and the failure to maintain supporting records as required is likewise punishable. Individuals responsible for signing reports on behalf of a union, or on behalf of employers and labor relations consultants, are *personally* responsible for the proper filing of the report.

Trusteeships. Trusteeship arrangements in which a parent union takes over a local or subordinate union structure and suspends its normal processes of internal goverance are governed by Title III of the LMRDA. The law seeks to protect locals against abuses, such as intervention for the purpose of suppressing opposition or of plundering the local's treasury, while protecting the right of a parent union to legitimately intervene to preserve the integrity and stability of a local.

Consequently, the law permits a union to create a trusteeship over a subordinate body only for specified reasons. These are:

(1) To correct corruption or financial malpractice;
(2) To assure the performance of collective bargaining agreements or other duties of a bargaining representative;
(3) To restore democratic procedures; or
(4) To otherwise carry out the legitimate objectives of the union.

A trusteeship may be imposed for any of these enumerated purposes only to the extent permitted by the union's own constitution or bylaws. The funds of a trusteed unit, other than normal payments and assessments, may not be transferred to the parent union.

The trusteeship organization or affected members who feel that a trusteeship has been wrongly imposed may either complain to the Secretary of Labor, who is empowered to bring a civil action against the parent union, or the aggrieved party may institute a private civil action challenging the trusteeship. The statue provides that a trusteeship in existence for less than 18 months is presumed valid, and any challenge must be supported by clear and convincing proof that its establishment and continuation fail to comply with the requirements of the law. A trusteeship that has been in effect for more than 18 months is presumed invalid. This shifts the burden to the parent union, which must show by clear and convincing proof that the continuation of the trusteeship is justified by a permissible purpose.

Elections. Title IV of the LMRDA governs the conduct of union elections. It requires that elections for officers be by secret ballot, establishes the maximum term a union officer may serve, requires a reasonable opportunity for members to nominate candidates, and governs the use of campaign literature. Title IV is enforced by the U.S. Secretary of Labor. An individual union member has no right to go into court to seek enforcement of any of the rights in Section IV (other than the right of access to membership lists). The conduct of an election can be challenged only after the election has been held. At that time, any union member may, after fulfilling a requirement of exhaustion of internal union remedies, file a complaint asking the Secretary of Labor to set aside an election because improper conduct has affected its outcome.

Officers of national and international unions must be elected at least once every five years by a secret ballot of the members in good standing or by a convention of delegates chosen by secret ballot. Local union elections must be held at least once every three years and must be conducted by secret ballot among the members in good standing. A union constitution or bylaws may require the election of officers more frequently than is required by the LMRDA. Election officials must preserve the ballots, the credentials of convention delegates, and all other records pertaining to an election for one year. The LMRDA also establishes standards governing eligibility for office and nominations, as well as campaign and voting procedures. A union's constitution or bylaws may impose additional or stricter standards so long as they do not conflict with the law.

Qualifications for Office. The LMRDA provides that all members in good standing are eligible to run for union office subject to reasonable qualifications. The term "reasonable," open to varying interpretations, has been an issue in litigation over the years. In *Calhoon v. Harvey* (1964), the union's bylaws provided that a member could not nominate anyone but him/herself for office. Further, a member was eligible for nomination or election only after five years of membership in the national union or after service of 180 days or more of sea time on a ship covered under a contract with the union in each of two of the three years preceding the election. The Supreme Court found these rules valid under Title IV's approval of reasonable qualifications. In *Wirtz v. Hotel, Motel, & Club Employees* (1968), a qualification requiring candidates for major elective offices to have previously held union office rendered 93 percent of the union's members ineligible. The Supreme Court found this rule to be an "unreasonable" restriction on the eligibility of candidates.

In *Steelworkers, Local 3489 v. Usery* (1977), a rule requiring candidates to have attended at least half of a local's regularly scheduled meetings for the three years preceding the election was also ruled invalid. The rule disqualified 96.5 percent of the local's members from running for union office and therefore, in the Supreme Court's opinion, impermissibly limited the rights of the union's membership to choose its leaders. This consideration was found to outweigh the concededly valid reasons the union offered in justifying the rule. This decision does not mean that all eligibility requirements dependent on candidates' fulfillment of attendance rules are invalid. The rule in this case was found to be "unreasonable" because its application made most members ineligible for office. However, a rule less harsh in its impact might well be found "reasonable." On an election question raised under Title I, the Supreme Court ruled in *Steelworkers v. Sadlowski* (1982) that the law does not preclude the membership of a union from adopting a rule that prohibits candidates from accepting campaign contributions from nonmembers. In the Court's view, Title I does not create rights for union members that strictly parallel those enjoyed by citizens under the First Amendment to the U.S. Constitution.

Congress has specifically excluded certain individuals from holding union office. Persons convicted of robbery, bribery, extortion, embezzlement, grand larceny, burglary, arson, violation of narcotics laws, murder, rape, assault with intent to kill, and assault that inflicts grievous bodily injury are barred for five years after the expiration of their sentence from holding most union offices and jobs. The same restriction applies to a person convicted under the criminal provisions of the LMRDA regarding the filing of reports and the establishment of trusteeships.

A provision of the LMRDA denying a person who is or has been a member of the Communist Party from serving as an officer or an employee of a union during or for five years after termination of party membership was ruled unconstitutional by the Supreme Court in 1965. The Court held in *U.S. v. Brown* (1965) that Section 504, which imposes criminal sanctions for willful violation of this restriction on holding office, was an unconstitutional bill of attainder. (A bill of attainder is a legislative act which inflicts a punishment upon a person supposed to be guilty of some offense without any conviction. The U.S. Constitutional prohibits such legislative acts.) However, the Court also implied that Congress has the power to deal with the issue of communists holding positions in labor unions by more narrowly and precisely drawn legislation.

Title IV election provisions are enforced by the Secretary of Labor and can be invoked only after an election has been held. A union member desiring to challenge an election must first exhaust the remedies available under the union's constitution or bylaws. If after three months no final decision has been made, the member can file a complaint with the Secretary of Labor. If a violation of law that may have affected the outcome of the election has occurred and has not been remedied by the internal union procedures, the Secretary must bring an action to set aside the election results. In *Hodgson v. Steelworkers, Local 6799* (1971), the Supreme Court said that the Secretary of Labor can sue only on those issues that the member attempted to correct through the union's internal proceedings. If a court finds by a preponderance of the evidence that a timely election has not been held or that violations of Section 401 may have affected an election's outcome, it must declare the previous election void and order a new one held under the supervision of the Department of Labor. Any local union member may also petition the Secretary of Labor if the local's constitution and bylaws do not provide an adequate procedure for the removal of an elected officer guilty of serious misconduct.

Financial Safeguards. Title V of the LMRDA creates standards aimed at safeguarding the financial integrity of a union. It imposes a fiduciary responsibility on union officers and union employees, requires bonding of all union agents and union employees who handle funds or property of the union, restricts loans of union money to union officials and union employees, and prohibits the union from paying fines of persons convicted of violations of the LMRDA. Persons covered by the fiduciary obligation may be both civilly and criminally liable for breaches of the obligation.

The government regulates virtually every aspect of the internal affairs of a union as well as circumscibes a union's relationship to its members. It is significant that this regulation aims not only to secure and protect the rights of union members but to protect the interests of the public at large in the free and democratic operations of unions. Curiously, the internal affairs of employers, whose practices have a greater impact on the public, have not been subjected to such sweeping regulation. Most of an employer's activities are not even amenable to public scrutiny because information concerning those activities is not available. For example, employers are not required to detail how they spend their money.

Unions do have a right to impose membership qualifications and under specific procedures to discipline members for a variety of offenses. However, the ability of members to resign and escape the union's authority effectively undercuts discipline as a method of achieving union solidarity.

The emergence of the duty of fair representation will continue to have enormous impact on the operations of unions, especially at the local level. This principle has, probably more than any other legal development, the potential for changing the way in which unions perform one of their primary functions—contract enforcement. The result likely will be greater emphasis on the technical and procedural aspects of grievance handling.

As the representation function becomes more complicated and unions are required to assume expanded legal obligations, the union as an institution acquires an identity and a role distinct from (and often incomprehensible to) its members. These developments encourage unions to become service delivery mechanisms rather than dynamic organizations whose vitality comes from their members.

Review and Discussion Questions

1. What is the legal foundation for a union's duty of fair representation?

2. Why should a union owe the duty of fair representation to all persons who are members of a bargaining unit it represents, regardless of whether a person is a union member or not?

3. What effect does the duty of fair representation have on the "finality" of arbitration decisions?

4. If a union loses a grievance because the aggrieved individual failed to make the union aware of all relevant facts, should the aggrieved individual have any right to charge the union with a breach of the duty of fair representation?

5. Suppose an employer, due to unexplained losses of materials, suspects dishonesty among a group of workers and threatens mass dismissal. To prevent mass dismissal, the union acquiesces in an employer's provisional layoff of five of the employees. There are no more losses, so the employer permanently discharges the five laid-off workers. Does the union have an obligation to grieve and arbitrate on behalf of the discharged workers? Explain.

6. Suppose an employer refuses to permit a worker who has been on sick leave from returning to her job unless she is willing to release her medical records to the employer. The employer wants to determine if the worker is able to do the job. In processing the grievance, the union requests either the records or, at its expense, an examination by another physician. The worker refuses to cooperate, and the union declines to ar-

bitrate the grievance. Has the union performed its responsibility of representation adequately?

7. Under what circumstances should a union have a right to discipline its members to compel certain behavior?

8. Should a union have greater authority in discipline when it relates to the union's relationship to the employer or when the matter is strictly one involving the internal operations of the union? Explain.

9. Should a union have any authority to compel certain behavior by nonmembers whom the union must nevertheless represent? Explain.

10. To what extent does the law permit a union to discipline a supervisor-member who works during a union strike?

11. What rules does the Labor Management Reporting and Disclosure Act establish concerning the ability of a union to discipline its members?

12. What are some reasons why the public (and not just union members) has an interest in assuring that the election of union officers is a fair and democratic process?

13. Why should unions, unlike most other social institutions, be required to report the details of their financial operations to the government?

14. Why should a union member who successfully sues the union in a claim under Title I of the Labor Management Reporting and Disclosure Act be entitled to recover attorney's fees from the union?

15. What impact does the Labor Management Reporting and Disclosure Act have on the right of a union to decide qualifications for membership in the union?

16. Why should the law make special provisions for union votes on the costs of union membership, *viz.*, dues, fees, and assessments, while allowing unions significant discretion in the making of decisions on other issues?

17. Are the regulations on the ability of a union to impose a trusteeship on a subordinate body too restrictive, too lax, about right? Explain.

18. Does enforcement of the election provisions only by the Secretary of Labor provide sufficient safeguards in union elections?

19. Why has the Labor Management Reporting and Disclosure Act encouraged unions to elect officers at conventions rather than by membership vote? Has this promoted or reduced union democracy?

20. What is the relationship of a union constitution and bylaws to the Labor Management Reporting and Disclosure Act in regulating internal union affairs?

11

Direct Governmental Regulation of the Employment Relationship

Governmental action affecting labor can logically be divided into two types of laws. One type is legislation which establishes procedures and a framework within which society permits certain activity to take place. The Labor Management Relations Act, which establishes a framework for labor-management relations in the private economy, is an example of such legislation. Its primary aim is to foster and to shape collective bargaining between employers and unions, who are free to agree on the substantive rules to govern their relationships. This process of collective bargaining over wages, hours, and working conditions between two private parties creates most of the standards governing the employer-employee relationship.

The second type of governmental legislation affecting employment is standards legislation in which the government itself fixes or prescribes a rule to apply to a particular aspect of work. Standards legislation is frequently referred to as "protective" legislation, because it establishes a minimum level of protection relating to a specific aspect of work. Much of the early organized activity of workers was centered in efforts to secure adoption of standards by government, *e.g.*, the battle for government-mandated shorter working hours. Some of the more dramatic instances in labor history, such as the Haymarket affair in 1886, involved the demand for a shorter workday.

Employment standards legislation represents a direct social ordering of a relationship. Such legislation is based on a philosophy that says that certain job conditions are a matter of concern to the society at large and cannot be left to the employer, the employees, or a union. For instance, the government has prescribed that cer-

194

tain machines can be operated only when equipped with adequate safeguards. This public intrusion into the private relationship between employer and employee is justified on the ground that there is a social interest in preventing workers from having limbs amputated in unguarded machines. The public's concern is both economic and humanitarian. An injured worker reduces the productive capacity of the society and is an economic burden on the society. There is also a widely held belief that workers ought not to have to sacrifice their health in order to make a living. All standards legislation, whether relating to the workplace, the environment, or the consumer relationship, is the result of a social concern that has found expression in public policy. Deregulation is a denial of a public concern. The policy is based on the view that the activity regulated ought to be left to or returned to private regulation and/or control of the parties affected by it. Collective bargaining is one form of private regulation.

Governmentally created standards are of critical importance to nonunion workers, who have limited ability to participate in the making of rules that govern their work lives. The importance of standards legislation to unionized workers is less direct and less obvious, but vitally important nevertheless. The lack of adequate standards in the nonunion sector undermines the ability of unionized workers to win and maintain higher standards for themselves. In addition, standards legislation establishes a foundation for collective bargaining goals and may supplement those protections which workers are able to win through bargaining. Consequently, organized labor actively promotes standards legislation, both to supplement protections for its members as well as to eliminate competition from substandard nonunion operations. Standards legislation is enacted at both the state and the federal level, and it applies to many aspects of employment.

Example: Workers' Compensation

Workers' compensation, one of the earliest protective laws, illustrates the varied goals that may be achieved by legislated standards. Workers' compensation is socially important because it improves working conditions and job rights of employees, lessens the burden on society caused by job-related injuries, and systematizes the responsibilities of an employer to employees injured on the job. Many other legislated standards serve such varied purposes as well.

The adoption of workers' compensation laws, preceding by 30 years the New Deal legislation relating to employment, was rooted in particular social and economic conditions created by the industrial growth that followed the Civil War. The industrialization of the United States is distinguished by its carnage of workers. For instance, the *monthly* average of railroad workers killed in the United States during the years 1888–1909 was 328. A story common to this period illustrates the principle of "profit before all." A worker responsible for damage to a piece of machinery would be fired; however, a worker responsible for the injury or death of a fellow worker would receive no sanction. The difference between the actions is that the first involved the destruction of capital value that required an outlay for repair or replacement. The death of a worker was a mere inconvenience, easily remedied by hiring one of the always available masses. *See* James Weinstein, "Big Business and the Origins of Workmen's Compensation," *Labor History* (Spring, 1967).

The common law applying to personal injury claims required an injured worker to sue the employer in a civil action and to show that the employer's negligence had caused the injury. Furthermore, the employer enjoyed several defenses that would defeat a claim, even if the employee successfully showed that the employer had been negligent. These defenses were:

(1) The assumption of the risk by the employee;
(2) The fellow servant doctrine (injury caused by co-worker); and
(3) Contributory negligence (on the part of the injured worker).

Predictably, few employees recovered any damages for job-related injury.

By the late nineteenth century, the inequities of a system that allowed employers to escape almost entirely the responsibility for job-related injuries sustained by their employees inspired a movement to reform. A new system was not without attraction to employers as well. Injured workers rarely recovered damages in civil suits against employers, but when they were successful, the jury awards were often large. The costs of such suits were totally unpredictable and, therefore, potentially ruinous, because employers were unable to plan for such contingencies. If skyrocketing insurance costs came to represent an undue proportion of production costs, an employer could be rendered noncompetitive.

Workers' compensation laws were attractive to employers because such laws statutorily defined the extent of the employer's liability. Employers could incorporate the cost of employee benefits into the price of the commodity or service produced and could routinely pass the expense on to the consumer. The principle of including the wear and tear on the capital structure, machinery, and equipment into production costs was a standard practice of good business management. Workers' compensation extended the same economic principle to anticipated costs occasioned by the injury to or the death of employees on the job. If all employers were a part of the scheme, then financial stability could be maintained because the cost of insuring employees against particular risks would be nearly the same. However, this financial stability could only be achieved if workers' compensation became the *exclusive* remedy available to injured employees.

In order for employees to accept a system that statutorily imposed a maximum amount of recovery, the system had to provide some incentive for them to give up a civil remedy which theoretically gave employees an opportunity to recover several times that amount. This incentive was provided by eliminating the requirement of proving that the employer was at fault in causing an injury. A further incentive was provided by the coverage of many injuries which previously had been viewed as due to conditions inherent in industrial production and thus outside the realm of recovery.

The "exclusive remedy" feature of compensation laws is currently the subject of controversy. Because they cut off the right of the injured worker to sue the employer, compensation statutes, critics argue, allow employers to avoid the economic burden of bad safety practices. A few states liberally interpret their compensation laws to permit suits against employers whose deliberate and flagrant violations of safety standards have caused injury to their employees.

In 1917, the Supreme Court found a compulsory compensation law to be a reasonable exercise by the state of its regulatory powers in *New York Central Railroad Co. v. White*. The Court noted that changed economic conditions had rendered the common law inadequate as a means of reconciling employer-employee interests in job-related injuries. In the Court's view, the public's interest in seeing that adequate provision be made for the victims of industrial activity overrrode the competing interests of the private parties.

Today, there are workers' compensation programs in all of the 50 states and the District of Columbia. Various federal acts provide coverage for federal and certain other employees. Significant differences exist among the states in the range of compensable disabilities, the level of benefits, and the procedures which must be followed to substantiate the right to receive benefits.

Labor and management both continue to support the compensation principle, but conflict over the details of implementation. An adequate system of compensation for workers that is simple, speedy, efficient, equitable, and self-enforcing has yet to be developed. A national commission report in 1972 gave state compensation systems a dismal grade in nearly all aspects of implementation: range of coverage, level and duration of weekly benefits, sufficiency of medical and rehabilitative services, promotion of safety, and effectiveness of claim mechanisms.

The commission urged that the states be given three years to voluntarily bring their programs into compliance with a set of 19 standards that the commission considered to be basic to an effective compensation program. Should voluntary compliance fail, the commission recommended that Congress mandate minimum federal standards to assure an adequate compensation program for all workers. However, the commission concluded that responsibility for administration of the standards ought to remain at the state level. The report stimulated dramatic improvement in the compensation law of many states. But according to the AFL-CIO, not one state had, by 1979, brought its law into conformity with all of the recommendations. In some cases, the AFL-CIO reports, states had actually cut back rather than expanded coverage.

One of the arguments against improvements is that they increase costs for business and handicap efforts to attract new employers. Whether or not that assertion is true, it has deceptive appeal. In all likelihood, federal minimim standards would ensure adequate compensation coverage and eliminate any actual or feared competitive advantage for states that refuse to improve their compensation programs. At the same time, states could offer their workers a greater level of protection than those provided in the federal standards, should they choose to do so. Some advocate federalization of the entire workers' compensation program as the only way to eliminate the disparities between the states in the administration of compensation programs.

Federal Standards Laws

The Fair Labor Standards Act. Enacted in 1938, the Fair Labor Standards Act was designed to guarantee a minimum wage and a maximum number of hours that must be worked before a worker becomes entitled to premium pay. Commonly this law is referred to as the minimum wage law. Contrary to popular myth, this law does not establish a mandatory limit on the workweek. It does not entitle a worker to refuse to work more than 40 hours per week. Such a restriction on compulsory overtime can be obtained via collective bargaining. Otherwise, an employer is free to require overtime so long as it is willing to pay at one and one-half times the regular rate.

"Employer" is defined broadly in the Fair Labor Standards Act to include most employers, regardless of the nature of the enterprise. There are still exemptions in the law for employees of small local retail and service establishments if their annual business is less than $362,500. Some agricultural employees, employees of some seasonal amusement or recreational establishments, and executive, administrative, and professional employees are also exempted from coverage. Special provisions apply to learners, apprentices, handicapped workers, and full-time students. Many of the workers not covered by the federal law are covered by state wage and hour laws in the individual states.

Currently, the labor movement has substantial interest in creating a "35-hour" standard workweek. There are two legislative routes to achieve this. One route would be to lower the statutory level at which the overtime rate becomes payable to 35 hours per week and/or to increase the overtime rate to at least twice the regular rate creating a financial incentive for employers to establish a 35-hour workweek. The other method would be to legislatively establish a 35-hour workweek with a worker right to refuse to work a greater number of hours. The economic aim of both of these changes would be to create additional jobs, reduce unemployment, and ultimately improve the strength of all workers vis-à-vis employers forced to compete for a labor force. Some unions, through private-sector collective bargaining, made progress toward achieving a shorter workweek by negotiating for longer vacations (*e.g.*, the United Steelworkers) and for a larger number of paid holidays and personal days (*e.g.*, the United Auto Workers).

The Davis-Bacon Act of 1931. As amended, the act mandates that all federally financed construction work be done by employers who pay wages and offer fringe benefits at a rate equal to that prevailing in the area for the particular type of work on similar projects. The Act also applies to federal assistance programs if the statute authorizing the assistance contains a Davis-Bacon requirement. This law guarantees the maintenance of wage standards which would be undermined if contractors were permitted to secure contracts by bidding low and then by meeting the bid through wage cuts. Federal construction contracts for dams, roads, bridges, buildings, defense facilities, etc., account for approximately 30 percent of the nation's entire construction industry. Construction also represents a major portion of all government expenditures. Obviously, the act's requirement for the federal construction business continues to have an enormous impact on the vitality and influence of unions in the construction trades and on the ability of unions to protect and advance the interests of their members.

Unemployment Compensation. Unemployment compensation protects workers in temporary periods of unemployment. The current unemployment compensation program has its roots in the Depression Era of the early 1930s. Premised on the belief that the economy could recover only if there was a sufficient level of demand for goods and services, unemployment compensation bolstered the demand level by maintaining at least part of the purchasing power of unemployed workers. The federal Social Security Act contained financial incentives for employers to participate in an unemployment compensation program. This stimulated the adoption of unemployment compensation schemes by all of the individual states. State administrative costs are subsidized by the federal government. Because unemployment insurance is a state program operating under minimum federal guidelines, the specific requirements vary from state to state. The Trade Adjustment Assistance Act of 1974 provides supplemental unemployment compensation benefits in terms of more benefits for a longer period of time for workers displaced because of the import of products or product components from foreign countries.

Only those persons who have previously been employed in a covered job for a specified period of time are eligible for unemployment compensation. A further typical requirement is that an applicant for benefits be able and available for work in any suitable job for which the individual is qualified by virture of his or her training or experience. Even though a person may be eligible in that he or she is able and available, many applicants for unemployment compensation benefits may be disqualified for a variety of reasons. Frequently, states either disqualify persons who were discharged from a previous job for misconduct, who voluntarily quit a previous job, or who are engaged in a strike or penalize them by reducing the amount of benefits they can receive.

The Employment Retirement Income Security Act of 1974 (ERISA). ERISA guarantees certain rights to the beneficiaries of pension and benefit plans. The law does not require that any plan be established; it simply governs the operation of those that exist. The law seeks to assure that workers are not required to satisfy unreasonable age and service requirements before becoming eligible for plan participation. Relatedly, the law assures a worker who has worked for a specified minimum period under a pension plan of at least some benefits under the plan. This "vesting" provision is important to the highly mobile work force in the United States, where workers may hold several jobs, each under a different plan, before retirement age.

A funding requirement mandates that money be set aside on a regular and continuing basis to cover a pension plan's potential obligations. A fiduciary provision requires that the assets of a plan be handled in a prudent manner. Other provisions require the reporting and disclosure of information concerning a plan's operation and insures certain plans in the event the plan is terminated.

The Social Security Act. The Social Security Act created a pension and insurance system operated by the federal government. Participation is compulsory for most workers, including self-employed workers. Federal employees are not covered. States may voluntarily choose to participate with regard to the employees of state and local government. The program provides retirement benefits to workers at age 65, with reduced benefits payable as early as age 62. It also includes benefits for disabled wage earners, benefits to minor and dependent children of a deceased wage earner, and under certain conditions, benefits to a surviving spouse. The social security program covers wage earners, and the program is financed by employees and employers through equal percentage contributions on earnings. Coverage becomes effective only after a qualifying period of work in covered employment. A worker becomes fully insured after 10 years of covered employment. A major amendment to the Social Security Act in 1965 created the Medicare program, a government-sponsored and -subsidized health insurance program. Medicare covers persons age 65 or older whether or not they are receiving social security benefits.

This chapter by no means exhausts the subject of public laws which have a direct effect on the employment relationship nor does it examine in detail the particular laws discussed. It does provide introductory information on some of the laws having a substantial impact on workers and it illustrates the breadth of the impact of law on the employment relationship. John Dunlop, former Secretary of

Labor, noted in a 1977 speech that the number of laws enforced by the U.S. Department of Labor alone had grown from 16 in 1940 to 134 in 1975. Various other Cabinet departments and independent federal agencies, as well as state enforcement agencies, also administer laws which have an impact on the employment relationship. And there will undoubtedly be additional future laws. For instance, a bill now under consideration in Congress is intended to restrict an employer's decision to close down and move a business operation to a foreign country. Another bill would mandate the standards under which employers maintain and use employment records. An increased federal role in workers' compensation has been urged on the Congress. These are examples of the potentially greater public involvement that could occur in the employment relationship. A catalog of all such possibilities cannot be compiled not simply because the list is too long, but because laws are adopted in response to the needs of society. A changing society, reacting to new socioeconomic circumstances, will continue to demand a changing governmental response to and role in regulating the employment relationship.

Key Words and Phrases

Davis-Bacon Act	Social Security Act
Employee Retirement Income Security Act	standards legislation
	trade adjustment assistance
Fair Labor Standards Act	unemployment compensation

Review and Discussion Questions

1. Why is the minimum wage law important to organized labor despite the fact that a large majority of its members earn substantially more than the minimum wage rate?

2. What impact do governmentally created standards have on collective bargaining?

3. How has the public's view of the role of government in regulating the economy via employment standards changed in the past 50 years?

4. Does any presently existing or proposed standards legislation change the basic pattern of management decisionmaking in the United States? Explain.

5. Respond to the argument that higher minimum wage rates increase unemployment among those who are marginally in the labor market, such as youth, particularly minority youth.

6. Is the principle of workers' compensation adequate in protecting workers suffering from occupational disease?

7. Compare the advantages of state workers' compensation programs, state-operated programs which must recognize minimum federal standards, and a federalization of the entire program. Which would best serve the needs of workers? Why?

12

Workers' Health and Safety

One of the most significant concerns of workers is their own health and safety at the workplace. The health and safety of workers is a matter of public concern as well, because poor health and safety practices have an impact outside the workplace on workers themselves, on their families, and on society at large. Although unionized workers via collective bargaining may create standards to protect their health and safety, Congress in 1970 adopted the Occupational Safety and Health Act (OSH Act) to assure that all workers enjoy "safe and healthful working conditions." This law represents the first comprehensive effort by the U.S. government to establish and enforce minimum standards to secure safe and healthful conditions in the nation's workplaces.

The OSH Act was the result of a number of factors. In adopting the law, Congress noted statistics such as an annual death rate of 14,000 workers due to job-related accidents, the disablement each year of nearly 2.5 million workers, and the incidence of 300,000 new cases of occupational disease each year. Unions had pushed the proposal as a major legislative goal, and the time was one of emerging public concern over environmental health. In addition, the rising cost of industrial injury and disease to industry and to the public could no longer be ignored. Ten times as many workdays were lost because of job-related disabilities as were lost from strikes. The cost in terms of lost production and wages, medical expenses, and disability payments caused by job-related injury and disease was an enormous burden on the economy. Over and above these arguments was the human suffering which lay behind the statistics.

Coverage of the OSH Act

The OSH Act covers all employees of employers engaged in a "business affecting commerce." The OSH Act is more extensive than that of the Labor Management Relations Act because it covers agricultural workers except those on farms which employ fewer than 10 people. Recently, there have been legislative attempts to exempt small employers from OSH Act coverage. The most significant gap in OSH Act coverage is its statutory exclusion of state, county, city, and federal workers, a total of some 15.9 million people—or, 17.5 percent of the total U.S. work force in 1979. However, Presidental Executive Order 12196, which became effective in late 1980, did create some protective measures in workplace health and safety for federal employees, including those of the U.S. Postal Service.

Prior to the OSH Act, the federal government had regulated safety—and to an insignificant degree, health—only in particular industries. Mining is one major industry which has been the focus of much legislative concern at different times throughout the twentieth century and which is still subject to its own specific legislation. The Coal Mine Health and Safety Act of 1969, as amended, established comprehensive federal regulation of the health and safety conditions in that industry. Protection and enforcement procedures under that law largely parallel those contained in the OSH Act. Enforcement is delegated to the Mine Safety and Health Administration within the U.S. Department of Labor. The atomic energy industry is also exempted from OSH Act jurisdiction. Other industries previously regulated by federal legislation, such as the Construction Safety Act, were placed under the jurisdiction of the OSH Act. For these industries, previously existing standards continued in effect until they were replaced by OSH Act standards.

The OSH Act permits states to develop state plans to ensure safety and health in the workplace and to enforce them in lieu of the federal plan. The state plan must be "at least as effective" as the federal plan, but states are free to adopt programs that provide greater protections to workers than those mandated by the federal statute. Otherwise, state regulations of health and safety that existed before passage of the OSH Act have been totally supplanted by the federal law. States may, however, offer consultative, technical, and advisory services in workplace health and safety.

Three different federal agencies participate in the administration and enforcement of health and safety law:

(1) The *Occupational Safety and Health Administration* (*OSHA*), located in the U.S. Department of Labor, was established by Congress as part of the OSH Act. OSHA is the enforcement agency for the OSH Act. The agency's primary functions are to maintain reporting and recordkeeping systems for job-related injury and disease, to establish rights and responsibilities of employers and employees under the act, and to set and enforce job health and safety standards.

(2) The independent *Occupational Safety and Health Review Commission* (*OSHRC*) consists of two administrative levels. The first level is composed of administrative law judges who conduct hearings on appeals of OSHA citations. The second level is a review board made up of three members which, upon appeal, reviews decisions of the administrative law judges. Review proceedings fall basically into two categories: appeals of citations by employers that have been found by OSHA to be in violation of either a standard or the law, and employee or union protests of the time period allowed to an employer to correct conditions which OSHA has found to be in violation of standards.

(3) The *National Institute for Occupational Safety and Health* (*NIOSH*), is an office within the U.S. Department of Health and Human Services. NIOSH has no enforcement powers. Its function is to conduct research on the effects of substances, to determine safe exposure levels, and to recommend standards to OSHA. NIOSH may, at the request of either an employer or an employee, conduct a health hazard evaluation of a workplace to determine the presence of hazards, but it cannot issue citations for violations of standards.

Standards Setting

The setting of standards—rules defining the manner and level at which certain conduct can be safely carried out—is a primary activity of OSHA. In the area of job safety, hundreds of OSHA standards have been adopted. However, the setting of permanent health standards is a very slow process. By 1980, permanent standards had been established for only a few of the multitude of substances to which workers are exposed daily. In the absence of permanent standards, OSHA applies interim standards. Temporary emergency standards which take effect immediately may also be adopted and remain effective up to six months if there is evidence that a condition poses serious danger to workers. OSHA has applied such emergency standards sparingly.

OSHA may begin the standard-setting process either on its own initiative or on the petition of another party, such as NIOSH, a union, workers, employers, or a trade association. If OSHA decides that a standard is needed, it generally refers the matter to an advisory committee to develop specific recommendations. Based on its research, NIOSH may also make a specific recommendation in the setting of a standard. When the proposed standard is developed, the public is given an opportunity to comment on it. OSHA may schedule a public hearing on the proposed standard and must schedule one if requested to do so by an interested party. Once this process is completed, OSHA considers the arguments and the data it has received before publishing a final standard.

After OSHA has adopted a final standard, any person who may be adversely affected by it may, within 60 days, seek judicial review of the standard by a U.S. circuit court of appeals. A party may appeal if it believes that a standard is inadequate or is too burdensome or does not reflect the data compiled in the standard-setting process. An appeal does not delay enforcement of a standard unless the court specifically stays its enforcement. If there is an appeal, the court is directed to approve the OSHA Secretary's decision in setting a standard if the court finds that the standard is supported by substantial evidence in the record. This means that a court should not invalidate a standard supported by evidence, even if the court might have made a different decision had it been setting the standard. In the past few years, several OSHA standards have been appealed by both industry and labor groups. The challenged standards have included those on lead, benzene, coke oven emissions, and cotton dust.

OSHA's standard for benzene, a highly toxic and widely used solvent known to cause leukemia and bladder cancer, was challenged by the American Petroleum Institute. The API argued that OSHA had to consider the number of lives likely to be saved by the standard against the economic burden to industry in complying with the standard. In its review of the case, *IUD v. API* (1980), the Supreme Court skirted the cost/benefit question. It found instead that a standard must be justified by showing that a reduction of "significant risk" is achieved by setting an allowable exposure at a lower level. The Court noted that OSHA's decision to reduce allowable exposure to benzene from 10 parts per million (ppm) to 1 ppm was based on "a series of assumptions indicating that some leukemias might result from exposure to 10 ppm and that the number might be reduced by reducing the exposure level to 1 ppm." Because OSHA had not shown that an actual reduction of risk would occur if the benzene standard was lowered, the Court found its standard of 1 ppm unsupported by appropriate evidence.

In its review of the cotton dust standard in *American Textile Mfrs. Ass'n v. Marshall* (1981), the Court rejected the application of cost/benefit analysis to the standard-setting process. The Court based its decision on congressional intent in the use of the word "feasible." Noting that "feasible" means "capable of being done," the Court found that,

> Congress itself defined the basic relationship between costs and benefits by placing the 'benefit' of the worker's health above all other considerations save those making attainment of the 'benefit' achievable.... Congress understood that the Act would create substantial costs for employers, yet intended to impose such costs when necessary to create a safe and healthful work environment.

This decision could, of course, be changed by congressional action.

Even after a lengthy standard-setting process establishes a permanent standard, employers may obtain a temporary variance. A variance is a legitimate excuse for failing to comply with the standard and may last for a period of up to two years. An employer can legitimately request a variance because of the unavailability of personnel, materials, or equipment or because there is insufficient time to accomplish necessary changes in facilities. An employer's economic condition is not supposed to justify a variance. If the employer uses an alternative method of dealing with a hazard that is equally as safe as the method contained in the standard, a permanent variance may be granted. Employees and their union are entitled to notification and an opportunity to comment if an employer applies for a variance from compliance with an OSHA standard. A decision by OSHA to issue a variance to the employer may be appealed to the Review Commission if the employees or their union disagree with the decision.

The Inspection Process

In order to enforce its standards and regulations, OSHA is authorized to inspect workplaces covered by the law. Inspections are to be conducted without advance notice to employers. The alerting of an employer by an OSHA employee of a projected inspection is a criminal violation punishable by a $1,000 fine and/or six months of imprisonment. Some special circumstances, however, do justify advance notice to the employer. These include imminent danger situations that require correction as soon as possible and inspections that are to be conducted after regular business hours or when certain persons must be present. OSHA inspectors, commonly called compliance officers, have the authority to inspect workplaces to determine compliance with the law even if there has not been a complaint. Generally, however, inspections result from a formal complaint filed by workers or a union. When the complaining party requests confidentiality, OSHA is required to withhold that information from the employer.

Even though an employer is not generally entitled to notice that an inspection by OSHA is planned, a Supreme Court decision in effect permits such notice. The Court ruled in *Marshall v. Barlow's, Inc.* (1978) that the provision of the law that authorizes inspection of a workplace is unconstitutional unless it is interpreted to require an inspector to obtain a warrant to inspect. This decision allows an employer to demand that an inspector have a warrant in order to enter the premises to inspect for OSHA violations. An employer may voluntarily permit inspection without a warrant. The Court's decision was based on the Fourth Amendment to the U.S. Constitution, which states:

> The right of the people to be secure in their persons, houses, papers, and effects, against unreasonable searches and seizures, shall not be violated, and no warrants shall issue, but upon probable cause, supported by oath or affirmation, and particularly describing the place to be searched, and the person or things to be seized.

The Court held that this amendment protects citizens in their place of business as well as their residence and that both ought to be safeguarded against arbitrary invasions by government officials. Further, the Court held that "probable cause" in the criminal law sense would not be required in order for OSHA to obtain a warrant. In most cases, obtaining a warrant is more a formality than an actual impediment to an OSHA inspection. However, by asserting that inspectors can enter only with a warrant, an employer can delay inspection and thereby, have time to "clean-up" its operation, eliminating the element of surprise that had been incorporated into the OSHA statute.

An employee or a union-selected representative is entitled by law to participate in every step of the OSHA inspection and the closing conference. The employee participation ensures that someone who is familiar with the operations of a workplace can point out hidden hazards or can inform the inspector how conditions at the time of inspection compare to those that normally exist. The OSH Act does not require an employer to pay an employee representative for time spent in OSHA inspection and enforcement activities. However, a collective bargaining agreement may require an employer to do so.

An inspection may include an examination of employer records, the taking of measurements, or other activities necessary to determine compliance with OSHA standards. In addition, the inspector may question employees other than the walk-around representative, during the inspection. If necessary, compliance officers may question employees privately. Employees also have a right to talk to inspectors and are protected by law from discriminatory or retaliatory measures for exercising that right.

After an inspection is concluded, a closing conference is held between the inspector, the employer, and the employee representative. The employees or their representative may request a private conference with the inspector to emphasize particular concerns. At the closing conference, the inspector describes conditions or practices that appear to be violations of an OSHA standard. The employer is informed of the right to appeal any citation or penalty.

The Enforcement Process

After an inspection of a workplace, the OSHA area director reviews the findings of the inspector and determines whether OSHA standards have been violated. If violations are found, a citation is issued to the employer, stating the nature of the violations and establishing a time period for their correction or abatement. In certain limited circumstances an inspector may, after consultation with the area director, issue citations at the closing conference. The citation also imposes penalties for the violations that are cited.

OSHA may cite several types of violations, with differing penalties based on the severity of violations and whether the employer knowingly and deliberately committed the violation. The types of penalties are as follows:

(1) For a *nonserious* violation, that is, one having a direct relationship to health and safety but which probably would not cause death or serious physical harm, the penalty is discretionary, and parties cannot be fined more than $1,000 per violation.

(2) For a *serious* violation, one where there is a substantial probability that death or serious physical harm could result and that the employer knew or should have known of the hazard, a penalty is mandatory. Fines can range from $300 to $1,000 per violation, but may be adjusted to as little as $60, based on an employer's good faith, history of violations, and the size of the business enterprise.

(3) For a *willful* violation that the employer intentionally and knowingly commits, punishment may be a fine up to $10,000, with downward adjustments accounting for size of business and history of violations. Willful violations that result in the death of an employee are also subject to criminal sanctions of fines not to exceed $10,000, or imprisonment for up to six months, or both.

(4) For an *imminent danger* violation, that is, a violation that poses, with reasonable certainty, the threat of death or serious injury before it can be corrected or eliminated through normal enforcement procedures, the penalties are the same as those imposed for serious violations.

(5) For *repeated* violations of a standard or rule that has been previously cited as a violation, the penalty is a fine up to $10,000.

Penalties may also be imposed for falsifying records, violating the requirement to post citations, and failing to correct a violation in accordance with a finally settled abatement requirement. An employer is required to post a citation near the place where the violation occurred for three days from the date of receipt or until the violation is corrected.

On an employee-initiated inspection, employees have a right to ask the area OSHA director for an informal review of a decision not to issue a citation and for a discussion on any issue raised by an inspection. Employees or their representatives may not formally question a citation itself or the severity of penalties. Employees may challenge the abatement period by submitting a written objection to OSHA within 15 working days of the employer's receipt of the citation. This review is conducted by the Review Commission.

Within 15 days after a citation is received, an employer may formally challenge all aspects of an OSHA citation—the finding of a violation, the proposed penalties, and the abatement period. This review is also the responsibility of the Review Commission. Such proceedings delay the correction of the cited hazards. Employees or their union must be notified of any formal objection to an OSHA citation made by the employer. The employees or union can immediately acquire "party status," which entitles them to formal participation in any subsequent consideration of the citation. Party status creates several important rights, including receipt of copies of all documents pertaining to the case, participation in conference and settlement negotiations between the employer and OSHA, and the right to present evidence at the formal hearing and to cross-examine company witnesses.

In practice, most contested cases are settled prior to formal proceedings. For instance, OSHA may agree to withdraw citations or reduce penalties. If there is no settlement, the Review Commission assigns the case to an administrative law judge who conducts a formal hearing. During the hearing, OSHA must prove the existence of the cited violations and the appropriateness of the action it proposes. A decision by the judge may be appealed by any party to the Review Commission. Commission members may also initiate a review. Rulings of the Occupational Safety and Health Review Commission are appealable to the U.S. courts of appeals.

Right To Refuse Unsafe Work

Special provisions in the OSH Act deal with situations that present an imminent danger to a worker's health and safety. An imminent danger is any condition where there is reasonable certainty that an immediate danger exists that can be expected to cause death or serious physical harm before the danger can be eliminated through normal enforcement procedures. A health hazard (distinguished from a safety hazard) may create an imminent danger even though it will not result in immediate harm. The test as to whether a health hazard creates an imminent danger is whether there is a reasonable expectation that a toxic substance or a dangerous fume, dust, or gas is present, exposure to which will cause irreversible harm to such a degree as to shorten life or cause a reduction in physical or mental efficiency.

When OSHA receives a report of an imminent danger and after determining that there is a reasonable basis for the allegation, the OSHA area director must order an *immediate* (no later than 24 hours) inspection of the workplace. If an inspection reveals that an imminent danger exists, the OSHA inspector must notify employees of that finding. The law requires an employer to immediately correct the condition, or the OSHA agent can request that endangered employees be removed from the area. If the employer fails to comply with the request, OSHA may seek an injunction ordering shutdown of the affected operation or area. OSHA has no authority of its own to order a shutdown or to remove workers from an imminently dangerous situation.

The imminent danger provision of the OSHA statute also permits an employee injured by OSHA's willful disregard of an imminent danger situation to bring a suit against the U.S. Secretary of Labor, who oversees OSHA. Situations where this might occur are the failure by OSHA to inspect the workplace on a timely basis or the refusal of OSHA to seek an injunction to shut down a workplace, with the result being injury to the affected employees. The purpose of this provision is to create an incentive for OSHA to do its job as directed by the law. Neither this provision nor any other provision of the OSHA statute creates any right for employees to sue employers to compel observance of OSHA standards. The right to enforce the OSH Act belongs strictly to the government.

While the OSH Act did not expressly create an employee right to refuse work because of the existence of an imminent danger, an OSHA regulation did create the right to refuse unsafe work. The validity of this regulation has been upheld by the Supreme Court, which reviewed a challenge by an employer arguing that the Secretary of Labor had exceeded the scope of his authority under the law when he adopted the regulation. In *Whirlpool Corporation v. Marshall* (1980), the Court held the regulation to be consistent with the underlying purposes of the law and to be a valid interpretation of the general duty clause of the OSH Act, which guarantees workers a safe and healthful workplace.

In refusing work believed to be dangerous, a worker needs to keep in mind the requirement that the condition must be one which a "reasonable" person would agree is dangerous. The right should be exercised only when other options do not exist or have been exhausted. A worker must also be available for other work, since there is no obligation on the part of the employer to pay a worker who has refused unsafe work. Employer retaliation against employees for invoking the right to refuse can be challenged by filing with OSHA a complaint of discrimination under Section 11(c) of the OSH Act within 30 days of the retaliation. The Secretary of Labor has final authority in deciding whether to investigate and prosecute a claim of retaliation for refusing unsafe work.

Section 502 of the Labor Management Relations Act specifically pertains to refusal to perform unsafe work. Section 502 states:

> . . . nor shall the quitting of labor by an employee or employees in good faith because of abnormally dangerous conditions for work at the place of employment of such employee or employees be deemed a strike under this Act.

On its face, this section appears to protect the right of workers to strike or to refuse unsafe work when they reasonably believe that abnormally dangerous working conditions threaten their health or safety. However, the vitality of this section was seriously undermined by a Supreme Court decision. *Gateway Coal Co. v. Mine Workers* (1974) concerned the availability of an injunction against a work stoppage over a safety matter which the union argued was protected under Section 502. The applicable contract contained a final and binding arbitration clause, but it did not include an express no-strike promise.

The Court's decision contained several significant points:

(1) Safety disputes are presumed to be arbitrable, and as a rule, they must be handled through the ordinary contract procedures unless the contract expressly excepts safety disputes from the regular grievance procedure.

(2) Since safety is an arbitrable issue, a strike over safety can be enjoined on the theory that the agreement to arbitrate implies a promise not to strike over anything arbitrable.

(3) If employees or a union can present "ascertainable objective evidence" (hard, cold facts) supporting their conclusion that an *abnormally dangerous* working condition exists, then employees can stop work, and an injunction should not be issued ordering the employees back to work.

Only those workers who are actually affected by the conditions can claim this right to stop work. This right is not affected by the fact that the applicable contract has a no-strike clause or a final and binding arbitration clause.

The *Gateway* decision in effect rewrote Section 502 of the LMRA. Rather than a "good faith" belief (as provided in the statutory language) that an abnormally dangerous condition exists, employees must be able to factually demonstrate that the condition "actually" exists in order to claim protection under Section 502. This may be a difficult task, particularly when the issue is health hazards caused by fumes or chemicals, where changing conditions can eliminate the evidence. A reliance on the right to refuse under the LMRA that results in employer retaliation must, like other violations of employees' rights under that law, be pursued through the unfair labor practice channels of the NLRB.

Given the uncertainty of legal protections, unionized workers may seek a firm contractual right to refuse unsafe work as a substitute, or as a supplement, to the law. Because safety and health are mandatory bargaining issues, unions are free to negotiate for the level of protection desired by their members. This may include the right of individuals to refuse unsafe work, a safety committee with the power to shut down operations which it believes to be unsafe, or the right to strike over safety grievances if specific language exempts such disputes from the usual grievance-arbitration clause.

Without a specific contractual right to refuse unsafe work, workers have little contract protection in refusing work. In some cases where workers have been disciplined for refusing to perform work that posed an immediate threat to their safety, arbitrators have overturned the disciplinary actions. These arbitrators do not consider the failure to obey the management directive as insubordination and therefore find the employee protected by the "just cause" clause of the contract. Such a decision is a limited exception to the ordinary rule applied by arbitrators that a worker must obey a management order and later grieve any matter believed to be a contract violation. However, decisions on this point are not uniform and as a defense to employer action taken against employees who refuse to perform work as directed, such decisions do not substitute for an affirmative contract right.

Recovery Right of Employee Harmed by Violation of OSHA Standards

The rights of workers who are injured or become sick because of job conditions are controlled by the workers' compensation law of their particular state or other relevant compensation statutes. In most cases, these laws do not provide greater benefits to workers injured because of an employer's violation of safety and health standards. Some states do, however, award an add-on, an extra percentage of benefits or additional weeks of benefits, if the worker shows that the injury resulted from the employer's violation of a safety or health standard.

Furthermore, workers' compensation laws generally cut off the right of an injured employee to sue an employer for a job-related injury regardless of the extent of the employer's fault in creating the condition that caused the injury. Thus, injured workers are entitled only to compensation benefits that are limited in amount and often in duration as well. However, the "sole and exclusive" remedy section of most workers' compensation laws is being challenged. For instance, the West Virginia compensation statute preserves the right of an injured worker to pursue a civil action if the injury resulted from the "deliberate intention" of the employer. The state Supreme Court has construed this language to include injuries that result when an employer engages in willful, wanton, or reckless misconduct. In *Mandolidis v. Elkins Industries* (1978), the court found that an employer is vulnerable to suit if the employer knowingly fails to abide by an established safety or health standard and understands that the breach creates a high degree of risk to the affected worker. This decision puts such cases beyond the reach of the "sole and exclusive" provision of the compensation statute and allows an injured worker to maintain a civil action for damages in addition to and in an amount substantially greater than the benefits due under worker's compensation. Such potential liability obviously creates a stronger financial incentive for an employer to observe OSHA standards. In addition to the remedy against the direct employer, employees may pursue civil actions against third parties whose negligence contributes to a job injury or a disease, for example, against manufacturers of malfunctioning equipment or protective gear, against subcontractors whose activities result in injuries to another employer's employees, and against producers of raw materials (*e.g.,* asbestos) who fail to inform users of hazards involved in the use of the product.

Access to Information

In order to have meaningful influence over workplace health and safety, workers and unions need access to information. The information required may be as simple as the identity of a particular substance to which workers are exposed or as complex as long-term data on the incidence of illness or disease within the workplace. There are several sources which give to workers and their unions a limited right of access to information pertaining to job health and safety. Workers and unions are entitled to certain information under the OSH Act itself. Other information is available pursuant to an OSHA regulation, generally called the "right to know" standard. Some state laws require employers to make information not covered by the federal OSHA law and regulations available. In addition, unions are entitled under the LMRA to information that is necessary for the intelligent performance of collective bargaining responsibilities. A contract may also create a further right to require an employer to supply information pertinent to health and safety issues.

The OSH Act requires that an employer maintain copies of OSHA standards, rules, and regulations at the workplace, keep certain records, and make reports concerning work-related deaths, injuries, and illnesses. Employers are also required to maintain records of employee exposure to potentially harmful substances. Employees and their representatives are entitled to inspect the records compiled under these requirements. The statute also requires that the implementation of each standard include warnings to apprise employees of hazards, symptoms resulting from exposure, appropriate emergency treatments, and precautions for the safe use of the substance covered by the standard.

In furtherance of the goal of informed worker participation in health and safety issues, OSHA has issued a "right to know" regulation. This regulation covers employee access to medical records, exposure records, and company studies based on these records. A worker has a right to a copy of virtually all medical records maintained by an employer or any other party, such as a doctor or laboratory, which contracts with the employer. A union has the right to examine individual medical records provided it has the written consent of the individuals concerned.

Both workers and unions have the right to examine and copy exposure records that include: monitoring records for physical agents such as noise and a wide variety of substances such as chemicals, gases, fumes, and dust; results of biological monitoring; material data safety sheets and other records regarding the hazards of particular substances; exposure records of other employees with similar past or present job duties or working conditions; and exposure records of conditions to which a worker is being transferred.

Both workers and unions have a right to review any study or analysis made of either exposure or medical records. Access under this rule must be granted within 15 days of the request. A proposed OSHA standard that would have required all materials used in a workplace to bear a label listing the contents by generic name was withdrawn.

Some states and municipalities have laws that supplement the right of access to health and safety data granted by federal laws. The New York Toxic Substances Act requires employers to inform employees if they work with any of several thousand chemicals by both generic and trade name of the effects of exposure, of the level of exposure considered hazardous, of symptoms and emergency treatment procedures, and of methods of proper use. The law provides for the monitoring of exposures, for penalties when the employer exceeds safe levels, and provides employees with the right to refuse to work with a substance unless the employer provides the information required by this law. Laws such as this substantially improve job-related health and safety protections to which employees are entitled. The success of unions and workers in obtaining state and local "right-to-know" laws has prompted employers' efforts to secure a uniform federal rule defining the employer obligation in providing such information.

Apart from information access provided for in laws which directly regulate health and safety, the LMRA permits collective bargaining agents to request certain information. While this law does not require an employer to collect and maintain any information, it does entitle a union to request and obtain any information pertinent to health and safety which the employer in fact possesses. In some cases, it also includes a right for a union expert or union representative to enter a workplace for the purpose of gathering data or making an evaluation of working conditions.

Current Issues Under OSHA

Unions and health and safety advocates are continually seeking to expand employee rights under OSHA. Such efforts are generally subject to controversy centered around the appropriate extent of power that government via OSHA ought to have over the operations of private enterprise.

Under normal principles of law and contract interpretation, employers generally are free to transfer, or even to terminate, a worker whose health interferes with the ability to perform a job, even if the employer's practices were the cause of the worker's impaired health. To most arbitrators, the "just cause" provision of a contract that limits employer decisions to terminate workers does not apply to decisions based on an employee's health. Employers are, therefore, generally free to require that a worker be healthy enough to perform a particular job unless there is a specific contract right allowing a worker to transfer to a different job.

Another concern of workers is whether they retain the same rate of pay if they must transfer to a less well-paid job. The organized labor movement has pushed hard for the adoption of a right to transfer and to retain pay levels and was successful in obtaining such protections under the lead standard adopted in 1978. A governmentally created right of transfer and rate retention will necessarily cause some dislocations and confusion in unionized workplaces, since it will create an exception to long-established principles of seniority, job bidding, and pay classifications. But such accommodation further denies an employer the opportunity to derive financial gain from poor safety practices. Such protections are also important in achieving safe workplaces in such a manner that workers do not sacrifice job security. A right to transfer and rate retention will shift this burden from the individual worker onto the employer and to some extent onto the work force as a whole.

Another issue of continuing importance is the impact of job exposure to toxic substances on the ability of workers to conceive and bear healthy children. Because the relationship of child to mother is more obvious and because there is a tradition of protective legislation affecting women, industry efforts have focused on creating special standards for women workers, especially those able to bear children. Special standards for women ignore substantial evidence that certain substances affect male workers' ability to have healthy children as well and that some substances render men sterile. Unions have vigorously opposed efforts to create differential standards that would in many cases exclude women from the best-paying jobs in their communities. In addition, unions argue that separate standards discriminate against men as well as against women, since such standards compel men to work in a less safe workplace. The recent adoption of the lead standard provided the context for significant debate on this issue. The standard as finally adopted makes no special provision for women workers but provides for mandatory transfer and rate retention rights if a worker's lead-in-blood level exceeds 80 micrograms or if a doctor so orders, based on findings of other adverse health effects of lead exposure.

A related point of interest is direct employer action in several cases against women workers exposed to certain hazards. In several instances, women of childbearing capacity have been excluded from certain jobs or have actually undergone a sterilization procedure as a condition of job retention. OSHA has penalized employers for such practices under the general duty standard requiring an employer to maintain a safe and healthful workplace. However, this policy has been rejected by the Review Commission.

Safety Under the LMRA

As discussed in the materials on collective bargaining, the duty to bargain applies to "wages, hours, and other terms and conditions of employment." In 1966, the NLRB held in its *Gulf Power Co.* decision that safety rules and practices were within the category of mandatory subjects over which an employer is required to bargain. This case established the right of unions under the LMRA to engage in full collective bargaining concerning safety. In *San Isabel Electric Services* (1976), the Board found that a management demand for a management rights clause that effectively stripped the union of its right to bargain over safety issues to be a violation of the duty to bargain. The Board has also ruled that the right to bargain on safety and health issues includes a union right to information in the employer's possession that will enable the union to more intelligently perform its bargaining function.

The ability to bargain over safety issues permits a union to supplement the right provided by the public law. Further, it allows a union to obtain protections that are specific to the needs of a particular workplace, and it permits bargaining to establish a union-controlled safety committee with powers specified in the contract. Even if the contract does no more than incorporate by reference the safety standards provided by the public law, the reference alone enables the union to actively enforce the standards through contract procedures.

In addition to being a mandatory subject of bargaining, health and safety activity is recognized as "protected concerted activity" under the LMRA. An employer's violation of the right, such as retaliation for engaging in such activity, is an unfair labor practice. For instance, the NLRB found in *Alleluia Cushion Co., Inc.* (1975) that the discharge of a person who had filed a complaint with a state safety agency was a violation. The Board viewed this act as advocacy with a potential impact on the working conditions of all and, therefore, as protected "concerted' activity, even though only one person was involved. However, in unionized workplaces, employee activity on health and safety issues which circumvents the official union structure can lose its protected status if the employees attempt to bypass the union and deal directly with the employer on the issue. Workers governed by a collective bargaining agreement generally must pursue available contract remedies on safety complaints and subordinate individual or subgroup rights to those of the union. Otherwise, employees are free to organize around such issues, communicate with fellow workers, distribute literature, and solicit support, and are subject only to the rules governing all such activity.

Key Words and Phrases

abatement	OSHA
citation	"right to know"
imminent danger	serious violation
inspection	standard
NIOSH	state plan
nonserious violation	variance
Occupational Safety and	warrant requirement
Health Review Commission	

Review and Discussion Questions

1. Why is a special law governing job health and safety necessary since workers have a right to engage in collective bargaining on the issue?

2. Does OSHA provide workers with significant rights? Explain.

3. Should the cost of compliance with a standard be considered in deciding the strictness of a standard? Explain.

4. Should an employer have constitutional rights, as was the decision in the *Barlow's* case? Explain.

5. Does OSHA's current enforcement authority create a sufficiently strong incentive for an employer to maintain a safe and healthful workplace? Explain.

6. To what extent does the law currently protect a worker who refuses to do unsafe work?

13

Equal Employment Opportunity Law

Discrimination against certain groups of workers has existed since the beginning of the free labor market. Different groups have been subjected to discrimination during different periods of time. During the nineteenth century, for instance, some job advertisements in the U.S. stated that "no Irish need apply." Today, Irish ethnicity is no longer a bar to seeking employment. Because discrimination is a social problem found in all aspects of our social life, it cannot be completely eliminated in the workplace while it still exists elsewhere. However, significant inroads can be made by increasing the opportunity of people to make a decent living, a key to their self-respect and full participation as citizens.

Although there are instances of discrimination against individuals as individuals, the discrimination that pervades our society is focused on groups. A person's membership in a group is usually defined by a characteristic over which the individual has no control, such as sex, ethnicity, or age. Where group discrimination exists, the individual characteristics of a group member are for the most part irrelevant. Traditionally, discrimination has been justified by people saying that members of a particular group are lazy, dirty, or immoral, and that it is their own fault if their position in society is so low. Typically, members of a group victimized by discrimination are found in jobs which have the least status and the lowest pay and which require strenuous effort and significant exposure to hazards.

Beyond the moral and human imperatives for eliminating discrimination in employment, economic considerations make its eradication an important goal for all workers. Discrimination undermines the wages and security of all workers, because it enables employers to pit worker against worker, a particularly acute problem in periods of economic decline when jobs are scarce. By fostering individual and group competition, discrimination forces workers to focus on immediate, individual concerns and obscures the basic issue of workers' long-term interests vis-à-vis the employer, such as the right to hold a job and efforts to minimize the effects of a system that already has, as a normal feature, the displacement of workers.

Historically, the immediate economic effect of discrimination has been to weaken all workers, as illustrated by the use of certain groups as replacements for strikers. Often the strikers have responded by directing their anger against the group from which replacements are drawn, thereby missing the fact that employers have taken advantage of artificial divisions in the labor force which have been purposefully created and maintained.

Although there are now public laws against discrimination in employment, they are generally of fairly recent vintage. Prior to the enactment of these laws, organized labor sought to eliminate certain kinds of discrimination through the collective bargaining process. Favoritism, a persistent problem for workers, was replaced by the seniority system entitling workers to promotion and other benefits based on years of service. This system, then as now, substantially deprives an employer of the ability to discriminate between workers with regard to their job rights.

Within the past two decades, numerous public laws, both state and federal, have been adopted that attempt to eliminate specific forms of discrimination in employment, such as those based on racial, sexual, religious, ethnic, age, and handicap factors. Generally, organized labor has encouraged and welcomed all attempts to eliminate artificial barriers that have denied full participation in society to entire segments of the population. It was the labor movement, for example, that demanded that a prohibition on job discrimination be included in the sweeping Civil Rights Act of 1964. Title VII, a provision of the Civil Rights Act, has become the most important piece of legislation in U.S. employment discrimination law.

No anti-discrimination law guarantees any person the right to a job. But in a shrinking economy where competition for jobs is intense, the importance of equal access to jobs is frequently obscured by uninformed rhetoric and a fear that one's own opportunity is lessened by such laws. Inarguably, equal access means that the previously preferred group will experience some impairment of short-term interests. But that does not make equal opportunity any less a moral and legal imperative for workers. The very nature of unions is predicated on the subordination of immediate individual interests to the long-term collective interests of the whole. Equal opportunity is clearly a part of that collective interest.

No law forbids discrimination in general. Each of the public laws forbids discrimination on a particular basis, such as race, sex, or age. Often, other laws that are not themselves anti-discrimination laws also forbid discrimination on a particular basis relating to the enforcement of that law. For example, the Labor Management Relations Act prohibits discrimination against an employee on account of union activity, and the Occupational Safety and Health Act forbids retaliation against a worker for exercising rights guaranteed under that law. Just as there is no legal right to a job, there is no legal right to be entirely free of unfair employer actions. The only legal right is to be free of specific forms of discrimination defined in the law as illegal. The best protection against employment discrimination in general is a union contract which limits the ability of an employer to make decisions that unfairly affect workers. For instance, a contract clause which forbids the employer to discharge a worker without "just cause" is protection against many forms of employer discrimination that are not illegal under any public law.

Unlike federal laws relating to most other aspects of employment, those on discrimination generally do not preempt or displace state laws. Some of these laws overlap in coverage, and the enforcement responsibility of different laws resides with different agencies. These factors have created some confusion and generally impede the effectiveness of discrimination laws. The anti-discrimination laws that have had the broadest impact on employment practices are discussed in the material that follows. The discussion is not exhaustive but simply introduces the reader to the field of federal employment discrimination law. Each state has its own set of laws with its own enforcement procedures, and these are not discussed here.

Title VII of the Civil Rights Act of 1964

The most significant public law relating to discrimination in employment is Title VII of the Civil Rights Act of 1964, which was effective July 1, 1965. This federal law prohibits discrimination on the basis of race, sex, religion, color, or national origin and applies to all personnel actions of employers, including hiring, promotions, work assignments, training, and wages. The prohibition against sex discrimination now includes protection from sexual harassment.

Whether the meaning of the law will be broadened to encompass the issue of comparable pay for different work of comparable value is a developing issue. There are some narrow exceptions in the law for employment decisions that are grounded on national security, based on professionally developed job-related ability tests, or justified by legitimate business needs which cannot be fulfilled in a nondiscriminatory manner. In earlier decisions, the Supreme Court held that employers could not claim inconvenience, annoyance, expense, or customers' preference as a business necessity that could be used as a defense of a discriminatory policy. Recent decisions, however, appear to be eroding this strict view of business necessity. The fact that a practice is discriminatory in a particular case does not mean that the practice is always unlawful discrimination. Each case has its own set of facts. Moreover, an employer may successfully raise a business necessity defense in one case that would be unsuccessful in a similar case.

Title VII does not prohibit employer actions taken pursuant to a bona fide seniority or merit system or employer actions taken to fulfill a bona fide occupational qualification. "Bona fide" means "in or with good faith." Whether an employer action meets that standard is determined in individual cases raising the issue. The law provides that race cannot be a bona fide occupational requirement, while sex, religion, and national origin are in some unusual circumstances considered legitimate job qualifications. The basic test as to whether a qualification is bona fide is whether it is necessary for the operation of an enterprise.

Title VII covers employers who have 15 or more regular employees. The law also applies to employment agencies, labor organizations, and joint apprenticeship programs. The law also covers both state and federal employees and supervisors. Thus its coverage is substantially greater than that of the Labor Management Relations Act. Title VII is enforced by an independent federal agency, the Equal Employment Opportunity Commission (EEOC).

Generally, a complaint is filed by an aggrieved person or group or by an organization acting on someone's behalf. However, unlike the NLRB's limited procedural authority, the EEOC may initiate a charge. After an investigation, the agency determines whether there is reasonable cause to believe that discrimination has occurred. If that determination is positive, the EEOC must attempt to conciliate the dispute before instituting formal proceedings against the accused. After a waiting period, the aggrieved party can institute a private civil suit if the EEOC has not initiated an action. In effect, the

EEOC has the priority right in enforcing the law and may also institute its own action subsequent to one filed by the party. There are several remedies which the EEOC may seek in conciliation proceedings or in a court action. These remedies include reinstatement, back pay, promotion, and injunctions against future discrimination. These remedies are of the type that "make the victim whole" for actual loss of economic benefits and status caused by illegal discrimination. Punitive damages simply to punish an employer for violating the law are generally not available. Another remedy included in a settlement agreement or imposed by a court may require an employer to develop a plan detailing the manner and time period for recruiting, hiring, and promoting persons who are members of a group protected by the law. Such a plan is called an affirmative action plan.

Unlawful discrimination can be proved by different methods. Overt, intentional discrimination was more common at the time Title VII was adopted than it is now. Today, the proof of discrimination is usually established by methods other than a showing of direct intent. For example, in *McDonnell-Douglas Corp. v. Green* (1973), the Supreme Court allowed a minority applicant to establish a prima facie case, *viz.,* a case which is established by sufficient evidence until contradicted and overthrown by other evidence, of discrimination by showing that : (1) he was black, (2) he had applied for a vacancy for which he was qualified, (3) he had been rejected, and (4) the employer continued to seek applicants. At this point, the Court held, the burden shifted to the employer to show a legitimate, nondiscriminatory reason for the rejection. Furthermore, the employee had the right to show that the reason advanced for refusal to hire was in fact a pretext, or a cover, for an actual discriminatory reason. Among the ways pretext can be established is the use of statistics, *e.g.,* showing a deficiency in the composition of the employer's work force as compared to the composition of the relevant labor market.

Another method by which discrimination can be established is to show that a job qualification which appears to be neutral actually has an adverse impact on a protected class of workers. For instance, height may appear to be neutral as a job requirement, but in the application of the requirement, it may disqualify a substantially greater number of women than men. Therefore, the use of height as a job qualification limits the opportunity of women to obtain the job to which the qualification applies. When a job qualification is shown to have an adverse impact on a protected group, the burden shifts to the employer who must show that the requirement is based on a business necessity. This method of proving discrimination was developed in *Griggs v. Duke Power Co.* (1971), one of the most significant cases arising under Title VII. The *Griggs* decision, a unanimous one, represents the most expansive view of Title VII ever taken by the Supreme Court.

The Duke Power Company required a high school education or a certain score on a standardized test as a condition of employment for, or transfer to, certain jobs. The jobs in question had in the past been open only to white workers under an employer policy preferential to whites. There was no apparent evidence that either qualification was significantly related to job performance, and both requirements disqualified more black applicants than white applicants. The question in *Griggs* was whether Title VII's prohibition against racial discrimination in employment could prevent an employer from utilizing job tests or educational requirements. A recitation of the facts in *Griggs* illustrates the common pattern of discrimination against blacks at the time that Title VII was adopted. Duke Power's effort to evade the objectives of the law is also a typical story.

The Supreme Court described the facts in *Griggs* in the following manner:

> The District Court found that prior to July 2, 1965, the effective date of the Civil Rights Act of 1964, the Company openly discriminated on the basis of race in the hiring and assigning of employees at its Dan River plant. The plant was organized into five operating departments: (1) Labor, (2) Coal Handling, (3) Operations, (4) Maintenance, and (5) Laboratory and Test. Negroes were employed only in the Labor Department where the highest paying jobs paid less than the lowest paying jobs in the other four "operating" departments in which only whites were employed. Promotions were normally made within each department on the basis of job seniority. Transferees into a department usually began in the lowest position.
>
> In 1955 the Company instituted a policy of requiring a high school education for initial assignment to any department except Labor, and for transfer from the Coal Handling to any "inside" department (Operations, Maintenance, or Laboratory). When the Company abandoned its policy of restricting Negroes to the Labor Department in 1965, completion of high school also was made a prerequisite to transfer from Labor to any other department. From the time the high school requirement was instituted to the time of trial, however, white employees hired before the time of the high school education requirement

continued to perform satisfactorily and achieve promotions in the "operating" departments. Findings on this score are not challenged.

The Company added a further requirement for new employees on July 2, 1965, the date on which Title VII became effective. To qualify for placement in any but the Labor Department it became necessary to register satisfactory scores on two professionally prepared aptitude tests, as well as to have a high school education. Completion of high school alone continued to render employees eligible for transfer to the four desirable departments from which Negroes had been excluded if the incumbent had been employed prior to the time of the new requirement. In September 1965 the Company began to permit incumbent employees who lacked a high school education to qualify for transfer from Labor or Coal Handling to an "inside" job by passing two tests—the Wonderlic Personnel Test, which purports to measure general intelligence, and the Bennett Mechanical Comprehension Test. Neither was directed or intended to measure the ability to learn to perform a particular job or category of jobs. The requisite scores used for both initial hiring and transfer approximated the national median for high school graduates.

In a landmark decision, the Supreme Court held that Title VII prohibits not only overt (or purposeful) discrimination but also prohibits practices that are fair in form but discriminatory in operation. If an employment practice adversely affects a protected group and cannot be shown to be related to job performance, the practice is prohibited. The Court emphasized that Congress had directed the thrust of Title VII to "the consequences of discrimination, not simply the motivation."

The *Griggs* decision does not prohibit the use of tests or the imposition of any job qualification as long as such standards are a reasonable measure of job performance. Even if a standard disproportionately excludes persons in a certain group, the standard may be used if it is job-related and no other less discriminatory job qualification can accomplish the employer's objectives. *Griggs* in effect prohibits the use of arbitrary standards that discriminate against protected groups. The case does not prohibit the use of all arbitrary standards, because Title VII does not prohibit all forms of discrimination. The reach of *Griggs* has been substantially restricted by a number of later Supreme Court decisions. Several of these decisions have been significant, because the courts have required a showing of intent to discriminate as a necessary element in proving that a facially neutral rule violates Title VII.

Equal Pay Act

The Equal Pay Act of 1963 was actually an amendment to the Fair Labor Standards Act. The act prohibits an employer from discriminating on the basis of sex in the payment of wages and fringes for jobs of equal skill, effort, and responsibility performed under similar working conditions *unless* the difference is due to a seniority, merit, piece-rate system, or some factor other than sex. Jobs need be only substantially equal rather than identical to provide a basis for establishing differential treatment between men and women in violation of the act. The Equal Pay Act provides that an employer may not correct a violation by reducing the wages or benefits of any employee but rather must comply with the law by increasing those of the lower-paid employees. This law covers only wage and benefit rates. To this extent, its coverage overlaps that of Title VII of the Civil Rights Act of 1964. It does not cover other employment practices such as hiring, job assignments, promotions, and transfers. The only remedy available to an aggrieved worker is back pay, or double back pay if the violation is willful.

Employees covered by the federal minimum wage law are also covered by the Equal Pay Act. No minimum number of employees is required for coverage under the act. There are, however, specific exceptions for small retail, service, and agricultural employers, seasonal recreational enterprises, domestic service, and a few other narrow groups. Public sector employees are also covered.

Age Discrimination in Employment Act

The Age Discrimination in Employment Act, adopted in 1967, makes it unlawful for an employer to refuse to hire, or otherwise discriminate against, a person between the ages of 40 and 65. In 1978 the law was amended to extend protection until age 70. The law permits preferential treatment based on age when age is a bona fide occupational qualification.

The Age Discrimination in Employment Act applies to employers with 20 or more regular employees. Employees of both the state and the federal governments are covered by the act. Labor organizations and employment agencies are also covered, but apprenticeship training programs are excluded. This law can be enforced both by the EEOC and by the aggrieved individual in a private civil action, which includes a right to a jury trial. However, a private action cannot be instituted until 60 days after a complaint has been filed with the EEOC, which in effect gives the government the first opportunity to enforce the law. Nearly all of the states also have their own law banning discrimination on account of age.

Executive Order 11246

Executive Order 11246 is a presidential order prohibiting discrimination on account of race, sex, religion, color, or national origin by contractors or subcontractors who perform work under a federal contract exceeding $10,000. Coverage includes all facilities of the contractor, without regard to whether they are used in the performance of the federal contract. The executive order is enforced by the Office of Federal Contract Compliance Programs (OFCCP), an office within the U.S. Department of Labor.

Executive Order 11246 is significantly broader than Title VII of the Civil Rights Act of 1964. It requires covered employers to take affirmative action to ensure that persons in the protected categories are recruited, hired, upgraded, and trained. Except for the affirmative action requirement, Executive Order 11246 forbids discrimination in generally the same manner as Title VII. To enforce the executive order the federal government has the authority to cancel existing contracts and to debar employers from future contracts for failure to comply with the order's requirements. Employers who have nonconstruction contracts for $50,000 or more and who have 50 or more employees must submit a written affirmative action plan setting goals and timetables for hiring, training, and upgrading workers in the protected classes. A compliance review of an employer's practices must be conducted by the OFCCP before a contract exceeding $1 million can be awarded.

Executive Order 11246 has had significant impact on the construction industry. Through the efforts of the OFCCP, employers have been alternately encouraged and coerced into compliance with the order. The OFCCP has encouraged employers in local communities to voluntarily formulate "hometown" plans that establish goals in the individual trades for the hiring of minority workers—whether for federally financed or federally assisted projects or for private work. Extending the coverage of hometown plans to private sector work is an organized effort to draw into the industry workers who might otherwise be overlooked because of the fragmented and sporadic nature of the industry. When the parties cannot agree on a hometown plan, they may be forced to accept an

OFCCP plan as a condition to a contract award. Goals and time-tables for compliance with the executive order are incorporated into bid conditions for federal contracts or subcontracts in excess of $10,000. The bidder is required to submit a letter certifying compliance with the goal and timetable requirements specified in the bid.

Vocational Rehabilitation Act

The Vocational Rehabilitation Act of 1973 is another federal anti-discrimination law that potentially can affect employment practices in as fundamental a way as have the prohibitions on race and sex discrimination. Like Executive Order 11246, this law applies to employers doing business with the federal government and is also enforced by the OFCCP. Any employer doing business under a contract for more than $2,500 must take affirmative steps to hire, promote, and train handicapped job applicants and employees. The law defines a handicapped person as one who: (1) has a physical or mental impairment that substantially limits one or more of his/her major life functions; (2) has a record of such an impairment; or (3) is regarded as having such an impairment. The affirmative action required under the Vocational Rehabilitation Act is significantly less rigorous than that under Executive Order 11246. Neither a statistical analysis of the relevant labor force nor goals and timetables for hiring handicapped workers are required. But, the OFCCP does have the authority—as it does under Executive Order 11246—to wield the ultimate sanction, that is, to deny employers the right to continue to do business with the federal government. Many states have similar laws; some of these directly prohibit discrimination on account of handicap without regard to the employer's access to public contracts.

In order to be considered for a job, a handicapped person must be capable, with reasonable accomodation to his/her handicap, to perform the job. In essence, this entitles the employer to use physical and mental requirements that are job-related and consistent with business necessity and the safe performance of the job. An employer must make reasonable accommodations to the limitations of handicapped employees or applicants. But accommodation that requires an undue hardship for the employer, particularly in terms of financial costs, will not be required.

The definition of a handicapped person is quite broad and includes not only those conditions recognized as handicaps but covers ordinary health problems as well. For instance, by 1978, the OFCCP issued administrative complaints against eight government contractors for failing to take reasonable actions to employ qualified handicapped individuals. The diversity of some of these cases illustrates the breadth of the law as interpreted by that office: An airlines employer was charged with discriminating against a former pilot who, after recuperating from a heart attack, was denied another job with the airline; a second case involved a person refused employment on the grounds that his previous back injury would be aggravated by the stress of desk work; another complaint was based on an employer's refusal to hire a construction worker with a congenital spine condition on the basis that the applicant would make a poor risk; and, a university was charged with dismissing a technical researcher after she returned from an operation for cancer and with failing to take affirmative action to find the employee a similar professional position.

If these broad interpretations set the standard, the law will have significant impact for workers in general. A long-standing problem for workers has been the practice of many employers to terminate older workers who have developed health problems on the grounds that they are no longer able to perform the work. Several reasons underlie this practice. Older workers may not be able to work as quickly as younger workers. The worker with a health problem may represent a potential for increased costs, such as medical care and sick leave. Even unionized workers have been vulnerable in this area, since arbitrators frequently hold an employer's decision to be within the range of employer actions permitted by the "just cause" clause of a contract. This is especially true when an employee has been absent from the job for a substantial period of time for health reasons, even where the absence was due to a work-related injury. Although its implication for the right of a worker to transfer to less strenuous jobs has not yet been tested, Section 503 of the Vocational Rehabilitation Act has enormous potential importance for all workers whose health is less than perfect. Section 503 says that health is relevant only if it relates to the ability to perform a job.

Equal Employment Opportunity and the Seniority System

Of major concern to unionized workers is the conflict between the ideals of equal opportunity of persons as enforced by the anti-discrimination laws and the job rights of workers as embodied in a contract, particularly those deriving from the seniority clause. Because the principle of seniority protects workers with the longest cumulative service, it has often been attacked as impeding the opportunities of previously excluded groups of workers. Seniority itself does not discriminate against persons on a prohibited basis. On the contrary, it treats all workers on a single basis—years of service—without regard to race, age, and so forth. A seniority system discriminates in the sense that it prefers persons with more years of service to those with fewer. However, this policy embodies a value in which most persons, at least in the abstract, believe—that those who have given more have earned a right to be preferred. Since unions in the manufacturing and service sectors (as contrasted to the building and printing trades) do not participate in the hiring process, these unions are not responsible for an employer's discrimination. By its nature, the seniority system protects those whom an employer chooses to hire and to that extent institutionalizes and perpetuates any original discrimination by the employer.

Many industrial unionists now believe that the broadest seniority system best serves the interests of workers, since it increases their job opportunities and increases their job security. Prior to the antidiscrimination laws, some unions had already begun to seek consolidation of narrow departmental seniority lines into more comprehensive systems. This move had been stimulated by the advent of automation, which frequently eliminated entire departments and displaced workers who had substantial service records. Under the narrow departmental system, these displaced workers could not bump less senior workers in other departments. At best, they could enter a new department when a vacancy occurred, assume low spot on the roster, and thereby become the most vulnerable to layoffs and the least entitled to benefits. Unions therefore sought to restructure the seniority system to protect those who had the greatest seniority with the employer.

The enactment of Title VII accelerated the trend toward broader seniority systems which unions had already recognized as in the best long-term interests of workers. Since Title VII went into effect, many unions and employers have voluntarily revamped their seniority systems to broaden the access of all workers to a greater number of jobs. Other seniority systems have been revised in EEOC conciliation proceedings or pursuant to court decrees. Narrow departmental lines of seniority are, however, sometimes approved in the interest of safety and efficiency. Many departmental systems have been eliminated in favor of plant systems, wherein *total time worked* for the employer is considered in awarding jobs. When seniority systems are combined, persons holding positions usually keep them regardless of the fact that workers from other departments now have greater seniority. The greater seniority cannot be used to bump incumbents except in lay-off situations.

Title VII provides expressly that it does not prohibit any actions taken pursuant to a bona fide seniority system. Therefore, the question is whether a particular system is bona fide. Generally, a seniority system must be based on years of service alone to withstand a Title VII challenge. But, systems operating on that basis may have advantages for certain workers that are based on past discriminatory practices. The conflict at its most basic level is between those persons who have actually earned seniority under a particular system and those who have been discriminatorily denied an opportunity to earn credit under that same system. Three major approaches to the problem which have been considered in cases are as follows:

(1) Freedom now—Workers who would hold jobs but for unlawful discrimination would immediately replace workers who currently hold those jobs.
(2) Status quo—The current seniority system would continue to operate without regard to whether it perpetuates past discrimination.
(3) Rightful place—Future jobs could not be awarded solely on the basis of seniority which was accumulated under a discriminatory system. Workers who would have had the requisite seniority but for discrimination would be permitted to move into future openings over workers with actual seniority.

This latter position was supported by the AFL-CIO and has been adopted by the Supreme Court. In *Franks v. Bowman Transportation Co.* (1976), the Court granted seniority for identifiable job applicants who were unlawfully denied employment because of their race retroactive to a date after the enactment of Title VII. In effect, these persons could receive "constructive" seniority greater than the actual seniority of other workers hired after the time the unlawful discrimination occurred. The Court found Section 703(h) of Title VII, which protects a bona fide seniority system, to be irrelevant in this case, because the central issue was not the operation of the seniority system but the employer's hiring practices.

In *Teamsters v. U.S.* (1977), the major question before the Supreme Court was whether a seniority system which perpetuates the effects of pre-act discrimination could still be a bona fide system. There was no argument as to whether discrimination had occurred. The issue was whether the law could require that such discrimination be corrected by granting constructive seniority to persons retroactive to dates prior to the enactment of Title VII. The seniority system in *Teamsters* was fair on its face and even in its intent, but it institutionalized and perpetuated past discriminatory employment practices.

In the case, the government charged a trucking company, TIME-DC with discrimination against blacks and Spanish-surnamed persons in its hiring and transfer practices for its most desirable driving positions, the over-the-road or "line" driver positions. The union also was charged with discrimination on the basis that the seniority system contained in its contract with the employer required an employee who transferred to a line driver position to forfeit all competitive seniority acquired in any previous job. The government charged that this system perpetuated discrimination, locking its victims into inferior jobs. This argument was based on the premise that a worker could not be expected to risk accrued seniority in one job by transferring to another job in which he/she had no seniority. Lacking seniority in the new position, the worker would be vulnerable to layoffs and to loss of employment altogether, as there would be no right to return to the previous job. Because job security is of overriding concern to workers, the government argued, the system discouraged workers from transferring by denying them the right to carry over their seniority. The crux of the argument was that the victim of discrimination who must forfeit seniority to obtain a preferred line driver's job would never be able to catch up to the seniority level of contemporaries who were not subject to discrimination. Because the seniority system incorporated and maintained this disadvantage, its operation allegedly constituted a continuing violation of Title VII.

In its review, the Supreme Court agreed that the government had proved systematic racial discrimination on the part of the employer and that discrimination had continued well beyond the effective date of Title VII. With regard to this post-act discrimination, the Court noted that persons who could prove specific occurrences of illegal discrimination after the effective date of Title VII were entitled to make-whole relief under the *Franks v. Bowman Transportation* rule. In other words, individual victims who had experienced discrimination by being denied line driver jobs after July 1, 1965, could be awarded retroactive seniority to the date the unlawful discrimination occurred.

A court could order this individual relief, however, without questioning the legality of the seniority system itself.

The Supreme Court stated that the seniority system under consideration would seem to be illegal based on the *Griggs* decision, which prohibits practices that are fair in form but discriminatory in operation. But, in the Court's view, Section 703(h), which protects bona fide seniority systems, made the system invulnerable to challenge.

Clearly, both the *Franks* and the *Teamsters* decisions focus on discrimination against individuals per se rather than on discrimination against groups. These and other recent decisions, like *American Tobacco Company v. Patterson* (1982), holding that for purposes of Section 703(h) it makes no difference whether a seniority system was adopted before or after the effective date of Title VII, disturb some civil rights advocates. They believe that these interpretations of the Court undermine the promise of Title VII to eliminate discrimination and all of its vestiges by permanently relegating certain groups to a "catch-up" position. Title VII, they assert, was addressed directly to discrimination against persons not as individuals but as members of a particular group. Civil rights leaders maintain that individual remedies cannot correct the persistent inequities that are rooted in historical patterns of exclusion and denial of rights to certain groups. Their argument is that the last-hired/first-fired practice has now been officially approved and that consequently, historically excluded groups, particularly blacks, will be denied the opportunity to assume an integral role in the workplace and our national life.

Affirmative Action

Probably no other single aspect of equal employment opportunity law engenders as much debate as does the concept of affirmative action. Opponents of affirmative action have been quite successful at propagating the view that affirmative action is "reverse discrimination." There is a persistent belief that the law actually guarantees certain groups of people the right to a job irrespective of their qualifications.

In its simplest terms, affirmative action means that active or positive steps are taken to correct imbalances that may exist in an employer's work force. For instance, advertising jobs in a Spanish-language newspaper is a positive and necessary method of communicating to Spanish-speaking workers. However, it is not this aspect of affirmative action that has formed public response to the concept. Rather, it is the goals in hiring, or "set-asides" for members of a particular group, that receive most of the attention. Actually, Title VII of the Civil Rights Act does not expressly require an employer to engage in affirmative action. Rather, Executive Order 11246 mandates that employers operating under contracts with the federal government incorporate affirmative action programs into their personnel policies. Executive Order 11246 is therefore a more powerful instrument for eliminating the historical pattern of imbalance than is Title VII, which merely permits a court to order affirmative action after a judicial finding of unlawful discrimination.

Basically, an affirmative action plan must include a comparison of the potential work force with an employer's actual work force in order to determine the extent of underutilization of certain groups of workers. The plan must also include a timetable and a method for correcting whatever deficiencies exist in the employer's work force. Some of the factors considered in determining whether an employer has a situation of underutilization are as follows:

(1) Minority population of the labor area in the plant locale;
(2) Size of the minority unemployment force in that locale;
(3) Percentage of minority work force compared with the total work force of that locale;
(4) General availability of minorities with the necessary skills, both in the immediate location and within a reasonable recruiting radius;
(5) Availability of promotable minorities within the employer's work force;
(6) Existence of training institutions capable of training minorities with the requisite skills; and
(7) Amount of training that the contractor is reasonably able to undertake to make all job classifications available to minorities.

The major enforcement power behind Executive Order 11246 is the ability of the Secretary of Labor to debar future contracts and/or cancel existing contracts with an employer who fails to comply with the requirements.

Title VII does not specifically require that affirmative action be taken by employers to improve the position of those groups which the law protects. Nonetheless, the Supreme Court in *United Steelworkers v. Weber* (1979), approved the use of voluntary agreements for affirmative action between a union and an employer, without any requirement that the favored individuals prove unlawful discrimination.

The case involved an agreement between Kaiser Aluminum and the United Steelworkers, which reserved half of the positions in a new craft training program for black workers until the percentage of black workers equaled the percentage of black workers in the local labor force. At the plant in question, only five of 273 craft workers were black, although the local labor force was 39 percent black. Brian Weber, a white Kaiser employee, was denied a position in the training program even though he had more plant seniority than some of the black workers who were selected for training. The Supreme court rejected Weber's argument that Title VII forbade all race-conscious affirmative action and asserted that such an interpretation would be "completely at variance with the purpose of the Act." Quoting from Senator Hubert Humphrey's comments in the legislative history of Title VII, the Court said that its primary purpose was "to open employment opportunities for Negroes in occupations which have been traditionally closed to them."

The Supreme Court focused on a provision in Title VII which states that nothing in Title VII "shall be interpreted to require any employer ... to grant preferential treatment." The Court read this to mean that voluntary programs were permissible. Otherwise, Congress would have stated, "Nothing in Title VII permits voluntary affirmative efforts to correct racial imbalances." Congress not having so worded the law, the Court inferred that it had not chosen to forbid such voluntary efforts. It is unclear at this point what impact or relevance this reasoning will have on court-imposed (in effect, "required") affirmative action plans.

The *Weber* decision did not define what a permissible and an impermissible affirmative action program should be. The Court did discuss the fact that the Kaiser program is only a temporary bar to the advancement of white workers, indicating that such a measure would be appropriate only until the racial imbalance in the work force was eliminated. It is uncertain whether the same reasoning would support an affirmative action plan favoring women in jobs from which they have traditionally been excluded (for historical reasons different from those relating to blacks). It is emphasized that the Supreme Court did not rule that all affirmative action in employment programs are valid, and *Weber* will presumably not be the final word on just how much affirmative action is permissible, or required, by law.

The temporary preference challenged in the *Weber* case has received significantly more attention than a permanent preference long-contained in the federal civil service law and the laws which govern public employment in most states. In *Personnel Administrator of Massachusetts v. Feeney* (1979), the Supreme Court upheld a veteran's preference statute giving veterans an absolute lifetime preference in state civil service jobs. The challenge to this permanent preference for veterans was based on an argument that this seemingly neutral preference has had an adverse impact on women (because of historical patterns, policies, and laws which deny women an equal role in the military) and thus denies them the equal protection guaranteed by the U.S. Constitution. The woman who challenged the preference had consistently received high scores on competitive examinations during her 12 years of employment with the State of Massachusetts. However, she had been frustrated in her efforts to advance because of the extra points given to male veterans who, because of their status, received jobs even though they had scored less than she on the competitive examination. The Supreme Court held that the system was neither inherently discriminatory nor intended to foster discrimination. Therefore, it was a legally permissible preference. Advocates of increased opportunity for women now seek legislative changes in the veteran's preference statutes, *i.e.*, to limit the application of the preference to a certain number of years or jobs. Legislation granting limited preference would recognize the sacrifice involved in interrupting the careers of those persons who have served in the armed forces and seek to compensate veterans for those sacrifices. Permanent preference significantly restricts the career opportunities of all other persons and advocates of limited preference seek to lessen that restriction.

Pregnancy-Related Discrimination

One of the most controversial Supreme Court decisions interpreting Title VII was that in which it held an employer's exclusion of pregnancy-related health and disability benefits from its insurance plan was not a violation of the law. In *General Electric v. Gilbert* (1976), The Court emphasized that the insurance in question did not afford any protection to men not afforded to women, and vice versa. Rather, the Court reasoned, the insurance package simply insured all workers for some medical expenses while excluding coverage of others—specificially, pregnancy-related medical expenses. Because the policy did not make a distinction between coverage for men and for women, the omission of coverage for pregnancy-related medical expenses was not a form of discrimination prohibited by Title VII. Thus, the Supreme Court was able to avoid a finding that discrimination on account of pregnancy is, of necessity, also discrimination on account of sex.

Following this decision with its potentially devastating consequences on the ability of a woman to choose both to work and to be a mother, Congress acted to clarify the meaning of the prohibition on sex discrimination. In 1978, Congress amended Title VII by adding Section 1701(k), which states:

> The terms "because of sex" or "on the basis of sex" include, but are not limited to, because of, or on the basis of pregnancy, childbirth, or related medical conditions; and women affected by pregnancy, childbirth, or related medical conditions shall be treated the same for all employment-related purposes, including receipt of benefits under fringe benefit programs, as other persons not so affected but similar in their ability or inability to work, and nothing in Section 703(h) of this title shall be interpreted to permit otherwise. . . .

Before this amendment, Title VII had been held to govern several of the job rights of pregnant female employees, such as the retention and accrual of seniority. The amendment extended this principle to all job benefits. Title VII does no require any employer to provide any type of benefits to a pregnant employee. Rather, it mandates that those benefits which are offered must be available to all employees on a nondiscriminatory basis.

Sexual Harassment

The EEOC issued broad guidelines prohibiting sexual harassment in the workplace in 1980, incorporating them into the earlier *Guidelines on Discrimination Because of Sex.* Both prior to and subsequent to the issuance of the additional guidelines, courts have generally found that employees have a Title VII claim if they are subjected to sexually harassing behavior or activity.

The prohibition against discrimination on account of sex includes protection from sexual harassment either by managerial employees or by co-workers. Sexual advancements, requests for sexual favors, and other verbal or physical conduct of a sexual nature may constitute sexual harassment. Such conduct is forbidden if submission to sexual advances is either explicitly or implicitly made a condition of employment; submission to or rejection of sexual advances is used as a basis for employment decisions; or if the questioned conduct has the purpose or the effect of unreasonably interfering with work performance or of creating an intimidating, hostile, or offensive work environment. The employer has an obligation to police the workplace and to take appropriate measures to protect employees from such conduct.

Comparable Worth

Because job segregation by sex is a predominant feature of the U.S. labor maket, the goal of equal pay for equal work, even when achieved, cannot eliminate sex discrimination in employment. Over 80% of women workers are segregated into "female" occupations that are different in content from "men's" jobs but frequently not different in the skill, effort, and responsibility required for effective job performance. Women, on the average, earn less than 60 percent of the wages paid to the average male worker, a differential that continues to grow. A 1981 report by the National Academy of Science concluded that "many jobs held by women pay less in large part because they are held by women." Thus, equal pay for jobs of comparable worth, or pay equity, has become the major issue in employment discrimination and efforts to eradicate it.

Comparable worth is receiving increasing attention in the context of collective bargaining as unions seek contract language to improve the compensation of "women's" jobs. For example, such a demand resulted in a strike by San Jose city workers in 1981. Comparable worth has also been the subject of legislation in various states and was incorporated into rules developed by the Department of Labor, implementing Executive Order 11246, rules withdrawn by the Reagan Administration after it assumed office. Comparable worth received its most prominent attention when the Supreme Court ruled in *County of Washington v. Gunther* (1981) that women bringing a claim of sex-based wage discrimination under Title VII are not required to satisfy the equal work standards contained in the Equal Pay Act, *i.e.*, that the jobs being compared are substantially equal. The case involved female jail "matrons" who were paid approximately 70 percent of the wages paid to male "guards." The matrons, in addition to their supervision of prisoners, performed clerical duties. Thus, their jobs were not strictly equal to those of the guards whose only task was the supervision of prisoners. Though ruling that Title VII is to be read broadly, the Court side-stepped the comparable worth issue stating that it was simply allowing the matrons an opportunity to show that they were the victims of intentional discrimination.

Undoubtedly, the *Gunther* decision will produce extensive litigation on the comparable worth issue. Whether Title VII will eventually be read to prohibit discrimination—between workers whose jobs are different in content but in the same general classification and of comparable worth to the employer; between workers who are performing work that is fundamentally different but which is of comparable value to the employer; or between employees who work for different employers but whose work is of comparable value either to the employers or to the society—depends on many factors, probably the most important of which is the political activity of women who seek to eliminate the economic inferiority of "women's work."

Discrimination on Account of Religion

Title VII prohibits discrimination against an individual on the basis of religion

> ... unless an employer demonstrates that he is unable to reasonably accommodate to an employee's or prospective employee's religious observance or practice without undue hardship on the conduct of the employer's business.

The law defines religion as "all aspects of religious observance and practice, as well as belief."

One of the major issues raised by this provision is the extent to which an employer is required to accommodate a worker's religious beliefs. An employee's refusal to work on the Sabbath, particularly a Saturday Sabbath, has been at issue in a number of discrimination suits. The issue of work on the Sabbath is further complicated where a collective bargaining agreement establishes the method by which scheduling is to be accomplished and typically gives senior workers the right to a preferred schedule. In *Trans World Airlines v. Hardison* (1977), the Supreme Court has interpreted the "accommodation" provision to require only slight accommodation by an employer. The case involved a person who, in observation of the tenets of his faith, did not want to work on Saturdays. The Supreme Court interpreted Title VII as not requiring an employer to take steps inconsistent with an otherwise valid collective bargaining contract or to deny shift or job preferences to senior employees. The employer had made reasonable attempts to accommodate the employee's religious beliefs by holding several meetings with the employee, by authorizing the union to find another worker to exchange shifts with the employee, and by trying to find the employee another job which would not require Saturday work. The Court stated that an employer need not bear more than minimal costs to accommodate an employee's religious practices and that to give the employee Saturdays off would impose an "undue hardship" on the employer. The issue, then, was whether Title VII could protect employees from discharge if they refused to pay union dues because of religious beliefs.

Another area in which the Title VII prohibition against religious discrimination has had a significant impact is union security agreements. One of the forms that employees' religious objections to union security agreements has taken is the refusal to pay mandatory union dues. Generally, the argument has been that the requirement to pay union dues violates the First Amendment freedom of religion guarantees.

The EEOC view has been that both the employer and the union commit a Title VII violation when the union demands a discharge and the employer discharges a worker for failure to pay dues, unless a reasonable effort to accomodate the employee's religious beliefs is first made. Decisions by courts of appeal have generally upheld the validity of union security agreements against Title VII challenges, but have differed in the level of accommodation required of employers. In a practical sense, the issue is moot because a recent amendment to the LMRA relieves employees who hold a bona fide religious objection to paying union dues from the obligation.

Anti-Discrimination Law and Contract Proceedings

Contract proceedings, particularly arbitration, are generally accorded a high degree of validity by both courts and public agencies. The text dicusses this policy extensively in the materials under contract enforcement. Certain matters that are violations of a contract may at the same time be violations of one or more of the anti-discrimination laws. However, unlike awards on virtually all other issues, arbitration decisions on discrimination claims are not given persuasive significance by the courts.

In *Alexander v. Gardner-Denver Co.* (1974), the Supreme Court held that an employee who obtains an adverse ruling in an arbitration proceeding can nevertheless institute a claim raising the same issue under Title VII of the Civil Rights Act of 1964. The Court noted that the rights under a contract and under the statute have distinctly separate sources. In its view, the right to be free of unfair discrimination is absolutely guaranteed by Congress and cannot be waived in the collective bargaining process. Therefore, in the Court's opinion, the prior use of contract processes ought not deprive an employee of the right to pursue an action under Title VII. The employee might, however, voluntarily waive the right to legal action in settlement of a contract claim.

Application of the LMRA to Employer Discrimination

The Labor Management Relations Act does not protect employees against most forms of discrimination or arbitrary treatment. It does specifically protect them against discrimination by employers and unions on account of union activity and on account of their resort to and participation in NLRB processes. To a lesser degree, the LMRA protects employees from discrimination by providing for the union's duty of fair representation, that is, the obligation of a union to represent all persons for whom it holds bargaining rights in a manner that is fair, nonarbitrary, and nondiscriminatory.

Employer discrimination on the basis of sex or race does not constitute an unfair labor practice. The NLRB has refused to interpret Section 7 of the LMRA to include a right to be free of discrimination in general. In *Jubilee Mfg. Co.* (1973), the Board rejected arguments that discrimination on account of sex was inherently destructive of employees' Section 7 rights. (See *United Packinghouse Workers v. NLRB* (1969), for a contrasting view.) In the Board's judgment, a violation only exists under the LMRA if there is a connection between the discriminatory conduct and an interference with employees in the exercise of their Section 7 rights. Therefore, claims of race and sex discrimination by an employer must ordinarily be based on laws other than the LMRA and taken to an enforcement agency other than the NLRB. However, the subject of discrimination is a mandatory subject of bargaining and refusal to bargain with a union on the subject does constitute an unfair labor practice, as does a refusal to supply information concerning employment and pay of workers in groups specifically protected by equal employment opportunity law. The policies developed by the NLRB recognize that discrimination is covered by other laws and agencies with specific guidelines, powers, and remedies to deal with an issue that is somewhat divergent from the basic labor-management issues covered by the LMRA.

Key Words and Phrases

Age Discrimination in Employment Act	Executive Order 11246
	Griggs v. Duke Power Co.
bona fide occupational qualification	OFCCP
	Title VII
EEOC	Veteran's preference
Equal Pay Act	Vocational Rehabilitation Act

Review and Discussion Questions

1. Does discrimination against certain workers or groups of workers adversely affect the working conditions of all workers within either a particular workplace or a society? Explain.

2. Defend the sanction used to enforce Executive Order 11246, that is, the denial of government contracts to employers who violate the Order's requirements.

3. What might be the philosophy of the Supreme Court's approval of a gender qualification denying jobs as correctional counsellors in maximum security prisons to women?

4. What are some ways of proving unlawful discrimination?

5. Discuss the conflict between equal employment opportunity and the principle of seniority. Do you agree with the resolution of that conflict embodied in the Supreme Court decision in *Franks v. Bowman* and *Teamsters v. U.S.*? Explain.

6. Does affirmative action fit in with the notion of collectivity, the basic principle of the organized labor movement in the U.S.? Explain.

7. What does discrimination law provide with regard to an employer's action toward pregnant employees?

14

Issues in Public Sector Employment

Since 1960, the overall number of public sector employees in the United States has grown dramatically as compared to the rate of growth in private sector employment. This growth is related to the perception of social needs as public concerns and to the enactment of legislation in response to those needs. Public employment doubled in the two decades between 1957 and 1977. By the end of 1979, public employment engaged 15,907,000 workers, or 17.5 percent of the total U.S. work force. Of this number, 13,147,000 were employed at the state and local levels of government. With this growth in the number of public employees, union organizing efforts in the public sector have also flourished.

As discussed in an earlier chapter, the National Labor Relations Act and its later amendments declared that employers covered by that law "shall not include the United States, or any State or political subdivision thereof...." This exclusion from the basic labor law has necessitated special legislation covering public sector labor-management relations. The federal government and many states and municipalities have adopted laws recognizing the right of public employees to organize and to bargain collectively. Nevertheless, public employee unionization has proceeded amid extensive controversy.

The debate over the appropriateness of collective bargaining for public employees has centered primarily on the nature of the employer. It is argued that unions infringe upon the "sovereign" power inherent to and necessary for the operation of government. Although this debate is largely philosophical, it also has a practical aspect. Basically, the public assumes that governmental decision-making should be accountable to the public. Because citizens pay directly for decisions made in public sector bargaining, they examine the legitimacy of those decisions closely. This scrutiny contrasts with prevailing ideas toward private employers who are free to make decisions both unilaterally and in collective bargaining that may be quite expensive to the public and may affect social life in fundamental ways. This employer freedom reflects the persistent idea that citizens have little or no right to regulate private conduct despite its impact on society at large.

The concerns of public employees that lead to unionization are similar to those of private employees. Publicly employed workers are concerned about wages and economic benefits, about job security, about fair treatment, and about complaint procedures when they believe their rights have been violated. Public workers organize unions so they can more effectively deal with these concerns.

Because the issues are similar to those present in the private sector, laws governing the public sector are similar to the National Labor Relations Act. The laws generally define the manner in which employees may relate to their employers through unions. The laws establish procedures by which workers choose a union; authorize collective bargaining; specify the issues subject to bargaining; create mechanisms to settle disputes the parties are unable to settle between themsleves; and prohibit certain conduct on the part of employers and unions as violative of workers' rights. However, the details of these laws vary widely between jurisdictions. For instance, municipal workers may have greater or fewer rights than state workers in the same state. Even within a single jurisdiction, provisions of a law sometimes differ for certain groups of employees such as police, firefighters, or teachers.

Collective Action and Impasse Procedures

States and localities with collective bargaining laws generally prohibit strikes with a penalty of discharge for employees who engage in strike activity. Despite their illegality, strikes by public employees are not uncommon, particularly by teachers and by school personnel. Lesser forms of collective action such as sick-outs, or blue-flu, are also favorite tactics of public employees. However, as a rule public employees pursue other legal forms of collective action, such as informational picketing, lobbying, and voting.

Because unsettled disputes threaten to interrupt public services and because direct economic action is forbidden, public employee collective bargaining laws generally establish procedures that apply when the parties are unable to settle disputes through bargaining. These impasse procedures may apply both to contract negotiations when labor and management are unable to agree on contract terms and to disputes arising during the term of a contract over its meaning and application. These procedures vary but usually include some combination of fact-finding, mediation, and arbitration. The national emergency provisions of the Labor Management Relations Act is an example of how peaceful governmental processes can be substituted for direct economic action. Fact-finding usually involves an investigation by a neutral individual or panel to determine the reasonableness of each side's bargaining position and may include recommendations for settlement. While usually not binding on the parties, fact-finding is important because a credible investigation can result in public pressure on the parties to resolve their differences. If one party's position is publicly found to be unreasonable, then its ability to maintain that position is undermined. Mediation, like fact-finding, is not a binding procedure that can achieve a final resolution. A mediator, while free to make suggestions on terms that might be acceptable to both parties, can only operate within the context of the agreement and the demands of each party.

The need for peaceful resolution of disputes and the ineffectiveness of nonbinding fact-finding and mediation have led some states to authorize arbitration as an alternative method for settling contract terms. Because the parties have no choice in whether they utilize such procedures, this kind of arbitration is called compulsory arbitration. The delegation of the power to write binding contract language to an arbitrator raises one of the same issues as that raised by public sector collective bargaining: whether the sovereign can give up its power and responsibility to govern. The state Supreme Courts of South Dakota and Utah have declared statutes delegating such authority to arbitrators as unconstitutional. An additional concern for the parties is the transfer of decisionmaking over contract terms to a third party—a practice generally met with strong resistance in private sector labor relations. Despite these philosophical and practical problems, arbitration is becoming widely used as a method of settling impasses in public sector contract negotiations.

Beyond the issue of whether to authorize arbitration, the use of arbitration raises other problems. In some instances, it has not prevented strikes and disruptions by public employees dissatisfied with the course of collective bargaining. Another criticism is that it chills collective bargaining because arbitrators "split the difference" between the parties' positions instead of examining the merits of their arguments. Critics argue that this splitting encourages the parties to maintain unwarranted positions to ensure that some of their demands will be met rather than engaging in the give and take of compromise, the essence of true bargaining. To counter splitting, some jurisdictions have restricted the arbitrator's authority. Instead of giving an aribitrator total discretion to decide on the final terms of a contract, variations of the "final offer" limitations have been imposed on the arbitrator. Final offer arbitration requires that the arbitrator award the final offer made by one of the parties. It may be conducted on an issue-by-issue basis, but it is sometimes done as a total package to prevent splitting between the issues. An example of the former is the Michigan law; the latter is provided in the Wisconsin law. Because final package arbitration means that one side wins all, this method is meant to encourage true bargaining between parties reluctant to lose everything by allowing the dispute to end up before an arbitrator.

Union Security

Most collective bargaining laws for public employees give exclusive representation rights to the union representing a majority of a group of employees. Although many states permit a dues checkoff deduction for union membership, only about one-third allow unions to negotiate a clause requiring any form of union security, *i.e.*, membership or payment of dues as a condition of job retention. Some states permit union security clauses which cover only certain groups of workers, such as firefighters in Kentucky and higher education employees in Maine.

The controversy concerning mandatory support of a union in public employment raises issues similar to those raised in the context of private employment. However, there are additional arguments against union security arrangements in public employment. One objection is based on the appropriateness of union security displacing the merit principle as a determining factor in job security. A second objection views the federal and state constitutional right to associate (or not to associate) as a limitation on a public employer's authority to bind itself to a union security clause. Under present legal interpretation, both of these arguments are political issues rather than legal impediments to the implementation of union security clauses, if they are permitted under state law.

In *Abood v. Detroit Board of Education* (1977), the Supreme Court rejected the constitutional objections to union security arrangements. Michigan law permitted the negotiation of an agency shop fee in an amount equal to union dues. Teachers seeking to avoid the obligation challenged the law. They argued that public employment is different from private employment because the Constitution is directly involved. A second argument asserted that public sector collective bargaining is inherently political and that to require public workers to give financial support to it is to governmentally require "ideological conformity." Compelling support of unions, they argued, was in violation of the First Amendment to the U.S. Constitution and to the Fourteenth Amendment, which forbids states to restrict rights guaranteed in the U.S. Constitution.

The Supreme Court held that both these arguments were insufficient to override the Michigan law. The Court stated emphatically: "The differences between public and private sector collective bargaining simply do not translate into differences in First Amendment rights." Although the Supreme Court ruled that the agency shop requirement was valid, it found that union use of required fees for purposes not related to collective bargaining to be an infringement of constitutional rights. While unions may engage in political or ideological activities, public employees cannot be compelled to subsidize such activities. Therefore, the implementation of a union security agreement must include adjustments for those employees who object to uses of fees paid to a union for purposes not related to collective bargaining and contract enforcement.

Participation in Political Activities

Another difference between the rights of public employees and private employees is that restrictions are placed on their participation in electoral politics. In 1940, Congress enacted the Hatch Act (5 U.S.C. 7324), which applys to all federal employees in the Executive branch of the government. The Hatch Act makes it unlawful for a federal employee "to use his official authority or influence for the purpose of interfering with an election or affecting the result thereof." It further forbids employees from taking "any active part in political management or political campaigns." Since the enactment of the act, these prohibitions have been interpreted in numerous rulings involving various situations, and certain general rules have been developed.

The major thrust of the Hatch Act is to limit involvement in partisan politics. The Hatch Act, therefore, restricts the constitutional rights of expression and association that federal employees would otherwise enjoy as citizens. The restrictions have been justified on the basis that there is an overriding public interest in ensuring the actual and the apparent neutrality of the federal service. The Supreme Court has twice upheld the Hatch Act as a permissible governmental limitation on the First Amendment rights of citizens who accept federal employment: once, in its *United Public Workers v. Mitchell* (1947) decision, and again, in *United States Civil Service Commission v. National Association of Letter Carriers* (1973).

Federal employees may not be candidates or hold office in any national, state, or local partisan political organization. Nor may they solicit funds for partisan political purposes or promote fund raising for a political cause. Federal employees cannot be a partisan candidate for any elected office and cannot endorse or oppose any partisan candidate in a political advertisement.

The Hatch Act is enforced by the Special Counsel of the Merit System Protection Board, one of the successor agencies to the U.S. Civil Service Commission. The ultimate penalty against an employee found to have violated the law is removal from the federal service. Public employee unions, unable to overturn the Hatch Act through challenges to its constitutionality, launched a legislative effort to change the law in the early 1970s. In 1976, Congress approved major amendments to the Hatch Act which removed most employee political activity from its reach. However, President Ford vetoed the changes and the Congress failed to override the veto.

Federal employees may vote in any partisan election, express opinions publicly and privately on political issues, display political paraphernalia, contribute money, and attend political gatherings. Federal employees may participate in nonpartisan activity. An election is defined as nonpartisan if none of the candidates represent a party for which a presidential elector received votes in the previous presidential election. A federal employee may seek and hold a nonpartisan elected office.

Many states and local governments have also adopted "little Hatch Acts" which cover the political activities of employees. However, some state courts have interpreted their state constitutions to permit only those restrictions on individual rights that are necessary to prevent actual conflicts of interest for a public employee engaged in partisan politics.

Constitutional Issues in Public Employment

Because the constitutions of the United States and of the individual states limit the governments which act under them, governmental employees have a source of protection not available to private employees. Constitutional issues are raised in a variety of contexts. One of the major areas of litigation concerns the rights of government workers to express views about the agency for which they work and to hold and express personal views as a citizen on matters that are not job-related. The First Amendment also becomes involved when employees are required to take loyalty oaths and to reveal organizational affiliations. The privacy of public employees is also a significant issue in constitutional litigation. Privacy rights cover a variety of personal issues. Questions of lifestyle, *e.g.,* sexual preference or cohabitation, grooming and appearance, as well as requirements for disclosure of personal financial data are examples of personal issues that have become subjects of litigation. The extent of constitutional rights has also frequently been raised in the context of job security. Constitutional challenges to public personnel decisions may involve a substantive issue such as a person's "right" to a job. For example, a tenure system may imply that such a right exists. Or, the challenge may be to a procedural issue, such as the right to a hearing when a personnel decision has a negative impact on the employee. The application of constitutional principles to public employees is extensive and complex, and cannot be adequately covered in a general text. Students interested in a detailed and a thorough treatment of the subject are referred to the American Civil Liberties Union guide on the subject: *The Rights of Government Employees* by Robert O'Neil.

Federal Employees

Although the right of federal employees to organize and join a union was statutorily recognized early in the twentieth century, it is only recently that a mechanism and procedures to faciliate exercise of that right have been established. The right of federal employees to join a union and to engage in collective bargaining was added to the already existing civil service system. Created by the Pendleton

Act of 1883, the civil service system was designed to insulate public jobholders from political pressures and to ensure hiring and promotions based on merit. Though the various functions once performed by the Civil Service System are in large part now accomplished through collective bargaining, portions of the system remain, and workers enjoy certain rights independent of those achieved through collective bargaining. These rights are enforced by the Merit System Protection Board.

Organization and collective bargaining in the federal sector was first systematized by Executive Order 10988 issued by President Kennedy in 1962. The order established rules governing the make-up of bargaining units and procedures for the selection of bargaining representatives. It imposed an obligation on the agencies of the federal government to bargain on a large number of working conditions and job rights of their employees. Implementation of EO 10988, however, depended largely on each federal agency's good will or the union's strength. EO 11491, issued in 1971, was based on recommendations by a Presidential Review Commission, and made substantial changes in the federal labor relations program. EO 11491 created the Federal Labor Relations Council (FLRC) to make policy judgments under the order and to supervise collective bargaining. The FLRC consisted of the heads of the Civil Service Commission, the Department of Labor, and the Office of Management and Budget. The order also established a Federal Services Impasse Panel to settle negotiation impasses. Later developments strengthened exclusive recognition rights of unions and broadened the scope of subjects covered by the bargaining obligation.

The Civil Service Reform Act of 1978 replaced Executive Order 11491 as the basic law governing labor-management relations in the federal sector. (*See* Public Law 94–454. The portion of the law relating to labor management relations can be found in 5 U.S.C. Sec. 7101, *et seq.*) For the first time, federal labor-management relations were rooted in statutory law. Although the law embodied many of the principles developed under the Executive Order, it did make significant changes, particularly in the manner of enforcement. Most important among the changes contained in the Act was the creation of an independent agency, the Federal Labor Relations Authority (FLRA), with authority similar to that of the NLRB.

The major functions of the FLRA are to decide representation and unfair labor practice cases, to decide whether an issue is subject to bargaining (negotiability disputes), and to review appeals from arbitration awards. Like the NLRB, the FLRA has the chief authority to interpret the law under which it operates. Its authority to review arbitration awards contrasts sharply with that of the NLRB. Also similar to the enforcement structure under LMRA, the office of General Counsel has the responsibility of prosecuting unfair labor practices. Prior to the creation of the FLRA, the burden of prosecuting cases had rested entirely on the complaining party. The Civil Service Act retained the Federal Services Impasses Panel and maintained the service's responsibility of resolving impasses between federal agencies and unions. The decisions of the FLRA, except for arbitration reviews and for unit determinations, are subject to judicial review. The FLRA was also granted authority to seek court enforcement of its orders.

The law requires that all collective bargaining agreements in the federal sector contain a negotiated grievance procedure *ending in binding arbitration.* A "presumption of grievability" was written into the law which mandates that all disputes—other than a few which are statutorily excluded—will be subject to the grievance procedure unless the parties negotiate to exclude certain matters from coverage. This provision radically changed the prior rule which had excluded from grievance procedures many matters which were instead subject to a statutory appeal procedure under the Civil Service Act. Although the Civil Service Reform Act strengthens collective bargaining in the federal sector, a number of important issues such as pay levels and pensions remain subject to Congressional discretion.

Postal Workers

After a nationwide strike by postal employees in 1970, the Post Office Department of the federal government was reorganized. The Postal Reorganization Act of 1970 (Public Law 91–375, codified in Title 39 of the U.S. code.) created the United States Postal Service, an independent quasi-governmental agency. The labor-management relations of the Postal Service were made subject to the LMRA, the same law governing private sector labor-management relations. The National Labor Relations Board was given jurisdiction to determine appropriate bargaining units, conduct elections, and enforce the unfair labor practice provisions of the LMRA. Strikes were prohibited, and fact-finding, mediation, and arbitration procedures were established to resolve contract issues not settled by collective bargaining. Union security arrangements were prohibited. Although postal unions bargain on wages, hours, and conditions in the same manner as private sector unions, certain job rights, such as pensions, remain subject to Congressional decision. Postal workers also retain statutory protection in certain personnel actions. They also continue to be subject to the restrictions of the Hatch Act.

Key Words and Phrases

Civil Service Reform Act of 1978	Federal Services Impasse Panel
compulsory arbitration	Hatch Act
Executive Order 10988	mediation
Executive Order 11491	Merit System Protection Board
fact finding	Pendleton Act
Federal Labor Relations Authority	Postal Reorganization Act splitting

---

Review and Discussion Questions

1. How might compulsory arbitration of unsettled contract terms affect genuine give-and-take bargaining?

2. Does the public have a greater stake in public sector labor-management relations than it does in those in the private sector? Explain using as an example the difference in rights of workers in a publicly sponsored child care center as compared to those in a privately owned child care center.

3. Should public employees have a right to strike? Would a requirement that a 2-week notice of any planned strike be an appropriate limitation?

4. Should public workers be compelled to join a union or pay money to a union that represents a majority of the employees in their workplace as a condition of retaining a job? Explain.

5. Do you think the Hatch Act is necessary to prevent politicians from exploiting public workers by forcing them to be politically active in order to keep their jobs? Explain.

6. Describe the differences between the Civil Service Reform Act of 1978 and the National Labor Relations Act as amended.

Table of Cases

V

W

Y

Glossary

AFL-CIO *See* American Federation of Labor—Congress of Industrial Organizations.

Age Discrimination in Employment Act A federal law, passed in 1967 and amended in 1978, which makes it unlawful for an employer, an employment agency, or a labor union to discriminate in employment opportunities against persons between the ages of 40 and 70. This law also applies to employees of federal, state, and local governments.

agency shop A contract clause which requires a member of a bargaining unit to pay a union a fee for services and benefits accruing to the employee because of a union contract.

allied employer An employer who, through an arrangement with another employer whose employees are on strike, agrees to perform the work previously done by the striking employees.

American Federation of Labor—Congress of Industrial Organizations A voluntary federation of about 105 national and international unions that have joined together for purposes of solidarity, shared resources, and effective political action.

anti-injunction laws State or federal laws that forbid or limit the power of courts within a jurisdiction to use injunctions in a labor dispute. The federal Norris-LaGuardia Act of 1932 is the best known and most important anti-injunction law.

anti-trust laws Laws designed to protect trade and commerce from monopolies, price fixing, and conspiratorial restraints on the marketplace.

arbitration A method of settling a controversy, upon which parties cannot reach mutual agreement, by submitting it to a neutral third party whose decision the parties agree to accept.

area standards picketing A form of picketing with the purpose of encouraging an employer to observe the standards in that industry in that locality. This kind of picketing is more clearly legal than picketing to force an employer to recognize a union or to afford employees noneconomic benefits.

authorization card A statement signed by an employee designating a union to act on his or her behalf in collective bargaining.

bargaining unit Employees who are grouped together for the purpose of collective bargaining. A unit may be established by mutual agreement of an employer and a union. In case of dispute, the NLRB has the legal authority to define the contours of a unit. The LMRA contains some specific restrictions on the structuring of bargaining units.

blocking An NLRB decision not to proceed with an election in a bargaining unit where there are pending unresolved unfair labor practice charges.

boulwarism A bargaining technique pioneered by the General Electric Co. which combined a "firm offer" containing proposals which the employer asserted were in the best interest of the employees and a massive publicity campaign addressing the public and the employees to convince them of the rightness of the company's proposals.

boycott A refusal to deal with an enterprise in order to exert pressure on the enterprise to accede to a certain position.

business agent A full-time paid official of a local union whose duties include ongoing contact with employees, as well as contract enforcement.

captive audience A meeting shortly before an election at which employee attendance is required by an employer, who then uses the occasion to make an anti-union speech.

cease-and-desist order An order issued by the NLRB requiring an employer or a union to refrain from activity which the NLRB has found to be an unfair labor practice.

certification The formal designation by the NLRB of a union as the exclusive representative of employees in a bargaining unit.

certification bar rule An NLRB rule insulating a union from all challenges to its representative status for either one year from the date of certification or one year from the date good-faith bargaining begins.

checkoff A contract provision which requires an employer to deduct union dues and fees from an employee'e earnings and to pay that amount directly to the union when authorized to do so by an individual employee.

Civil Rights Act of 1964, Title VII A law forbidding employers, labor unions, and employment agencies in industries in interstate commerce to discriminate in employment or union membership against any individual on account of race, color, religion, sex, or national origin. The 1972 amendments to this law extended its coverage to state and local governments and to the federal government. The law is enforced by the Equal Employment Opportunity Commission, an independent federal agency.

closed shop A contract clause which restricts the employer to hiring only members of the union which is a party to the contract. Union membership is also a condition of continued employment. This type of union security clause is illegal and unenforceable.

collective bargaining The process by which employees as a group deal with an employer concerning the terms and conditions under which the employment is to be performed. Collective bargaining, as it is practiced in the United States, involves a union acting as an exclusive representative for a unit of employees.

collective bargaining agreement   A formal agreement, usually written, fixing the conditions of employment for a period of time. This agreement is usually called a contract.

commerce   Historically, a term used to describe the exchange of goods. In modern usage and law, the term also describes labor, transportation, communication, intelligence, and the media of exchange, all of which have assumed the character of commodities.

common situs   Term describing a site on which more than one employer operates, particularly in reference to construction sites where a general contractor and several subcontractors all operate at the same time. Each of these contractors is considered to be an entirely independent employer under the law.

company union   Usually a union which represents only the employees of a single employer, which has a "sweetheart" relationship with the employer, or which is dominated by the employer.

compulsory arbitration   Governmentally mandated use of arbitration to settle labor-management disputes. In the private sector, all arbitration is voluntary. Some laws applying to public employees provide for compulsory arbitration.

concerted activities   Activities undertaken jointly by employees for furthering collective interests or for "mutual aid for protection." Concerted activities are protected by Section 7 of the LMRA.

conciliation   A form of dispute settlement in which a third party neutral seeks to reconcile the opposing viewpoints of the parties so as to effect a voluntary settlement.

consent election   A representation election in which the employer and the union agree to date, place, voter eligibility, etc.

conspiracy   A combination of two or more persons who join together to pursue a course of action deemed to be harmful to the interests of society.

consumer picketing   Picketing of a retail establishment that is legal if directed toward getting *consumers* not to buy a particular product of a supplier or of a producer with whom a labor dispute exists. Such picketing is illegal if it is aimed at getting customers to stop shopping the store or at other parties, such as store employees or delivery personnel.

contract   *See* Collective Bargaining Agreement.

contract-bar rules   Rules applied by the NLRB in determining when an existing contract between an employer and a union will bar a representation election in the covered unit.

cooling-off period   Period during which employees are forbidden to strike. The Taft-Hartley Act's national emergency provisions, which override the legal right of employees to strike, is an example.

coordinated bargaining   Joint or cooperative efforts by several unions in dealing with an employer that has employees represented by each of the several unions. Also called coalition bargaining.

Davis-Bacon Act   A federal law passed in 1931 requiring the payment of prevailing wage rates to workers on federally financed construction work.

deauthorization election   An election conducted by the NLRB to determine if the majority of the members in a bargaining unit desire to take away their union's authority to apply a union security clause to the bargaining unit.

decertification election   An election conducted by the NLRB among the employees in a bargaining unit to determine if they desire continued representation by the same union. Such an election is conducted only when 30 percent of the employees in a unit petition the NLRB for such an election. A majority of those voting determine the union's status.

deferral   An action by which the NLRB declines to exercise its jurisdiction over certain unfair labor practice charges until contract methods for resolving the claim have been exhausted.

double-breasted employer   A unionized employer which establishes a separate, competing enterprise which it operates on a nonunion basis.

economic strike   A strike against an employer over an issue other than an unfair labor practice. A sympathy action is usually not considered an economic strike, because it is not directed against the employer's treatment of participating employees.

election bar rule   A rule stated in the LMRA prohibiting any representation election in a unit in which a valid election has been held in the preceding 12 months.

Employee Retirement Income Security Act of 1974   A law providing for mandatory vesting and funding of employee pension plans. The law entitles an employee who works a certain number of years to pension benefits and requires pension plans to have money set aside to pay the benefits. This law is enforced by the U.S. Department of Labor.

Equal Employment Opportunity Act   *See* Civil Rights Act of 1964, Title VII.

Equal Pay Act of 1963   An amendment to the Fair Labor Standards Act making it unlawful for an employer to pay wage differentials for the same work solely on the basis of sex.

excelsior list   A list of the names and addresses of all employees in a bargaining unit who are eligible to vote in an NLRB election.

Fair Labor Standards Act   A law passed in 1937 establishing a minimum wage and overtime rates for employees of enterprises engaged in interstate commerce. The law also limits child labor.

featherbedding   A contract clause requiring an employer to pay for work not performed. This type of clause is forbidden in Section 8(b)(6) of the Taft-Hartley Act.

free speech   Under the LMRA, the right of an employer to express views hostile to unionization, so long as these views do not include threats of reprisal or promises of benefits.

General Counsel   An office within the NLRB whose main responsibility is to investigate charges of unfair labor practice and to issue and to prosecute formal complaints when appropriate. The General Counsel also oversees the operation of the regional offices of the NLRB.

good-faith bargaining   The standard of bargaining that parties must meet to fulfill their obligation to bargain, which includes a willingness to meet with an open and sincere desire to reach a resolution on points of contention.

grievance   A complaint by an employee or a union that a right contained in a collective bargaining agreement or other job rights of employees has been violated. The range of complaints subject to a contract grievance procedure will be defined in the contract but may be expanded by mutually recognized past practices.

grievance procedure   A method set out in a labor contract which the parties agree to use to resolve any disputes between them as to the meaning and application of the contract.

hiring hall   An agreement between a union and employer under which the union agrees to serve as a source of employees, either through a referral service or by maintaining an actual "hall." This practice is common in industries where employment is casual or intermittent, such as construction.

hot cargo agreement   An agreement whereby an employer agrees not to handle, use, sell, transport, or otherwise deal in the products of another employer. Such a clause is expressly forbidden in Section 8(e) of the Taft-Hartley Act.

illegal subject of bargaining   Any subject forbidden by law, which cannot be incorporated into a contract irrespective of the desires of the parties to the contract.

impasse   The point in bargaining at which further negotiations would be fruitless. Once an impasse is reached, the duty to bargain is suspended on those subjects to which the impasse applies.

implied no-strike   An obligation not to strike that is judicially read into every agreement containing a grievance procedure that ends in arbitration. The no-strike obligation covers any matter subject to the arbitration clause.

informational picketing   Picketing for the purpose of advising the public that a picketed employer either does not have a union contract or is engaging in labor practices offensive to a union and its members.

injunction   An order by a judge which mandates that the enjoined party either perform a certain act or refrain from certain activity.

interest arbitration   The process of settling unresolved disputes in contract negotiations by submitting them to a third party for a decision. This method of arriving at new contract terms is used infrequently in private sector disputes, but it is sometimes required by public employee collective bargaining statutes.

international union   A union representing employees both within and outside the United States (usually in Canada). The term is loosely applied to unions operating on a nationwide basis in the United States.

interstate commerce   Trade or commercial relations between parties in two different states, or if contained within one state, trade or commercial relations which has an impact in other states.

intrastate commerce   Activity carried on totally within the boundaries of a single state and having no impact on commerce beyond that state's boundaries.

irreparable harm   A condition necessary for the granting of an injunction which requires that the activity will cause harm that cannot be repaired, if it is not enjoined.

jurisdictional dispute   A controversy between two unions over which union has the right to organize a particular group of workers or over which union's members should be employed to do a specific type of work.

jurisdictional standards   A dollar standard in the annual volume of business that an enterprise must exceed before the NLRB will exercise jurisdiction over its labor-management relations. There are different standards for different types of businesses.

Labor Management Relations Act of 1947   The basic law regulating private sector labor-management relations in the United States. It is commonly known as the Taft-Hartley Act.

Labor Management Reporting and Disclosure Act   A 1959 federal statute establishing rules concerning the internal operation of unions and standards of conduct for union officers, employers, and labor relations consultants. It also made some significant amendments to the Taft-Hartley Act, particularly in the rules on secondary boycotts. This law is popularly known as the Landrum-Griffin Act.

laboratory conditions   The conditions which the NLRB requires in election campaigns so that an employee may freely exercise the right to choose or reject a union.

Landrum-Griffin Act   *See* Labor Management Reporting and Disclosure Act.

lockout   A form of economic pressure by which an employer discontinues business activity and refuses to allow employees to perform their usual work.

maintenance of membership clause   A contract provision requiring an employee who voluntarily becomes a member of the union to remain a member as a condition of continued employment.

management rights clause   A clause in a collective bargaining agreement expressly reserving to management certain rights which are not subject to the grievance procedure when exercised. Even without the reservation of specified rights, management is assumed to have unilateral authority in a variety of matters. This authority derives from the fact of ownership and can be limited only by specific contract language which creates a union right.

mandatory bargaining subject   Any subject pertaining to "wages, hours, terms and conditions of employment." These are the subjects over which the parties to collective bargaining *must* bargain.

mediation   A form of dispute settlement in which a neutral third party makes proposals for settlement that have not been already proposed by the parties. Conciliation differs in that the third party cannot make proposals which differ from those the parties have discussed.

merged-product rule   A rule that limits consumer picketing when the picketed product is integrated with a product of a secondary employer in such a way that it loses its independent identity.

minimum wage law   *See* Fair Labor Standards Act.

multi-plant unit   A bargaining unit consisting of employees who work in two or more plants or operations owned by a single employer. Multi-plant units are common, for example, in the supermarket business.

multiple employer unit   A bargaining unit consisting of employees of more than one employer.

National Labor Relations Act (NLRA)   The first comprehensive law regulating labor-management relations in the United States. Passed in 1935, the law was popularly known as the Wagner Act. The NLRA was substantially amended by the Taft-Hartley Act in 1947 and has since been known as the Labor Management Relations Act.

National Labor Relations Board   A quasi-judicial federal agency created by the National Labor Relations Act and charged with the responsibility of enforcing that law. The two main functions of the NLRB are to supervise the selection of bargaining representatives by employees and to prosecute and adjudicate unfair labor practices.

National Mediation Board   A federal agency set up under the Railway Labor Act to mediate disputes in the railway and airlines industries and to conduct representation elections among employees in those industries.

national union   An organization comprised of a number of affiliated locals, or subordinate bodies, that engage in collective bargaining with different employers.

Norris-Laguardia Act of 1932   A federal statute which stripped the federal courts almost entirely of their ability to issue injunctions in labor disputes. Much of its vitality has been eroded by later legislation and judicial decisions.

no-strike clause   A provision in a contract in which a union agrees not to strike over any issue covered by the contract during its term.

Occupational Safety and Health Act of 1970 A law guaranteeing workers the right to a safe and healthful workplace. The law provides for the setting of standards for both work practices and exposures to physical and chemical agents in the workplace. It created the Occupational Safety and Health Administration in the U.S. Department of Labor to inspect workplaces for violations and to enforce the law.

open shop A workplace where employees are not bound by a union security clause and are free to join or to not join the union which represents their workplace.

past practice An employment practice which, through sanction or use, becomes an enforceable standard even though not included in a contract.

permissive subject *See* voluntary subject of bargaining.

per se **bargaining violation** Bargaining conduct, considered to be so destructive of the true give-and-take implied in bargaining, that it is a violation of the duty to bargain without regard to the good faith of the party engaging in the conduct.

picketing A physical presence at or near a place of business to advertise the existence of a dispute or of a fact, such as an employer's nonunion status.

pre-hire agreement An agreement between an employer in the building and construction industry and a union which contains a union security clause, even though the union has not established that it represents a majority of the employer's employees. Pre-hire agreements are authorized in Section 8(f) of the Taft-Hartley Act.

primary employer An employer with which a union deals concerning the rights of the employees of that particular employer.

probationary period A stated period of time during which a newly hired employee can be terminated at the will of the employer; the period of time before the employee is protected by the just cause provision of a contract. A probationary employee may not be entitled to other benefits in a contract, *e.g.*, holiday pay, insurance coverage.

protected concerted activity Certain collective activities by employees that are protected by Section 7 of the LMRA.

Public Contracts Act *See* Walsh-Healey Act.

quid pro quo Latin phrase meaning "this for that" used in law to describe a trade-off of rights.

Railway Labor Act (RLA) A law passed by Congress in 1926 recognizing the right of railroad employees to join and to form unions and to engage in collective bargaining under federal supervision. Today, the RLA applies to both railway and airline employees.

recognition Employer acceptance of an organization as exclusive representative for a unit of employees.

recognition picketing Picketing for the purpose of compelling an employer to recognize the union as a bargaining agent for the employer's employees.

re-opening clause A contract clause providing for the renegotiation of certain contract terms under specified conditions during the term of the agreement.

representation election An election in which employees vote on whether to empower a union to act on their behalf for the purpose of collective bargaining.

reserved gate An entrance at a place of employment designated for the exclusive use of certain subcontractors of the main employer on the site. The term may apply to both industrial and construction workplaces.

right-to-work laws State laws forbidding the application of an union security clause to workers within that state. Such state laws are permitted under Section 14(b) of the Taft-Hartley Act.

secondary boycott An action against an employer other than the employer with whom a dispute exists. The second employer is frequently a customer or a supplier of the first employer, and boycotters seek to exert pressure on the second employer, which will then act to exert pressure on the first employer.

secondary employer An employer which a union involves in a labor dispute even though there is no question or dispute concerning that employer's own employees.

self-determination election An election in which skilled employees vote on whether they wish to be included in an industrial bargaining unit. This kind of election is not permitted under present NLRB policy.

seniority An employee's status based on years of service within a workplace, department, or job. Included in many contracts as the standard for deciding job rights, such as protection against layoff, promotion and bidding rights, choice of vacation dates, etc.

sit-down strike A work stoppage in which employees take occupancy of the employer's premises.

Social Security Act of 1937 A law providing for a payroll deduction and an equivalent employer contribution for a pension and disability program operated by the federal government.

statute of limitation The period of time during which any legal claim may be brought. The time for an action is usually stated in the law which creates the right to institute such action. In the case of unfair labor practices, the statute of limitations is six months from the time the alleged violation occurred.

stranger picketing Picketing conducted by persons who are not employees of the picketed employer.

strike A concerted stoppage of work by employees who seek to force concessions from the employer by economic pressure.

struck work clause A contract clause permitting covered employees to refuse to do work that is "struck work" and which they would not be asked to do but for the strike. Such a clause is not a "hot cargo" agreement. A struck work clause is legal.

subcontracting   An arrangement by an employer to have certain work performed by another employer.

successor employer   An employer which acquires an already existing operation and which continues those operations in approximately the same manner as the previous employer, including the use of the previous employer's employees.

superseniority   Seniority granted by a contract clause that is greater than actual seniority. Superseniority may be granted to certain groups of employees, such as shop stewards, to assure their continued presence on the job for contract enforcement purposes. Superseniority can apply to layoffs but not to other job rights, such as job bidding or preferred vacation schedules.

sympathy strike   An action whose purpose is to affect the outcome of a dispute that does not involve the "wages, hours, terms and conditions" of the employees engaging in the sympathy action. A sympathy action may be against the immediate employer which is involved in a dispute with another group of workers.

Taft-Hartley Act   The popular name of the Labor Management Relations Act of 1947. It is the basic law regulating labor-management relations in the private sector in the United States.

unfair labor practice   Types of employer or union conduct that is outlawed by the Taft-Hartley Act. The term does not apply to all unfair conduct which may be in violation either of some moral codes or of some other public law or a collective bargaining agreement. It refers only to particular activities described in the LMRA.

unilateral action   An action taken by an employer without bargaining; action without bilateral decisionmaking.

union security agreement   A negotiated contract provision requiring union membership or payment of money to a union as a condition of employment.

union shop   A contract clause which requires an employee, after a grace period of not less than 30 calendar days, to join the union and remain a member of the union as a condition of employment. This is the highest form of union security permitted by the Taft-Hartley Act.

voluntary subjects of bargaining   Subjects of bargaining *other than* those considered to be wages, hours, terms, and conditions of employment. Either party may propose discussion of such a subject, and the other party may voluntarily bargain on it. Neither party may insist to the point of impasse on the inclusion of a voluntary subject in a contract.

Wagner Act   A popular name of the National Labor Relations Act of 1935.

waiver   A release of an employer from the obligation to bargain by the union's failure to request bargaining or by the union's conscious concession of certain bargaining rights in contract negotiations.

Walsh-Healey Act   A law establishing minimum wage and overtime standards for workers engaged in the manufacture or furnishing of materials, supplies, articles, and equipment to any agency of the United States government under a contract exceeding $10,000. Also known as the Public Contract Act.

Welfare and Pension Plans Disclosure Act of 1958   A law requiring administrators of employee welfare and pension plans to make reports to participants and to the U.S. Department of Labor. It also makes kickbacks, false entries, embezzlement, and conflicts of interest by fund officials or participants a federal crime. This law was repealed and replaced by the Employee Retirement Income Security Act of 1974.

whipsawing   A union stratagem seeking to obtain benefits from a number or group of employers by applying pressure to one, the objective being to win favorable terms from the one employer and then use this as a pattern, or perhaps a base, to obtain the same or greater benefits from the other employers, under the same threat of pressure (including a strike) used against the first one.

wildcat strikes   A strike by employees without the authorization or consent of their union.

yellow-dog contract   An individual contract of employment in which an employee was required to affirm that he or she was not and would not become a member of a union while an employee of a particular employer. Such contracts were outlawed by the Norris-LaGuardia Act of 1932.

zipper clause   A contract clause that fixes all terms of employment for the duration of a contract, stating that the agreement is "complete in itself."

Bibliography

Aaron, Benjamin; Grodin, Joseph; and Stern, James L., eds. *Public Sector Bargaining*. Washington, D.C.: The Bureau of National Affairs, Inc., 1979.

Anderson, Howard J. *Primer of Labor Relations*. 21st ed., rev. Washington D.C.: The Bureau of National Affairs, Inc., 1980.

Ashford, Nicholas. *Crisis in the Workplace and Occupational Disease and Injury*. Cambridge, Mass.: MIT Press, 1976.

Berman, Daniel. *Death on the Job*. New York: Monthly Review Press, 1978.

BNA Editorial Staff. *The Comparable Worth Issue: A Special Report*. Washington, D.C.: The Bureau of National Affairs, Inc., 1981.

———. *Grievance Guide*. 6th ed., rev. Washington, D.C.: The Bureau of National Affairs, Inc., 1982.

———. *Sexual Harassment and Labor Relations: A BNA Special Report*. Washington, D.C.: The Bureau of National Affairs, Inc., 1981.

Brodeur, Paul. *Expendable Americans*. New York: Viking Press, 1974.

Clark, Elisse. *Stopping Sexual Harassment: A Handbook*. Detroit: Labor Education and Research Project, 1980.

Coulson, Robert. *Labor Arbitration—What You Need to Know*. New York: American Arbitration Association, 1978.

Elkouri, Edna A., and Elkouri, Frank. *How Arbitration Works*. 3rd ed. Washington, D.C.: The Bureau of National Affairs, Inc., 1973.

Grune, Joy Ann, ed. *Manual on Pay Equity: Raising Wages for Women's Work*. Washington, D.C.: Committee on Pay Equity, 1980.

Hricko, Andrea, and Brunt, Melanie. *Working for Your Life: A Woman's Guide to Job Health Hazards*. Berkeley: Labor Occupational Health Program, 1976.

Knapp, Andrea S., ed. *Labor Relations Law in the Public Sector*. Chicago: American Bar Association, 1977.

Lynd, Staughton. *Labor Law for the Rank and Filer*. San Pedro, California: Singlejack Books, 1982.

Morris, Charles J., ed. *The Developing Labor Law: The Board, the Courts, and the National Labor Relations Act*. With Supplements. Washington, D.C.: The Bureau of National Affairs, Inc., 1971–1982.

National Lawyers Guild. *Guide to Labor Law for Employees and Union Members*. New York: Clark Boardman Co., Ltd., 1981.

O'Neill, Robert. *The Rights of Government Employees: The Basic ACLU Guide to Government Employee Rights*. New York: Avon Books, 1978.

Schlossberg, Stephen I., and Sherman, Frederick E. *Organizing and the Law*. Washington, D.C.: The Bureau of National Affairs, Inc., 1971.

Stellman, Jeanne M. *Women's Work, Women's Health: Myths and Realities*. New York: Pantheon Books, 1977.

Stellman, Jeanne M., and Daum, Susan M. *Work is Dangerous to Your Health*. New York: Random House, 1971.

Stone, Katherine Wetzel. "The Postwar Paradigm in American Labor Law," *Yale Law Journal* 90 (1981): 1511-1580.

Treiman, Donald, and Hartmann, Heidi I. *Women, Work, and Wages: Equal Pay for Jobs of Equal Value*. Washington, D.C.: National Academy of Science, 1981.

U.S. Commission on Civil Rights. *Affirmative Action in the 1980s: Dismantling the Process of Discrimination*. Washington, D.C.: Government Printing Office, 1981.

U.S. Department of Labor, Women's Bureau. *Brief Highlights of Major Federal Laws on Sex Discrimination in Employment*. Washington, D.C.: Government Printing Office, 1980.

Topical Index

A

Administrative law (*See also* Government regulation; names of federal agencies) 4-5, 6
Administrative law judges 30, 47, 206, 212
Affirmative action
  affirmative action plans 226, 230
  enforcement 237-39
  requirements 236-37
AFL-CIO (*See also* American Federation of Labor; Congress of Industrial Organizations) 56, 186, 198, 234
Age discrimination 229-30, 232
Age discrimination in Employment Act 229-30
Agency shop arrangements 100
Agricultural workers 23, 26, 205
Airline industry 13, 23
Allied employer doctrine 160-61
American Federation of Labor (AFL) 55
American Petroleum Institute 207
American Railway Union 127
Antitrust law 11-12, 13
Appeals (*See* United States courts of appeals)
Arbitration
  adverse discrimination rulings, right to civil action 243-44
  awards
    judicial enforcement of 114-16
    overriding legal rights 116-17
  duty of fair representation 176-78
  fees charged to nonmembers 101
  grievance arbitration 95, 110
  injunctions to enforce arbitrable issues 127-33
  interest arbitration 95-96, 110
  judicial deference to contract procedures 112-13
  NLRB authority relative to 118-22
Arbitration
  postal workers' contracts 22, 250
  presumption of arbitrability 113-14
  principles and scope 109-10

public employment, in 248-49, 254
safety issues, arbitrability 114, 215
strikes creating national emergencies 152
Arbitration Act of 1888 13
Area standards picketing 167-68
Authorization cards 50-51, 66-67

B

Back pay 43, 226
Balloting (*See* Elections, union representation
Benefits (*See* Health and disability benefits; Pension and benefit plans; Unemployment compensation)
Bill of Rights (U.S. Constitution) 3, 184
"Bill of rights" of union members 16, 184-87
Blocking 53
Boulwarism 78
Boycotts
  political boycotts 162-63
  secondary boycotts
    allied employer doctrine 160-61
    common situs questions 157-60
    consumer picketing 161-63
    Moore Dry Dock standards 158-59
    political boycotts, as 162-63
    prohibition of 16-17, 140, 170
    reserved gates 159-60
    unprotected activity, as 154-57
    union liability for damages 11
Building trades (*See* Construction industry)
Burger, Warren 21

C

California 26
Captive audiences 63-64
Carter, Jimmy 151
Certification (*See* Unions)
Certification bar rule 51-52, 62

279

About the Author

Betty Justice graduated from Pikeville College, Pikeville, Kentucky; in 1975, she graduated from the Antioch College of Law. From 1976 through 1982, she worked as a labor educator for the Institute for Labor Studies at West Virginia University. Currently, she works as a freelance labor educator and editor. Prior to attending law school, Ms. Justice was a public school teacher. She has also held a variety of service and clerical jobs. With Renate Pore, Ms. Justice edited *Toward the Second Decade: The Impact of the Women's Movement on American Institutions,* published by Greenwood Press in 1981. She has authored numerous professional and popular articles on issues concerning women, labor, and Appalachia.